THE EARTH EXPERIMENT & OUR E.T. PROGENITORS

Conversations with Quan Yin Vol. 1

Alison Chen

Daniel Scranton

Printed in the United States of America

ISBN 979-8-28925-354-5 (sc)
ISBN 979-8-28927-685-8 (hc)

2025.06.22

CONTENTS

Part II
E.T.s and the Earth Experiment

ACKNOWLEDGEMENTS

This book is a co-creation between Ascended Master Quan Yin, myself, and Daniel Scranton, a renowned channeler of higher-dimensional beings. I ask the questions, Quan Yin gives the answers, and the conversation is enabled by Daniel, who channels Quan Yin and then conveys the message to me. The book only came into existence thanks to this unique mode of collaboration. While it is unusual, it brings forth wisdom and truth that is crucial at this juncture of our evolution on planet Earth.

The team also includes our editor Anya Hurd, graphic designer Petra Ra, and format editor Alfredo Sarraga Jr.

As an editor, Anya is meticulous and encouraging. She sharpened the clarity of the content by pointing out concepts that needed explanations or clarification and by revising material as necessary throughout the book. She also asked insightful questions and identified areas that warranted further amplification or refinement. She always did her job with a calm temperament and cheerful enthusiasm.

Petra is as artistic as she is spiritual. The design of the cover is a rendition of the book in artistic form. The amazing and touching images were created from her artistic as well as channeling talents.

Alfredo is the ultimate professional, patient, and efficient, and provides excellent advice on getting a book published on Amazon.

There is another invisible member on the team, my higher self. As Quan Yin tells me, my higher self is part of my soul, as I am part of my soul. So my higher self is not a separate being, but a higher consciousness within my soul that I'm connected to. I sense their gentle guidance steering me to the most pertinent knowledge to explore. I also feel their helping hands lifting me over my writer's block when I ask for assistance.

So much help and support have been extended from both the physical and nonphysical realms to make the creation of this book possible. However, all responsibility for this book in its physical shape and form rests with me. I know the book is blessed because of its intention and the service it is meant to offer for all who wish to know the higher purpose of our being here on Earth.

MESSAGE FROM QUAN YIN

Humanity is at a crossroads in terms of your politics and your policies. You are at a crossroads spiritually as well. Many people are calling into question at this time their own beliefs, beliefs that they had held to be as truths in every portion of their lives leading up to this moment, and that is why it is important to know your history. It is important for you to know where you came from, why you are here, and where you are potentially going.

This book addresses all of that and more, as it gives you a perspective, my perspective as an Ascended Master, on how you got to where you are and why, and what choices lie ahead of you. As an individual, you can always make a choice that is for the good of the many, and you can always make a choice that exemplifies the love that you really are. And while you cannot control what choices other people in your society are making, you can choose to respond to what they're doing and saying differently. You can always choose a path of unity consciousness, and you can look back at the mistakes of the past, made both by humans and extraterrestrials, to see that it is important to take everyone into consideration.

In the course of reading this book, you will be exploring humanity's relationship to that which you call extraterrestrial. And some of what you read might frighten you, and some of what you read might anger you. It is important for you to process those feelings and to understand that each and every E.T. race has made mistakes just as humans have, and one of the mistakes they've made is in how to relate to you all as human beings. Many E.T.s have attempted to help you, but have hindered you instead, and some have come to Earth for very selfish reasons. It is all very important for this to become known to each of you because as you move forward now into this time where each E.T. contact will be very open and a part of just about everyone's life, you need to have forgiven, processed, and moved beyond what has been done by the E.T.s who have been involved in your history.

It is important for you to see the future with your extraterrestrial friends as one that is bright and filled with collaboration, filled with an enormous array of wonderful teachings that they will hand down to you. And it is important for you to know that even when they land their ships, which they will in the future, they will not be there to interfere this time. They will be there to help, they will be there to unite, and they will be there to inform. And you will benefit from these interactions much more in the future than you have in the past.

It is also important for you as individuals and as a society to see how your actions impact the whole and the future. And by looking at your past and the mistakes that have been made in the past, you can make more informed choices. You can learn from the past. You are not destined to repeat the past. And even though you are seeing some of what has been a part of your past coming up again, it is coming up again so that you can approach these same scenarios and these same challenges differently.

And that's what this Ascension is all about. You are there to shift not only to another dimension of reality, but you are there to shift yourselves. You are there to shift your thoughts and your beliefs. You are there to shift your overall vibration so that the better thoughts make more logical sense to your minds. Thoughts that are more inclusive and that benefit everyone are the ones that will make more sense to you as you move forward, because you are a part of a Universal shifting consciousness, and humanity on Earth is playing its part in that Universal Shift.

So please look at your collective past with the knowing that you're not just there to repeat past mistakes or feel bad about what went wrong in this scenario or that scenario. You are there to become more, because of what has transpired and not in spite of it. You are there to have all the possible experiences and all the possible emotions, and that is why you have such a unique history on planet Earth and a history that needs examining. Most importantly, it's a history that most people would not accept as being true.

But if you are reading this book right now, then you are ready for these truths to come to light for you, and you are ready to see this version of history as the version of history that you accept as your timeline. And as you do that, you benefit from it, and you will grow through the reading of the words of this book. And I am very happy to have been called upon to participate in it, just as I continue to participate in your consciousness evolution in all the ways that I am allowed to.

You are beautiful beings, beautiful human beings, and you have so much support from here in the higher realms where I now reside as an Ascended Master. Please call upon me at any time when you need help dealing with the challenges of today's modern Earth. I love you, I am here to help you, and I appreciate all that you are going through in your lives.

With many blessings,
Quan Yin

~ Channeled by Daniel Scranton, March 2025

INTRODUCTION

ABOUT THIS BOOK

I began receiving guidance from Ascended Master Quan Yin in 2020 with the help of Daniel Scranton, a renowned channel of higher-dimensional beings. I had embarked on a spiritual awakening brought forward by the difficult challenge of being a caregiver for my dementia-stricken parents. Adversity can be an effective trigger of a search for the meaning of everything.

In the beginning, I asked questions about my parents and why everything happened the way it did. I was graciously given answers about karma and my life purpose for this seven-year journey that was as grueling as it was transformational. Gradually, I became more intrigued by the truth of our existence, and I expanded the questions I posed to Quan Yin. Are we souls incarnating as humans on Earth? What is our purpose in coming here? Is "Ascension" a true cosmic event for Earth and humanity to move up to a higher plane of existence?

After both of my parents passed away, I finally had a chance to review all the information I had gathered. To my surprise, I realized I had assembled an incredible amount of spiritual knowledge ranging from soul purpose and soul family structure to the true meaning of karma, as well as the upcoming Ascension of Earth and humanity. I contemplated what to do with the content, and I felt the call from within to share it. So many of us are searching for the higher truth of our being on this planet, particularly at this time when we have so many questions and so few answers. Quan Yin's guidance has been immeasurably valuable to me, and it will be for many others as well.

In 2023, I started to work on creating a book based on the content I had, and I asked Quan Yin additional questions to amplify and clarify what I had already learned. Unexpectedly, we went in a new direction when I accidentally inquired about the identity of "starseeds." Starseeds are generally recognized as people from other star systems who have volunteered to come to Earth to assist humanity with Ascension. Quan Yin corrected this assumption and told me that literally all on Earth are starseeds in origin, and we as earthlings all have extraterrestrial lineages. It's just that those who call themselves starseeds are more aware of their star connections and their intent to help with the evolution of consciousness on Earth.

I was captivated by this revelation. From then on, I wandered into a different course of questions and answers with Quan Yin. I began to trace back our journey in the cosmos before arriving on Earth, and I delved into our current journey on Earth and our E.T. connections.

The process of creation was organic. I had no idea or outline of the stories we would tell because I didn't know what I didn't know. But one question led to another, and one answer led to another question as well. In about 18 months, I accumulated a new body of content that touched upon our cosmic origin, our cosmic journey, and our history and purpose on Earth.

The idea of the "Earth Experiment" was brought forward in the conversations. It was a grand design of a melting pot for species in the galaxy to come together and experience diversity in the fullest way possible. E.T.s have been the architects and implementers of the plan, and they have been closely involved with our creation and evolution. They are our ancestors, and they have co-created these major Earth experiences with us.

I explored many essential questions about our existence as a soul, as a starseed, and as a human being. But more importantly, I found that we, the earthlings, are standing at a culmination point where we are revisiting and making peace with our past and readying ourselves to graduate from this Earth experience in the upcoming cosmic Ascension.

Thus, the book *The Earth Experiment and Our E.T. Progenitors, Conversations with Quan Yin Vol. 1* was born. As Quan Yin put it simply, it is a history of humanity that we have not been privy to, and she gave her perspective on how and why we got here and what lies ahead of us.

As she explained, we need to know our past in order to understand what challenges and opportunities we are being presented with now. And this past was very much interwoven with the influence and participation from E.T.s.

This book is a co-creation between Quan Yin, myself, and Daniel Scranton. I ask the questions, Quan Yin has all the wisdom, and Daniel acts as a bridge between Quan Yin and me to enable the conversation. Channeling is the ability to access higher realm consciousness and energy, and Quan Yin supports it by reaching down from the realm of the Ascended Masters. In a channeling state, Daniel converts Quan Yin's higher-dimensional energy into human thoughts and language for me, and he also turns my verbal questions and written content into higher-level energy for Quan Yin to answer and review.

Even if I assume the role of asking questions in this co-creation, I know I've been guided and nudged toward the knowledge that will be most relevant and beneficial to the readership of this book.

As an accomplished channeler, Daniel is key to conveying clear messages without bias or filtering. Daniel channels many higher-dimensional beings. He is also an energy healer, a Reiki master, and a spiritual teacher. He publishes a daily channeling from the Ascended Masters and the ninth-dimensional Arcturian Council. He offers many online classes and regular group channeling events, as well as one-on-one channeling and healing sessions.

For readers who are not familiar with Quan Yin (1), Quan Yin is an Ascended Master from the twelfth dimension, where many other Ascended Masters reside. Some of the familiar names include the Buddha, Yeshua, Lao Tzu, St. Germain, Mary Magdalene, Sanat Kumara, and Melchizedek. All Ascended Masters are enlightened master souls who have had experience in the entire Universe. They have incarnated as great teachers, sages, and healers in our world and many other worlds. They hold the highest vibration of love and wisdom in this Universe.

Many in the world would know Quan Yin as the Buddhist bodhisattva of infinite compassion and wisdom. A bodhisattva is an enlightened, higher-dimensional being who is on a path to Buddhahood. In Buddhism, Quan Yin is known to deliberately remain a bodhisattva until all sentient beings are set free from suffering in this physical realm. People pray to Quan Yin in times of distress, and they assiduously practice Quan Yin's teachings in search of enlightenment. The role in Buddhism is one of Master Quan Yin's emanations on Earth, and the most profoundly influential one.

Quan Yin is revered and worshiped throughout the Buddhist world. In many East Asian cultures, Quan Yin represents divine feminine energy in relieving people's pain and guiding them to a higher state of being. In Chinese culture specifically, Quan Yin's influence is not confined to Buddhism and is felt deeply in the intricate fabrics of Chinese society. This is even more the case in Tibet, where Quan Yin is known as Chenrezig in male form and Green Tara in female form, and honored not only in temples, but in the shrines at homes and shops. In the West, Quan Yin is not only well-known to Western Buddhists but also followed faithfully by those who recognize Quan Yin as an Ascended Master.

My experience speaking with Quan Yin through Daniel Scranton is one with an Ascended Master. Quan Yin gives enlightened teachings and guidance beyond the boundaries of religions or spiritual movements. She has shown me infinite love and patience.

It is with gratitude and elation that I receive the wisdom and guidance from Quan Yin and share it with anyone who has a desire to expand their heart and mind. The expansion is not just achieved by gaining precious new knowledge, but it is made possible by opening up to feelings and perceptions beyond cognitive faculties, such as deep memories about our past, intuition, synchronicity, and an affinity for the nonphysical realm.

We want to know ourselves not as limited, finite, vulnerable physical beings, but free, powerful, eternal souls who are partaking in an adventurous journey in this Universe. Earth just happens to be our current stop, but it is a significant stop. In the evolution of Earth and humanity, we need this awakening and expansion to break through to a much brighter future for all of us.

A pivotal moment to expand our minds and hearts can come from the knowing of E.T.s' consistent presence, seen or unseen, in humanity's evolution. This has been a well-kept secret. E.T.s have made great contributions as well as presenting obstacles on our evolutionary path. As our galactic family, E.T.s have brought both love and discord into our relationships. Knowing their past and present involvement with us, I feel deep warmth and affection towards the ones who will be landing on our planet in the foreseeable future. I look forward to their arrival to help us transform our world and to integrate us back into the galactic community where we belong.

There is much information in this book that does not easily fit into the system of thoughts and beliefs that are prevalent in most human societies. Some of the concepts may also lie outside of the intellectual framework of our physical reality. When new information or knowledge is contrary to existing thoughts and beliefs, it is natural to develop skepticism or simply confusion. Such knowledge can be challenging to process, but not resisting and opening to it has the potential to elevate us intellectually and spiritually.

Staying open-minded and focusing on what resonates is the best way to read the book. It is more important that we find ourselves inspired by the new ideas and knowledge that we're introduced to, rather than seeking full comprehension of them using our rational mind. What excites and enchants us quickly expands our minds and hearts, giving us access to a higher perspective. Our state of being as a soul and our state of being as a human are different, and it is our work now to take more of a soul's perspective of our current life and purpose on Earth.

As we expand and evolve, we'll acquire higher intelligence and awareness. Receiving new concepts from higher realms is like planting seeds within us to grow and blossom later. Once we uplift our consciousness to an advanced level, we can transmute a mindset of ingrained limitations and become empowered as creator beings to weave together the reality we prefer to experience with more love, peace, harmony, and unity. And we are approaching that possibility every day in the upcoming Ascension, a most anticipated and exciting cosmic event in our soul's journey. The journey to Ascension is ongoing, and it is addressed in part two of the Introduction.

Note

1) Quan Yin is alternatively known as Guanyin, Guan Yin, Kwan Yin, Avalokiteshvara in Sanskrit, and Chenrezig in Tibetan.

INTRODUCTION

WHAT IS ASCENSION?

My spiritual awakening was prompted by personal challenges in my life, but it was also sparked by an enthusiasm about "Ascension." Messages about Ascension are published daily on many websites and YouTube channels. These messages have resonated with me deeply and sent me down the path of exploring our existence as cosmic beings. The intellectual and spiritual quests expressed in this book are indeed very much anchored in the perspective of Ascension.

For those who are not familiar with the concept of Ascension, here is a brief introduction based on Quan Yin's teachings and other available information in the public domain. (Please see more resources below.)

Ascension is essentially a raising of consciousness and vibratory frequencies for planet Earth and all life forms on it. This upward movement will lift all on Earth to the fifth dimension from the third and fourth dimensions, where all life forms presently dwell. This is a gigantic undertaking set forth by the Universe, and it will result in a complete transformation of life on Earth as we know it.

A dimension in the Universe is expressed through the level of vibratory frequencies and its physical or nonphysical nature of existence. Lower vibrations are associated with denser physicality, and vice versa. What comes with the level of vibrations is also the level of consciousness of objects, life forms, and beings existing in a dimension. Higher vibration is synonymous with higher intelligence and consciousness, or awareness, which is invariably linked with love and spirituality.

Throughout human history, we have primarily existed in the third dimension, which is a dense physical plane of solid materiality and lower vibrations. Our spiritual connections, and specifically connections to God, Source, or our cosmic origins, were shrouded by this density. The capability to connect with the higher and nonphysical realms is fully natural in the fifth dimension and above in this Universe. On Earth, it is not as straightforward.

Some people deliberately preserve this ability and have kept their spiritual connection open since birth. Some people activate it later through diligent spiritual practices. But most will remain behind the veil of forgetfulness. It is a forgetfulness about our true identity as cosmic soul beings and not just humans in the flesh. This is by design in order to have the experience we wanted to have on Earth.

The third dimension is also noted for intensified duality or polarity with the co-existence of good and bad, love and hate, and light and darkness. It is a difficult environment to navigate because of the lack of knowingness and the disempowerment caused by not being able to feel the connections to higher realms. These challenges keep us in a lower level of consciousness and vibration. Our lives, as a result, can become very difficult at times.

According to Quan Yin, Earth shifted into the fourth dimension on December 21, 2012. We have been slowly but surely making progress toward the fifth dimension since then. Currently, our body, awareness, and beliefs, along with our systems and institutions, still reflect a third-dimensional legacy, but this is changing and changing rapidly.

In Ascension, we rise to the fifth-dimensional frequencies, which restore our connections to higher realms and bring forth more love, harmony, peace, joy, unity, abundance, and freedom. Those of us living on Earth will experience this Shift more and more consciously as we get closer to the point of Ascension. The Shift and Ascension refer to the same monumental changes that are coming upon us, and Quan Yin has used these terms interchangeably.

Physically, our body will transform from a carbon-based to a crystalline constitution that holds and conducts much more light energy. Spiritually, our human self will become our higher self, the part of us holding a higher perspective from the fifth dimension and guiding our human experience. We will reactivate our Divine connections and many innate capabilities such as telepathy, self-healing, teleportation, seeing into the future, accessing Universal knowledge, and communicating with our soul family and higher-dimensional beings. These capabilities are not always available or easily retrievable in a third or fourth-dimensional body and consciousness. As we raise our vibrations, we open ourselves to all kinds of potentials.

In addition, all systems, institutions, and our ways of living will evolve to reflect the fifth-dimensional consciousness, which emphasizes love and service to all. During this process of transformation, negativity and darkness on our planet will seem to intensify at times. This is because the higher frequency energy is sweeping up all that is incompatible with a higher consciousness in order for it to be rooted out. Many smooth changes and peaceful transitions can also be seen happening at the same time.

To many, this may sound too good to be true, and a fantasy that will never materialize. This notion is an exemplification of the third-dimensional belief system. Indeed, we have had a long string of hardships and disheartening experiences on Earth that still haunt us today. But it is time to open our hearts and embrace the higher truths being revealed to us. It is different this time. Our third and fourth-dimensional reincarnations are coming to an end. We are ready for the next level of experience. This is a plan by the Universe.

A continuous influx of cosmic energies has been entering Earth to facilitate these changes. These energies are being sent from higher realms and our sun, and other star systems, or they are engendered by eclipses or astronomical alignments. For us humans, a heart opening and awakening to love and truth is a good first step. We also need to heal our innermost and deepest wounds and traumas from eons of incarnating on this planet. We need to release the darker emotions before we can ascend.

Incredible Divine help from the nonphysical realm is available to us if we are open to it, merely by asking for it and allowing it to come to us. Another form of help comes from the extraterrestrials. Some E.T.s in the higher dimensions have been working with us energetically. In the foreseeable future, we can also expect to see physical E.T.s arriving peacefully and landing their ships around the globe. They will be here to support us through the Shift and to welcome us back to our galactic family.

We'll see negative energies receding both within us and on the planet. We will witness fundamental changes in every aspect of our lives. We can expect some disruptions as part of the change process, but many conversions will be bright and beautiful, such as medical innovations and the rendering of peace on our planet. This is a very challenging but very exciting time on planet Earth. It is a monumental milestone in our soul's journey. According to Quan Yin, Ascension is not a distant dream in the indefinite future, and we can look forward to seeing Ascension happen in our lifetime!

More and more people become believers and followers of Ascension every day. They are frequently referred to as lightworkers, light holders, or light bearers, as Ascension necessitates the continuous streaming of light onto Earth. But anyone is a lightworker if they hold love and compassion and a genuine intent to help self and others to rise to a higher consciousness and vibration. Religious or spiritual affiliations are not relevant here as they tend to be human-affixed labels. True love and spiritual connection reside in every single one of us and represent who and what we really are.

The information on Ascension is voluminous. Please see the resources below for a few examples to further explore this important subject of our time.

Resources for Ascension

"What is Ascension?" by Sandra Walter www.ascensionpath.com

"What is #Ascension?" by Christabel Zamor & Sandra Walter on YouTube

Council of Love (COL) Golden Library of channeled messages from the Divine Mother, Archangels, and Ascended Masters by Linda Dillon www.counciloflove.com

Ascension messages from Ascended Masters and 9D Arcturian Council by Daniel Scranton www.danielscranton.com

PART I

OUR COSMIC JOURNEY AND EARTH ADVENTURE

CHAPTER 1

OUR COSMIC ORIGIN AND JOURNEY

A perennial existential question for many on this planet is why we are here, living the life that we do. We tend to ask this question when we are challenged by misfortune or faced with trauma in life. But many would also ask this question innately while witnessing the beauty of nature and the wonders of life. The question can be the starting point leading to a quest for the meaning of life and a path of spirituality.

Religion may be the first stop to find an answer. At the risk of gross simplification, we can either believe that there is an omnipotent God that put us here, that there are many gods who control our destiny, or that we are trapped in reincarnation cycles until we clear all our karma. Outside of the context of religion, some people may feel fully in tune with nature and accept our life cycles as essentially part of nature. Then there are others who decide life is a mystery, and there is simply no higher purpose for our existence than coincidence or natural evolution if the person leans more toward rational thinking.

With or without an answer or religious belief, many brave individuals keep a strong faith and conviction that our life is meaningful, and we go through all experiences to find wisdom and self-growth. These individuals are able to face all that life has to offer with calm, acceptance, and appreciation. Societal or family acculturation doesn't usually help to forge this attitude toward life. Do these individuals have an inner voice or a knowing that sets the tone for how they experience their reality?

I am one of those who often think about and ask these existential questions. And as I mentioned in the Introduction, I have been privileged to have many of these questions answered by Master Quan Yin with the help of channeler Daniel Scranton. I have received extraordinary insights and guidance as to where we come from and why we are here on Earth. Life is not entirely a mystery, even if it has many mythical qualities to it.

I am a believer of Ascension, the upcoming Shift of the Earth and humanity from the third/fourth dimension to the fifth dimension. I read and listen to Ascension messages regularly. I came upon the idea of "starseeds" often and understood they are people who originated in other star systems and came here on a mission to assist humanity with Ascension. A casual question about the starseeds kicked off a new and inspiring series of conversations with Quan Yin about our cosmic origin and our collective purpose here.

Our Cosmic Origin and Purpose

I posed the question of starseeds to Quan Yin to learn more about the "special forces" from other stars and planets in service to Ascension on Earth. But Quan Yin's answer caught me by surprise.

Alison: There has been a fascination with starseeds in the lightworker community. Many lightworkers call themselves starseeds from other star systems on assignment here on Earth. Did they volunteer to come to Earth?

Quan Yin: Most humans on Earth are starseeds who have incarnated on other star systems. Those who claim to be starseeds are aware that they have had incarnations on other planets and star systems, not just on Earth, and are fascinated with E.T.s and other star systems.

Alison: Oh. Is it true that they are on Earth to help with the evolution of consciousness?

Quan Yin: It is true that many souls came to help with the evolution of consciousness on Earth. It is true that many, many souls incarnated. However, did they all come from another star system and have not had any Earth incarnations prior to this one? No.

Alison: Ahh, I see. So we have all been incarnating on Earth. Perhaps the starseeds are more consciously aware of their connections to other star systems and their intention to help with our consciousness evolution?

Quan Yin: Correct, but most on Earth are starseeds as you all came from different star systems.

Alison: Wow, I'm utterly amazed. If that's the case, have I been on another star system?

Quan Yin: You came from a different star system before coming to Earth. Plejades was the last one.

Alison: "The last one" means there were others. Which other star systems have I been on?

Quan Yin: You have been on Arcturus, Orion, Pleiades, Cassiopeia, and Antares (1) for your old or previous fifth-dimensional experiences.

Alison: I'm utterly amazed again that I have been in the fifth dimension and in so many star systems.

Quan Yin: There are a lot of different star systems in a galaxy.

Alison: So those star systems I've been on are in the fifth dimension, and I know Earth was in the third and is now in the fourth dimension. I hear about dimensions all the time, but I'm not sure if I fully understand what a dimension is.

Quan Yin: It is a manifestation of a vibration.

Alison: What does that really mean?

Quan Yin: It means the experiences that one could have in that dimensional plane would only be of a certain range of vibrations. For instance, you're not going to have abject fear, you're not going to stay in a state of despair once you get out of this dimensional plane you're on, and you move up to a higher dimensional plane where the lowest experiences vibrationally you could have would be boredom.

Alison: So, vibrations define different dimensions and offer specific experiences that we could have. Do vibrations come from energy?

Quan Yin: Yes, the Universe is made up of energy.

Alison: So a dimension is not a different physical space, but more an energetic sphere. We don't physically travel to it.

Quan Yin: You're just vibrating on a different frequency. When you go to a higher, less physical, or nonphysical dimension, you go to a higher plane of existence, a higher level of consciousness, and you have light bodies you're vibrating in.

Alison: How do we move around different dimensions?

Quan Yin: People can understand Source as the highest dimension, a nonphysical one, where everything exists as love, as energy, as thought, vibration, and feeling, but not hard solid matter. That's where you started. And if a being decides to move from Source into density, into dense physical forms, they have to go through a process of descension. They have to move through various dimensions that will eventually land them in a physical one, and each of those dimensions is slightly more dense, with more polarity.

Alison: I see the reference to Source all the time in my spiritual reading, and it is often used interchangeably with God or the Creator. Is that who Source is?

Quan Yin: People in the New Age use the word Source because the word God is associated with a man with the long beard, a white tunic or robe or something, sitting on a throne, very old, a king-like being who judges and says this is good, this is bad, you belong in my kingdom, and you do not. So we are moving away from that concept of God. Source, God really is *all that is*. *All that is* encompasses all of creation. So Source, God, and *all that is,* really is love. It is love expressing itself.

Alison: You mentioned that a move from Source into density is descension, a downward movement across the dimensions. When a being decides to do this, do they usually do this sequentially?

Quan Yin: Yes, to have experiences that each different dimension can offer.

Alison: So we go from a higher dimension to a lower one, and eventually into the physical realm with more density. I also hear people talking about the polarity or duality on Earth, which is about the two contradictory ends of something or a state of existence. Does the level of polarity increase in lower dimensions like density?

Quan Yin: Yes. You could use the idea of a pyramid or triangle to illustrate this. At the base of the triangle, the two points are farthest they will ever get from one another. That can be seen as the first dimension where there is the biggest extreme of polarity. And as you move up in the pyramid structure, you have those two points on those diagonal lines getting closer and closer together until they meet at the point where there is no separation. So the very tip of the pyramid is the Source energy dimension. And if you are building any structure, you can have the top of the pyramid be glass, whereas the bottom has to be stronger, denser, and more solid to be the foundation. So the pyramid structure itself is less dense and hard as you move up in it. You can use this type of analogy to think about the dimensions.

Alison: So the bottom of the pyramid represents lower dimensions, which are more dense, physical, polarized, separate from Source, and in lower vibrations. The tip represents Source and has all the qualities opposite to the bottom.

Quan Yin: Correct.

Alison: How were we born into existence before we started to move down the dimensions?

Quan Yin: You came from Source in the thirteenth dimension, the dimension of Source where there is only love and consciousness. After being born from Source, you initially existed in the highest dimensional plane, the twelfth dimension, in this Universe. Then you decided to go into physical form, meaning you had to gradually take on more and more density, descending through the dimensions while traveling through other star systems.

Alison: So when we were born, we didn't have a physical form. We were nonphysical, and we were just our souls.

Quan Yin: Correct.

Alison: What you've just said is breaking new ground for me. I'm curious as to why we were born in the first place.

Quan Yin: Originally, we are all a thought of Source. We are all that which Source decided one day to experience as Source's self. And we decided we would individuate in that sense and have different experiences in different realms. And each realm is a Universe, and each Universe has a different set of rules. It's a free will Universe or it's not a free will Universe; it's polarity, duality, or it's triality or quadrality. You have all kinds of different ways of imagining existence to be in all these Universes.

(Note: According to Wordnik.com, triality means "a union or junction of three… and it is a word invented after the model of duality." Wiktionary defines quadrality as referring to "a relationship between four objects.")

Alison: So when we entered the twelfth dimension, we entered the Universe we're in now, and we decided to descend to experience physicality.

Quan Yin: Yes.

Alison: Do we move back to Source after we complete descension into physical dimensions? And how do we do that?

Quan Yin: The feeling of love you have is the closest thing you have to knowing Source. That feeling is also telling you, "Move toward this, move toward this" because we are all going home to Source, and if you want to go home faster, you follow the yellow brick road, you follow that trail of love. And if you want to stay in the physical, you get caught up in the trappings of the physical, which are more about physical pleasure than they are about love, romantic love or love of an animal, love of a friend, or love of this thing you like to do expressing yourself in some way. So those are the paths that lead you closer and closer to the love that you truly are.

Alison: I see. It feels like we move away from pure love, and then we go back to it.

Quan Yin: Yes.

Alison: At the end of descension, we begin to ascend back to the Source dimension. This is the path we are on now, and we will hit a major milestone when we reach the fifth dimension?

Quan Yin: Correct.

Entering a Universe of Our Choice

Quan Yin said that we entered this Universe through the twelfth dimension. We had just left the Source dimension, and we were scoping this realm where our experiential journey would unfold. Quan Yin also said there are different Universes. Did we have a choice in which Universe to go into? How different are the rules for each Universe?

Alison: Did we consciously choose to go into a free-will or a no-free-will Universe?

Quan Yin: Yes.

Alison: What is an example of a life in a no-free-will Universe?

Quan Yin: Everything would have been laid out for the souls to have certain experiences, and they would have those experiences no matter what, and they would feel the feelings as a result of those experiences no matter what. So there is no choice. If a person wants to get to that Universe, they will be on a slightly different track.

Alison: Is my soul in a no-free-will Universe?

Quan Yin: Your soul is completely at this time in this free will Universe. It's more diverse, really. To go to another Universe and have different experiences is a big transition that you'll make someday.

Alison: Our Universe is a free will Universe and one of duality or polarity?

Quan Yin: Yes.

Alison: Is it correct that duality or polarity means two extremes, such as good and bad, light and darkness?

Quan Yin: Sometimes not as extremes, like right and left. They are not extremes. They're just opposites.

Alison: I see. What would be an example of triality or quadrality that you mentioned?

Quan Yin: Well, you'd have right and left, and a third choice in that equation would be straight. So you really do have triality if you're thinking about directions. You really do have it, but not everything can be expressed that way. For example, you have hot and cold, and you have warm. See, you really do have three right now, but the third choice in a triality would be much different than the other two choices that are opposites. So it's hard for you to imagine what would be different from hot and cold as a third opposite. It'll have to be something else that will also give you an opposite experience of temperature, which would be the third choice.

Alison: And it's not warm?

Quan Yin: It's a way of wrapping your mind around how there could be three choices, but the third choice would be something different, markedly different from hot or cold, and you can't imagine what that would be because you don't live in that type of Universe.

Alison: I see. That third choice just doesn't exist in our Universe, so it's not even possible to use any analogy from our world to describe that third temperature choice. Warm is something in between hot and cold, but this would need to be something completely different.

Quan Yin: Yes.

Alison: And same thing for quadrality?

Quan Yin: Yes, more possibilities and experiences.

Alison: Does duality exist throughout our Universe or is it more a phenomenon in the third dimension?

Quan Yin: No, everything in this Universe has a duality in it, even if it is so subtle, say in the twelfth dimension where you'll hardly be able to notice it. You'll not be able to notice so much of it as being the opposites or extremes. It'll be so subtle in the twelfth dimension that the opposites are almost unified, almost to the point that they're a singular option, which is pure unconditional love.

Alison: I see, because the twelfth dimension is near the tip of our dimensional pyramid where polarity disappears?

Quan Yin: Yes.

Alison: Bashar (2) said there is trinity in everything on Earth. Is trinity different from triality?

Quan Yin: There is the neutral point in trinity as we were discussing. There is warmth. There is neutral in addition to positive and negative.

Alison: What is the significance of that neutral point?

Quan Yin: It's your free will. It's the point from which you get to choose one or the other.

Alison: Ahh, I see.

Our Vibrations

Each dimension has a range of vibrations that offer different experiences and different consciousness levels. Each one of us vibrates within that range of vibrations in a dimension. Knowing we are on our way to ascend to the fifth dimension, I became intrigued by our vibratory level on Earth. How far do we have to go?

Alison: You've said that Earth moved from the third to the fourth dimension on 12/21/2012. What is the general range of frequencies or vibrations for humans on Earth right now?

(Note: This question was asked in mid-2024.)

Quan Yin: Around 80,000 cycles per second to 250,000 cycles per second.

Alison: That's a wide range. Is there a definitive point for the fifth dimension?

Quan Yin: Those who are hitting the 250,000 mark, but they aren't staying there.

Alison: They come back down and stay here to help out?

Quan Yin: Yes.

Alison: So right now, there are people whose vibrations have already reached the fifth-dimensional level, and then there are people vibrating at 80,000 cycles per second. Would that be a third-dimensional consciousness having third-dimensional experiences?

Quan Yin: That is a third-dimensional consciousness, yes.

Alison: What would be the vibrational range for the third dimension?

Quan Yin: 80,000 to 160,000 cycles per second.

Alison: Oh, okay. So there are still people in lower third-dimensional vibrations.

Quan Yin: Yes.

Alison: What about the fourth dimension?

Quan Yin: 160,000 to 250,000 cycles per second.

Alison: Is there any instrument available to measure human vibrations?

Quan Yin: There are many instruments that can use a variety of ways to measure an overall vibration, yes. But you're never going to get a fully accurate reading, and the fact that it's being read in that moment will alter the person's vibration.

Alison: Ahh, like measuring blood pressure. Are there people trying to measure human vibrations now?

Quan Yin: There are. There are all kinds of tools being used and all kinds of ways, and psychic ways as well, of people using their gifts to measure another's vibration.

Alison: So going back to our vibratory levels, what percentage of people on Earth are actually in fourth-dimensional vibrations?

Quan Yin: That's a good question. Sixty-five percent are fourth-dimensional.

Alison: And being fifth-dimensional would be a much smaller number, I suppose.

Quan Yin: Less than 1%.

Alison: Then the rest 35% are still third-dimensional.

Quan Yin: Yes, third-dimensional.

(Note: Earth being in the fourth dimension means it can accommodate vibrations from the first to the fourth dimensions.)

Alison: At least there are more people in the fourth-dimensional range than in the third. We are making progress.

Quan Yin: Yes.

Alison: In terms of the vibrations in higher dimensions, especially the twelfth dimension, I'm curious about it, but I get a feeling that's just not something we can measure or comprehend from fourth-dimensional cognition.

Quan Yin: Correct.

Alison: But is there an exponential increase of vibrations when we go from a physical to a nonphysical dimension?

Quan Yin: Yes.

Alison: And that's probably all we need to know at this point?

Quan Yin: Yes, just focus on raising your vibration by being in peace, joy, or love as much as possible.

Notes

1) Arcturus, Orion, Pleiades, Cassiopeia, and Antares are all star systems in the Milky Way galaxy. Based on what Quan Yin told me, I, as an aspect of my soul, have spent time in the fifth dimension in these star systems. These star systems can span across multiple dimensions above and below the fifth dimension, just like Earth supports dimensions one through four.

2) Bashar is an extraterrestrial being from E'sassani, a planet in the fifth dimension. He is a first contact specialist, a being trained to assist a less advanced civilization to evolve into higher consciousness. His messages have been channeled by Darryl Anka for close to four decades. More information can be found at https://www. bashar.org. Darryl Anka produced a documentary, *First Contact*, (https://www.youtube.com/watch?v=e-CoNQm5hjc) introducing Bashar and his teachings. He also published a channeled book on behalf of Bashar, *The Master of Limitation: An E.T.'s observations of Earth*, available on Amazon.

CHAPTER 2

✧

LAUNCHING THE DESCENSION JOURNEY

In the previous chapter, we learned that we came into existence because of a thought of Source to experience itself through its aspects, and we are all aspects of Source. We also learned that after being born from Source, we chose to enter this Universe of free will and duality. We are here on behalf of Source to experience this wonderful playground of twelve dimensions, which represent a wide range of vibratory and consciousness levels. Quan Yin told us that descension was a natural choice because we desired to experience physical reality. So, how did we plan for and embark on this exciting journey?

Beginning the Journey of Descension

Venturing into any journey requires a clear motif and some planning and mapping. The journey we are contemplating here is one through the cosmos, and there is a genuine process of conception that creates the ultimate experience of our choice.

Alison: We chose to be in this free-will, dualistic Universe for our soul's journey. How did it start after our initial entry?

Quan Yin: So in our Universe that we chose to come in, first to create it and then to play in it, we knew that to have a type of experience of growth, to have an experience of evolution, there would have to be a descension and an ascension. So we all started out in that twelfth dimension where we knew ourselves as some sort of collective, nonphysical consciousness.

(Note: A collective in higher dimensions is comprised of many souls who are closely connected and united as if it is one entity, one massive being of consciousness.)

Alison: Okay, we were not only nonphysical, but we were a collective consciousness. How did we as a collective approach descension in the first half of our cosmic journey?

Quan Yin: As you are descending from the 12th to the 11th to the 10th dimension, it's more of a time of anticipation to come to where you are now because you know you're descending, so you know you're going to be in physical form. So you're planning, and you're setting up those experiences, those planets, those moons, those suns, those lifetimes. You're planning what this galaxy would be about, what this planet would be about, what that star system would be about. You get excited about what costumes you are going to wear and what roles you are going to play, what imaginings you can partake in, and what adventures you will go on. And you begin descending and starting to have these experiences. This is all a story that's being told very linearly, even though it really does happen without any sense of time, a before and after.

Alison: It's surprising that descension in the higher realms is more about planning and anticipation of future lifetimes in the physical.

Quan Yin: It's creating a lot of experiences that you're going to have, just like you're planning a vacation. You think about where you are going to go, what you are going to do, what you are going to feel through the experience, and who you are getting together with in these different places. In many ways, the physical realm is like a vacation from the nonphysical. It's different from the dimension where we all started. It is pretty much something we create and plan for ourselves, so we get to experience what we want to.

We plan all that out even before we start incarnating into the first physical body. So it's not just in between lifetimes we are making these choices, but it's from the highest of high dimensions in the Universe that we began to explore what we were going to do.

Alison: What would be an example of us creating the experience we'll have in the physical from a higher realm?

Quan Yin: It's about deciding what it is that will give you the greatest opportunities to explore, that you want to explore as a soul in the physical.

Alison: That's planning work then.

Quan Yin: Yes.

Alison: Since we did so much work in the nonphysical to plan our lifetimes in the physical, is the focal point of descension really in the physical dimensions?

Quan Yin: Yes.

Alison: Is it because that's where we'd get more important experiences?

Quan Yin: It is because you want variety, you want experiences, and there are experiences you can only get in the physical, as you complete the journey to the physical.

Alison: Aside from planning for our lives in the physical, what types of experiences do we have in higher dimensions that serve us in our evolution?

Quan Yin: Teaching, helping those that are in the physical.

Alison: We are helping lower-dimensional beings while descending?

Quan Yin: Yes.

Alison: Anything else we're experiencing that's valuable to us in the higher realms?

Quan Yin: Opportunities to know the self in different ways.

Alison: Is this about self-expression in different vibrations?

Quan Yin: Yes.

Alison: You've said that we are primarily a collective consciousness in higher dimensions. Is our planning work done in more of a collective or individual way?

Quan Yin: It's always done in a collective way.

Alison: Then we individuate more when we reach the physical dimensions?

Quan Yin: Yes.

Alison: Are there many collective consciousnesses in the higher dimensions and each group will make their own decisions, and there isn't one set of decisions for all?

Quan Yin: Correct.

A Close-Up of Twelfth to Ninth Dimensions

Quan Yin told us that our work in the higher dimensions is planning for the physical lifetimes while teaching lower-dimensional beings and enjoying self-expression. Since each dimension is vibrationally different, the way we experience them should be different as well.

Alison: When we went from the twelfth to the eleventh to the tenth and the ninth dimension, what would be the major differences?

Quan Yin: There are a lot of Oversouls in the eleventh dimension, whereas there are more of the angelic and ascended master type of collectives in the twelfth dimension. And then in the tenth dimension, that's when you start to move into different star systems, where there are collectives of Arcturian groups, Pleiadians, and other advanced E.T. groups. And you also have in the ninth dimension different star system collectives like the ninth-dimensional Arcturian Council (that Daniel channels regularly).

(Note: According to Quan Yin, an Oversoul is a massive soul being and consciousness that oversees and nurtures a collective of individuated but connected souls and soul aspects, and it absorbs and integrates all experiences from the soul aspects traveling down the dimensions. There were originally 144,000 Oversouls in this Universe, and because the Universe has expanded, the number of Oversouls has reached around 300,000. We each belong to an Oversoul group. All soul aspects in all dimensions in this Universe connect back to their Oversouls in the eleventh dimension, consciously or unconsciously. Therefore, the Oversoul in the eleventh dimension can be considered a central hub for the soul's journey in the Universe.)

Alison: So, in the eleventh dimension, what are we experiencing as it relates to our Oversoul?

Quan Yin: You are part of your Oversoul. You know yourself more as the totality of who you are. You know yourself more as the Source energy aspect that you are, as your Oversoul. And yes, it's a different type of experience than what you're having now. You do feel yourself as a collective in the eleventh dimension. It's like you get instant access, instant benefit from all the different experiences that your Oversoul is having in all of these other dimensions. It's plugging yourself into the supercomputer and knowing yourself more as a collective consciousness that is being filled with more energy and more knowledge and more experience. It's a blissful experience to be one with your Oversoul.

Alison: Wow, it is a very different and amazing experience being part of an Oversoul, something we can only imagine in our dimension. And then, in the tenth dimension, what does it mean to be a collective for a particular star system?

Quan Yin: Well, it has a lot of meaning to it in the sense that you have custodians for the land there on Earth. You have beings there who decide that they are the ones who are going to care for that land, care for that particular piece of planet Earth. And if you think in terms of macro and micro, what the tenth-dimensional Arcturians are doing is at the macro level. They focus on their star system as a whole and how to best be the guardians of that star system through energetic alignments and transmissions. These are transmissions of knowledge and wisdom, but also of love and compassion, healing energy, and so on. On the other hand, what the ninth-dimensional Arcturians are doing is a microcosm when they are working with a particular group of all of you, as an example.

Alison: So that is the difference, macro and micro, between the tenth and the ninth-dimensional collectives.

Quan Yin: In the tenth, those councils and collectives are acting more like an overseer of that particular star system. And in the ninth, those collectives and councils are playing more of a role as helpers, teachers, and guides, and are more likely to be channeled.

Alison: Are the ninth-dimensional collectives and councils engaged more directly with groups of lower-dimensional beings?

Quan Yin: Yes.

Alison: I can see that the level and scope of oversight get more specific as the soul collectives move down the dimensions.

Quan Yin: Yes.

Alison: And in the ninth dimension, is it still purely nonphysical?

Quan Yin: Correct.

Alison: So, the ninth-dimensional Arcturian Council that Daniel channels regularly is in the nonphysical. Is it just their lineage that they named themselves after because they no longer live on a physical star or planet?

Quan Yin: Correct.

Alison: They can be anywhere they want once they're not physical?

Quan Yin: Exactly. Because there's nowhere to be when you're nonphysical. But it's easier for people to imagine them in the Arcturian system because they still hold a similar frequency that the Arcturian star system holds.

So in that sense, if you're wanting to connect with them, it's easier to do so when you're aiming yourself, or aiming your awareness towards the Arcturian system.

Alison: They are offering a lot of teaching and guidance for us through channeling here on Earth, and I assume elsewhere as well. Are they still very much aligned with the beings in the Arcturian system in the lower dimensions?

Quan Yin: Yes, in the lower dimensions, there are more soul family, soul group connections there. So the Arcturians are more likely to be reaching up to the Arcturian Council that Daniel channels, for instance, than any other group of beings throughout the galaxy would.

Alison: And this council is a collective.

Quan Yin: It is, yes.

Alison: Okay. And is the Pleiadian Council that Daniel also channels not a collective since they call themselves the Pleiadian Council of Seven?

Quan Yin: It's not really seven beings. It's more of a number that represents a vibration. In other words, they wanted to use a number system to identify who they are to avoid confusion with any other Pleiadian group that is being channeled. And the number seven has a particular vibration to it that they aligned with.

Alison: That's really interesting because I have always assumed that there are seven of them sitting on a council.

Quan Yin: They're actually all collectives, and it's much bigger than seven who comprise that collective if you think in terms of souls.

Alison: We do receive a lot of channeled messages from the ninth-dimensional collectives.

Quan Yin: Yes, you do, and they're close to where you are, closer than the tenth or the eleventh dimension. But there are also plenty of collectives in those dimensions who want to help.

Alison: Currently, we're also seeing much of that help and guidance coming from the twelfth-dimensional beings.

Quan Yin: Yes, and that's to give you an even higher perspective with beings that you can relate to, and in a lot of ways beings that routinely visit Earth, either in incarnations or visions or dreams, like the angels who are seen and felt and experienced by many different people.

Alison: I see. Is the guidance from the twelfth dimension abundant these days because of Ascension?

Quan Yin: They've always been, well, I should say we've always been involved from this dimensional plane, but there's more awareness of us now and the help that we're giving.

Alison: When we receive messages from the higher realms, especially the twelfth dimension, do we receive them from beings who have been on Earth, or not necessarily?

Quan Yin: Not necessarily.

Alison: Okay. So sometimes we heard messages that said, "We have walked in your shoes, we have walked on Earth." That would be coming from the Ascended Masters who have incarnated on Earth.

Quan Yin: Yes, indeed.

Alison: And so in terms of Ascended Masters, is each of you a collective?

Quan Yin: Yes.

Alison: Daniel also channels the 12D Creators. What would be the difference between 12D Creators and Ascended Masters?

Quan Yin: The difference is that Ascended Masters are identifiable. We are beings that you know of existing in this dimension, but not like the Creators who weren't a known group before Daniel here started channeling them, or Abraham who were also not a known group before Esther started channeling them (1). There are a lot of collectives in this twelfth dimension, in this highest realm of the Universe, and we are all assisting other dimensions, realms, and beings within this Universe.

Alison: I think I get it. The Ascended Masters are among the most evolved souls in the Universe, who have incarnated on Earth as master teachers and sages. And we know you through religion or history.

Quan Yin: It's a name you have for those humans who've lived those lives that have touched so many.

Alison: And we are talking about incarnate humans such as Yeshua, Buddha, Lao Tzu, yourself, Mary Magdalene, St Germain, and many others.

Quan Yin: Yes, indeed.

Alison: When my soul and other souls entered the twelfth dimension, were we all in a collective that played a role similar to that of the 12D Creators?

Quan Yin: Yes.

Alison: And there are many collectives in the twelfth dimension who would be Ascended Masters to beings on other planets and stars?

Quan Yin: Yes.

Alison: What would be the role of Archangels? How would it be different from the 12D Creators or Ascended Masters?

Quan Yin: It's a different point of focus. It's a different desire of experience. The Archangels are looking over all of creation and helping all of creation. The Creators are creating creation.

Alison: Would collectives like the Creators start a descension journey? Is that how they create creation?

Quan Yin: Aspects, soul aspects will. In other words, there will be the feeling that it's time now to go and play in the lower-dimensional planes from some of the beings amongst that collective. So there will always be a collective within the twelfth dimension that is nonphysical and is expressing as nonphysical, but some of those individuated consciousnesses within the collective will want to move on and into lower-dimensional planes, and they will make that choice to do so.

Alison: So my soul then is still part of a collective in the twelfth dimension. And aspects of my soul and of the souls within that collective are or have been traveling down the dimensions for creation and experience.

Quan Yin: That's correct.

Alison: And these soul aspects first move to the eleventh dimension as a collective, as an Oversoul collective, and these are the ones that continue to descend the dimensions?

Quan Yin: Yes.

Alison: Are the Archangels collectives too?

Quan Yin: Yes.

Alison: Okay. So this is going to sound funny, but are the Archangels the oldest of all souls who left the 13th dimension?

Quan Yin: Not the oldest, but the highest. In other words, there's no real difference in terms of beings that have been here in this Universe since the dawn of this Universe in terms of age. There are different experiences and choices of experience within this Universe that different souls have made. But you don't have to think in terms of time or age.

Alison: And the Archangels are the highest in the sense that they are closest to Source?

Quan Yin: Yes.

Alison: And their aspects do not journey down the dimensions.

Quan Yin: No, they do not.

Alison: You said once that when my soul entered the twelfth dimension, one soul aspect joined the Archangel Michael Collective and is still there.

Quan Yin: That's right.

Alison: That aspect of my soul wanted to have that experience there. Does that happen with other souls as well, that their soul aspects would go into different Archangel collectives if they desire that experience?

Quan Yin: Yes.

Alison: Okay. I see. That's fascinating. And then, once we are done descending from the twelfth to the ninth dimension, what is the eighth dimension going to be like?

Quan Yin: The eighth is a transitory dimension, from physical to nonphysical or from nonphysical to physical.

Alison: What does it mean to be in a transitory dimension between physical and nonphysical?

Quan Yin: Well, in the eighth dimension, both options of physicality and non-physicality are available. It depends on whether the being wants to be experiencing physicality or not, because in the eighth dimension, it's more of a choice of what you're experiencing. The eighth dimension exists because the transition from physical to nonphysical or vice versa is such a big transition. And so the dimension is used to aid souls in that enormous transitioning.

Alison: So in descension, it is a trial run for physicality but still offers an option to switch back to the nonphysical whenever desired?

Quan Yin: Yes.

Touching Down on the First Physical Dimension

If the primary purpose of descension is to experience physical reality, we begin to fulfill that promise when we leave the eighth dimension and go into the seventh dimension.

Alison: While descending, which dimension is considered the first dimension to have a full physical experience?

Quan Yin: If you come down from the nonphysical, the first physical dimension is the seventh. In fact, the seventh dimension is the first place a being will experience full physicality when descending, and it is the last place a being will experience physicality when ascending.

Alison: Is the seventh dimension all physical?

Quan Yin: There are, of course, different vibratory levels within each dimension. So in the seventh dimension, there are physical and nonphysical levels determined by the level of vibration. There are realms within a dimension as well, such as a star system, which souls incarnate into or project their energy to. And so if you're incarnating on a planet with a sun and a moon, then yes, it's in the seventh dimension, and you're in a realm where there's physicality. And in certain realms, it'll be all nonphysical. But you can also experience both physical and nonphysical in certain realms in the seventh dimension.

Alison: I see. We are given options for gradual transitioning in the seventh dimension. Is the physical experience more real in the seventh compared with the eighth?

Quan Yin: At a certain point in the seventh dimension, if you're descending, it's going to be not more real, but you're going to be dealing with solid objects. Now, you're still seventh-dimensional, so you can still instantly manifest what you want to. So it's very different from your current experience of physical reality. But it is physical reality.

Alison: So, I assume instant manifestation comes from being in a higher vibration, much higher than where we are. Are all the beings immortal in the seventh dimension, even in the physical realms?

Quan Yin: Yes.

Alison: I guess we must still have a strong connection with Source there. We are immortal and we can choose willfully between physical and nonphysical realities.

Quan Yin: Yes, indeed.

Alison: But is it more likely that we'll start out being nonphysical and then move towards being physical in the seventh dimension?

Quan Yin: If you're descending, yes, you would start out in the seventh still as nonphysical and then quasi-physical and then physical.

Alison: What else characterizes our experience in the seventh dimension?

Quan Yin: In the seventh dimension, you know yourself as a collective, and you don't forget you're a collective. You are part of a collective consciousness even if you can have a physical body. As people mentioned, there is really a "seventh heaven". It is really the best of both worlds because you're not forgetting who and what you are, but you still get to have those physical experiences that you all like to have.

Alison: Do we have a very different body in the seventh dimension than what we have now?

Quan Yin: It doesn't have to be. A soul can choose humanoid, can choose avian, can choose aquatic, can choose to be an orb, can choose to be whatever it wants.

Alison: It seems like we can choose to be in solid form, which is less dense than lower dimensions but still solid. We can live on land or in the air, or water, but we can also be fluid and flexible like an orb.

Quan Yin: You can choose whatever you want.

Alison: And we can manifest different bodies and jump into different lives since we don't experience death?

Quan Yin: Correct.

Alison: So once we are in the seventh, we are not doing the practice runs for experiencing physicality like we were in the eighth. It is now our objective to create experience in the physical realm.

Quan Yin: That's what it is. It's more of a choice that you continually make to be physically expressed and expressing with physical objects.

Setting Foot on the Fifth Dimension

So we have our first full physical expression in the seventh dimension while descending. With a higher vibration, we still connect to the nonphysical realm, are immortal, and can manifest our physical form and reality instantaneously.

The fifth dimension would be the next major destination and landmark in our descension journey. It is an entirely physical dimension where we are presented with many firsts in our physical experience, some fun and exciting, and others quite disagreeable. It's all a matter of perspective, as "good and bad" are subjective and all part of the experience in the physical. With this descension, we begin to operate less as a collective, and we lower our vibrations further. The fifth dimension is a higher version of the third dimension. This is where we commence some of the same challenges that we carry into the third dimension.

Alison: What happens as we go into the sixth and fifth dimensions? I mean, what do our souls have in mind for the incarnate beings in those dimensions?

Quan Yin: You start to individuate more, you start to have more of a personal type of agenda, you start to think about what you're going to do when you are completely individuated. You still know you're part of that collective consciousness, but you start to feel more like you have your own ideas, your own agenda, things that you want to explore that are perhaps different from what other people in the collective consciousness where you are a part of want to explore. So you start to create the idea of separation, separate agenda and focal points, and themes you want to explore. And you feel a little denser, a little heavier in your bodies as well.

It's not a huge difference from the seventh to the sixth, because the sixth is also a transitory dimension. Now from the sixth to the fifth when you were descending, that was a large descension because in the fifth, of course, you had the Orion Wars, you had beings really wanting to get into the experience of themselves, being individuated and breaking away from the collective knowing and collective consciousness.

(Note: The Orion Wars were an intergalactic war waged by beings on the Orion Constellation against other star systems in the fifth dimension millions of years ago. According to Quan Yin, it was the biggest war that happened in our galaxy, and it had a monumental impact on the evolution of our collective consciousness. Not surprisingly, it was also the true story and inspiration behind the Star Wars movie series.)

Alison: So, separation is separation from Source and separation from each other. Were the Orion Wars a watershed event?

Quan Yin: There was a lowering of consciousness that occurred during the Orion Wars in this galaxy, which of course affected the entire Universe. So the Orion Wars helped to descend the consciousness that was fifth-dimensional into a fourth-dimensional state of really having this relationship to time and space that's different.

Alison: Was it in the fifth dimension that we experienced wars for the first time?

Quan Yin: Yes.

Alison: When was the first time we had a sense of time during our descension?

Quan Yin: In the old fifth dimension.

(Note: The old fifth dimension means the fifth dimension that we incarnated into and experienced in our descension journey.)

Alison: Was time in the fifth dimension more fluid compared with what we have now?

Quan Yin: Actually, it's very similar to what you have now.

Alison: Was it measured in the same way?

Quan Yin: The fifth dimension you've moved from had a similar keeping of time to what you have now.

Alison: Did we have a year as a unit of time there?

Quan Yin: You did, because you still had planets revolving around a star like the sun.

Alison: Is time moving at a different speed there? Is one year in the previous fifth dimension longer in our dimension?

Quan Yin: That's right.

Alison: So it is moving faster. Since we had time in the fifth dimension, did we start to experience death?

Quan Yin: Yes, there was a death experience in the fifth dimension that was ultimately changed by the Orion Wars as well. People were cut down much younger by the weapons being used. So there was more awareness of one's mortality because you could be killed at any age by these weapons that were created by technology.

Alison: How long could we have lived in the previous fifth dimension? What was the average lifespan for an incarnate soul in the fifth dimension?

Quan Yin: It really depends on the star system that you're talking about and whether there is a war going on. The Orion Wars cut the average lifespan considerably, but in a peaceful star system where there's no war going on in the fifth dimension, the average lifespan was around 400 years.

Alison: Is that fifth-dimensional or third-dimensional time?

Quan Yin: In a third-dimensional time, in the way that you look at it right now, yes.

Alison: What is the conversion between fifth-dimensional and third-dimensional time?

Quan Yin: About 3.5 times.

Alison: I see. So, a longevity of 400 years in third-dimensional time would equal about 114 years in old fifth-dimensional time. Did we choose to die when we felt we were done with a lifetime, or was it pre-determined for us in the fifth dimension?

Quan Yin: There was more of a feeling of being done with a life. There was more of an understanding of a death experience and why that was necessary. But not everyone chose their death at that time. Some were more conscious than others around it. Some thought, because they could still have this type of thought, that they were needed, and there was more for them to do. So some really had to be nudged out of their body, while others did feel a sense of completion and desire to move on to the next experience.

Alison: Did we have karma in the old fifth dimension?

Quan Yin: Yes.

Alison: I see. It started in the fifth. Did we experience our lives and ourselves in the fifth dimension similarly to the way we do here on Earth?

Quan Yin: Yes, but people had more awareness of their chakras, more awareness of their soul, more awareness of who they really are as Source energy beings. That allowed them to tap more into their gifts and abilities.

Alison: Did that ability to tap into these gifts and abilities change during our tenure in the fifth dimension?

Quan Yin: Yes, it was a use of technology to take the beings away from the inner technology capabilities that they had access to all the time. And the reliance on technology and seeing technology as the most important aspect of life is what gradually took people away from the inner knowing of who they are and their ability to create and manifest.

Alison: So the fifth dimension is indeed between the seventh and third dimensions. We kept certain spiritual connections there, but became mortal and moved away from a collective consciousness. The Orion Wars introduced premature deaths and physical vulnerability, and technology dulled our spiritual abilities. Our consciousness was lowered, and we then continued on this path into the fourth and third dimensions.

Quan Yin: Right.

Alison: How long did we generally spend in the fifth dimension?

Quan Yin: It varies from soul to soul.

Alison: If I'd been on five star systems in the fifth dimension, it must have been a long time for me, especially if time needs to be multiplied by 3.5 to equal Earth time.

Quan Yin: Yes.

(Note: In Chapter One, Quan Yin told me I had lived in the Pleiades, Arcturus, Orion, Cassiopeia, and Antara star systems.)

Alison: I wanted to go back to the topic of individuated consciousness. It seemed individuation took a giant leap in the fifth dimension, and a sense of separation and experience of wars were two of the results. How did we begin our individuated consciousness back in the twelfth dimension?

Quan Yin: Individuated, yes, but not as an individual, still as a collective, a much larger being than you think of yourself as an individual.

Alison: So that more clearly individuated consciousness doesn't come about until we hit the fifth dimension? Or is it just more concrete in the fifth dimension?

Quan Yin: It becomes much more concrete when you have a physical body. But it's a gradual sense of wanting to know yourself more as a singular being that began really at that inception point into the Universe. It then continues in its continuation of that experience of not being your full and whole self as Source, that you are only one perspective of Source, one lens through which Source is seeing Source's self.

Passing Through the Fourth Dimension

The fourth dimension was another transitional dimension before we descended into the third dimension. It is also currently a transitional stop before we ascend to the fifth dimension. It is where we are now.

Alison: You said the other day that by descending to the fourth dimension, we began to have a different relationship to time and space. Could you say more about that?

Quan Yin: Fourth dimension is really when you get into the idea of mortality, and start to think about it in terms of how much longer do I have, how much more do I want to do here, am I going to live for this amount of time or that amount of time? So yes, that becomes more of an awareness of the consciousness, because you did have death in the fifth dimension, but it wasn't as feared as it is in the third and in the fourth. That just shows you how more people are stressed about time and mortality in the third and fourth dimension, because again, you're separating yourself from the truth of who you are as eternal beings to have all these gifts and abilities to do what you want with your physical body.

This separation started in the fifth dimension, but in the fourth, people stopped recognizing they had gifts, and they started to feel they had to work toward something, like they had to use physicality, gadgets, and technology to get things done. People started to get lazier and not want to go within to use their ability to teleport, because it takes more time to focus oneself into that experience. So then machines were created to do it, so people didn't have to do as much focusing and meditating on being in a different location. You have no doubt seen technology in the Star Trek series being used to teleport bodies to different locations. People started to use that type of technology rather than focusing and meditating because it was faster and easier.

Alison: I didn't realize teleportation on Star Trek was a technology. I guess that's why Captain Kirk always said, "Beam me up, Scotty."

Quan Yin: It is a technology, yes. Just like time travel can be accomplished through the use of a machine rather than through the use of one's consciousness.

Alison: But we could have done teleportation or time travel on our own, using our innate capability?

Quan Yin: Yes, you have done it, but as you've descended, what you've also done is you've relied more on technology than on the inner abilities, the powers that you have within you.

Alison: Where did we spend our time in the fourth dimension?

Quan Yin: In other star systems. The fourth dimension is all about transition. You were transitioning to the third. But you were doing so in other planets and other star systems, moving from the fifth to the fourth, ready to come to the Earth for the third-dimensional experiences you'd have there.

Alison: What is the positive highlight of this transitional experience in the fourth?

Quan Yin: The highlight is really coming to that knowing of who you really are and making that decision to have a different experience of who you really are in another dimension, whether it's a higher or lower dimension. As you descend to the fourth, you realize there is a lot to gain through continuing descension, and you get excited about the forgetting (of who you are as an eternal soul), because it's like you'll get to know that and experience everything again for the first time when you start ascending the dimensions, and you know that.

Alison: I see. That's the soul-level experience we get to have from these incarnations. And we are getting ready for the big drama of remembering who we really are before heading back to the fifth dimension.

Quan Yin: Right.

Creating Exciting Adventures in the Physical

As we've learned, being in the physical dimension is considered a "vacation" from the nonphysical by our souls. Physicality is not the norm for a soul, and it wants to take advantage of the opportunity to have a kaleidoscope of experiences.

Alison: What is really the allure of the physical realm in the experiences it offers?

Quan Yin: Once you get to a physical realm, you realize there is this possibility for an exciting adventure, and there is this possibility for creation, and I can know myself in this way and that way, and you basically learn through doing and learn through experiencing all that you can become and all that you can experience.

Alison: So it's about different possibilities. According to Bashar, the ability to experience movement and change in a linear way helps us to directly experience creation, and it is a major reason to be in the physical.

Quan Yin: It's all part of it.

Alison: Adventure and creation are high points in the physical realm. Do we not get these in higher dimensions?

Quan Yin: It is because of the way you experience them differently with different feelings. It's not so much that the experiences will vary so greatly in terms of the physicality, but in terms of the emotionality and the thoughts. The thoughts that you think will be markedly different in the third dimension.

Alison: Such different thoughts and emotions start in the seventh dimension and become more accentuated as we descend.

Quan Yin: Yes.

Alison: But the fifth, fourth, and third dimensions also offer serious challenges as part of the adventures. I feel it is the soul's perspective that these are exciting adventures because most humans would think of an exciting adventure as a fun, exotic excursion with no pain.

Quan Yin: Correct.

Alison: Are the fifth, fourth, and third dimensions the toughest dimensions in that regard?

Quan Yin: Yes, they are.

How Long Has It Been for Us to Get to Where We Are?

As physical beings, we do have a finite lifetime in each incarnation. But as souls, we are timeless and eternal. We have descended to the physical, and we are now at the bottom portion of the imagined pyramid. How long has it been since we made our entrance into the twelfth dimension in this Universe? Quan Yin has told us that time only starts to exist in the fifth dimension, but is there a way to gauge the length of this journey so far?

Alison: How long has it been for our souls to move from the twelfth dimension to where we are now on Earth?

Quan Yin: Billions of years.

Alison: Wow! Since we started preparing for lower dimensions while in higher dimensions, have we stayed much longer in the physical dimensions even if time is the wrong word to use here?

Quan Yin: Time is experienced differently, so you don't really have a way of counting time in the nonphysical.

Alison: You said it took billions of years for us to descend from the twelfth dimension to where we are now. Was it approximating Earth years to account for all the experiences we have had, and perhaps we have had more experiences in the lower dimensions proportionately?

Quan Yin: Certainly it feels that way, doesn't it? It's your experience of time that's important here because again, time doesn't really exist, and everything really is simultaneous. I understand why you are asking the question, but really, it's not a relevant question because it is your experience of time that matters.

Alison: So, time is something we experience in the lower dimensions starting in the fifth, and it doesn't exist independently in this Universe. When I was in higher realms, I wouldn't know or experience time.?

Quan Yin: You would know everything is happening now, and that's how you would experience everything. You wouldn't be saying yesterday, today, tomorrow, last year in a nonphysical realm. The Universe is billions of years old. That has to be the answer to that question because it is billions of years old, and because you were at the creation of the Universe.

Alison: I'm actually not sure if I understand what that means.

Quan Yin: There is a creation point, there is an imagining of this Universe that brings it into its viability as a place to explore within Source. And that's the birthing of the Universe as it is today. It has changed since it first came into being, through our experiencing of it, but that is certainly something that came into existence with a thought.

Alison: There was a starting point of the Universe, and much has happened, much has been experienced, and we have an equivalent to the human years of time. In fact, that's what our scientists have estimated as well (2).

Quan Yin: Yes, it's the equivalent.

Notes

1) Abraham is a twelfth dimensional collective channeled by Esther Hicks. Their website is www.abraham-hicks.com.
2) According to NASA, the Universe is nearly 14 billion years old. Please search "NASA, age of the universe."

CHAPTER 3

∞

DECIDING TO COME
TO EARTH

Knowing our identity as eternal souls traversing this Universe of our choice invokes a sense of awe. When I look up at the night sky and see stars and constellations, I realize they really aren't that far away. They aren't unreachable and a mystery that can never be solved. They have been our home, just like Earth is home to us now.

In the descension journey, we progressed steadily to the physical realm, and ultimately the lowest dimensions of this Universe. We had envisioned our lives in physical realities while still in the higher dimensions. There are many stars and planets in the Universe that offer the experience of lower dimensions. So why Earth? It is the only habitable planet in the solar system for our form, and it is surely the most beautiful one seen from space. But life on Earth is also complicated and challenging, as we all bear witness to it. It stretches us to many extremes from happiness to pain, excitement to fear, and hope to despair. Why did we choose to come here? How is our purpose served by this blue planet?

So I asked Quan Yin why we decided to come to Earth. And again, I received a dynamite answer. Quan Yin described an ancient Earth where the "Earth Experiment" was put in place and set in motion. This piece of antiquated history sheds light on the Earth experience that attracted us here. It will also prove to be a powerful affirmation of our undeniable galactic heritage.

What's So Special About Earth?

So the first question to ask is obviously how Earth stood out in the choice of planets we had for the third-dimensional experience. The answers blew my mind. We were not looking for an easy ride at all.

Alison: How did we decide to come to Earth?

Quan Yin: Well, you see the opportunity laid out for you there, and you choose it. You choose to squeeze yourself down, lower your vibration down to being in a tiny physical body. As a soul, of course, you're choosing lots of experiences simultaneously. It's just like saying "I'm going to Vienna" for you as a soul. It's not like that vacation to Vienna is so important that you must take that vacation or else, because that's the way people tend to look at this, that you're on a mission, you have to go, there is so much at stake, etc. As a soul, you don't look at it in that way at all. You simply wanted the experiences you could only have on Earth.

Alison: What is the opportunity and experience that drew us to Earth?

Quan Yin: Separation from Source, from each other, emotion, creativity, humor, diversity. These are some of the main components that set it apart from the other planets where you have the ability to explore all of these aspects.

Alison: If I look at this list, separation is a big one because you mentioned once that the feeling of separation becomes complete in the third dimension. And the feeling of separation is really the root cause of our fear, vulnerability, or lack of self-love. The rest of the list could be positive or negative in its effect. Let's take emotion as an example. What is the opportunity to experience emotion here that's so different from the other planets?

Quan Yin: You won't be able to experience emotions in exactly the same way on any other planet as you experience them on Earth, because they are unique to the Earth experience, the emotions that you have.

Alison: No other planets or stars can offer the same emotions?

Quan Yin: Not exactly the same, not exactly the way you would experience those emotions. But of course, there is fear, hate, anger, etc. throughout the galaxy, and they can all be experienced the way they are experienced on those worlds, just like gravity is going to be different in each and every place. Even if it's similar from one planet to another, it'll still be slightly different.

Alison: Is it the range or the intensity of emotions on Earth that is unique?

Quan Yin: Both.

Alison: Ahh, I see. In terms of the range of emotions, are there any emotions that are only available on Earth, or is it just that Earth has them all?

Quan Yin: Earth has them all and has them in greater intensity.

Alison: We had emotions in the fifth dimension too, but not in the same intensity?

Quan Yin: Correct.

Alison: What are the most intense and difficult emotions we face on Earth?

Quan Yin: Abject fear and despair.

Alison: And we can't experience these emotions in the same way on other worlds?

Quan Yin: Not in the same intensity as on Earth. Of course, in this Universe of duality, in order to have ecstasy, you also have to have despair. So really, the height of ecstasy on the other end of the spectrum is very fleeting usually, whereas those experiences on Earth that you have about fear and despair can be much drawn out in terms of how long you feel them for.

Alison: So the most extreme emotions on Earth are fear and despair on one end of the spectrum and ecstasy on the other.

Quan Yin: Of course there is fear and ecstasy in other parts of the Universe, but what I said was abject fear and despair because I'm talking about extremes now, extreme feelings of them that can only be felt in a very polarized experience of reality.

Alison: So this intensity applies across the entire spectrum of emotions. It's just these two extremes are off-the-charts difficult, and they are only available on Earth?

Quan Yin: Yes, indeed. But most emotions are temporary, and they are meant to be temporary.

Alison: But on Earth, difficult emotions can last a long time?

Quan Yin: They last for a lot longer for a variety of reasons. There is a lot there for you to explore. There are a lot of themes that souls want to experience and explore there on Earth. So the only way to do that is to give themselves the opportunity to really feel such strong emotions.

Alison: Sometimes the emotions continue for way too long and become detrimental?

Quan Yin: The problem is that the emotions are not allowed by the human being who finds them to be so off-putting. It's like they're on fire. They try to put the fire out as quickly as possible, rather than being curious about the feeling of it and the knowledge in it and seeing it as part of the journey and accepting it and embracing it, which is what we teach you to do when you come to us. And when I say us, I mean all the beings that are teachers. You say to us, "I've had this for a long time, and I don't know why, but it's a physical, mental, emotional condition." And usually, it's the same answer. "You haven't been feeling the emotion, and it's the frustrating side of you that has to get louder and to present itself in a different way to get your attention."

Alison: So it's the resistance and not feeling the emotion fully?

Quan Yin: Yes, not feeling it, or suppressing it, or numbing yourself to it or denying its existence. Any of the above will create the problem in the body. Then the person will have to deal with it one way or another.

Alison: I see. Does intense polarity mean that if we are happy, we can be wildly happy but not for very long?

Quan Yin: Usually you are wildly happy because of something, usually because you've been reunited with someone, you're falling in love, you've won a lot of money, you achieved a goal that has been something you've worked on for 10 or 20 years, but usually conditional and not lasting. The very good-feeling emotions, which you'd like to have lasting longer, the reason they don't last is because they are conditional. They are based on some set of circumstances that you can't maintain, or you get what's called habituated in psychology to that experience in the sense that now it doesn't have the same emotional impact on you anymore because you've experienced it so many times.

Alison: I guess that means we need a new set of circumstances to find happiness again. So it works very differently on the two ends of the spectrum, and this makes it even tougher for us. We can't maintain our happiness for long, but we tend to be soaked in our fear or sorrow for an extended period of time.

Quan Yin: They work in very different ways, yes. Now eventually the person does get habituated to the lower frequency emotions as well. Even though they can still think of the death of a loved one 10 years later and it can still hurt, it's not hurting quite as much as it did the moment they lost that person.

Alison: Is that a good thing?

Quan Yin: In a way it's a process thing. It's the way the person has processed the emotion to an extent, not to the fullest extent that they could, but they processed it enough so it doesn't hit so hard. They also realized after 10 years that life does go on, that they do still get to experience comfort sometimes, and joy sometimes, and peace sometimes, and so it's not the end of the world experience that they felt at that moment. And they realized that intellectually and experientially as well.

Alison: So we knew how tough the emotional game would be on Earth, and we willingly came for the experience?

Quan Yin: Yes.

Alison: What about the diversity that you mentioned? Is it diversity about the racial, ethnic, cultural varieties and the number of species on the planet, or is it more about the experiences we get to have, physical, mental, or emotional?

Quan Yin: Yes both.

Alison: I see. I know such diversity adds to our unique experience. What about humor? Is this a way to offset the heaviness of our emotions?

Quan Yin: Yes, it's everywhere.

Alison: Could you say more about the opportunities of creativity on Earth?

Quan Yin: You have specific experiences that you can have there, given the unique variety of beings on Earth. You have specific emotions that you would only feel on Earth based on the unique mix of energies and DNA and all that exists on Earth at this time. And of course, when you can have unique experiences and unique expressions brought by emotions, you can have unique creations.

Alison: We think of creativity often as artistic work, or a major invention or solution to a big problem. Does the creativity you're referring to have a broader definition?

Quan Yin: So it may just be a problem in your life that you're experiencing, but you come up with a unique creative solution to the problem, and you've had that experience of creativity as a soul.

Alison: I see. How about intellectual work such as philosophies, scientific and economic theories, and many isms of political or social movements? They all represented the human desire to understand our world, our existence, and ourselves. Even if some are just thoughts and may never lead anywhere, they can still be an expression of creativity?

Quan Yin: Yes.

Alison: You talked about diversity and its challenges, and how it would lead to tolerance and acceptance. How does that factor into the creativity concept?

Quan Yin: Well, they are necessary steps because if you're not in acceptance, allowing, tolerance, whatever you want to call it, then you're in resistance. And when you're in resistance, you cannot receive the download that's required for the creativity to emerge.

Alison: Ahh, I see. Resistance stops the flow of intuition. And thus, in the broadest sense, when we make choices and decisions, we create. Depending on what choices are made, we can have great creations or nothing or even dreadful creations. And that's how unique experiences and expressions become a canvas for unique creations?

Quan Yin: Yes indeed.

Polarization and Darkness

Duality or polarity tests our emotional capacity, and it can amplify darkness as well. People can create darkness and/or suffer from darkness. We can be tempted to make bad choices, and we can also be inflicted with the bad choices others make. Our reactions to these choices determine how our reality is experienced. In the darker moments of polarization, we can find ourselves in an abyss: scared, depressed, and hurting. We can also reach a high point where we feel powerful, winning, and self-gratified, but intensely empty or unloved inside.

As bad as any situation can be, whether we are mistreated or we mistreat others, it can always serve a purpose. We can always rise above darkness and reach for light. It is like a rubber band effect. When we are stretched to the max, we bounce the farthest and we create and grow the most. It feels like another "Earth special." I explored this rationale with Quan Yin.

Alison: If our Universe is a Universe of duality, all the planets would have duality built into their energy fields. Is the pull of duality or polarity on Earth much stronger than on other planets?

Quan Yin: It's able to be explored to a greater extent.

Alison: In that sense, does our creation on Earth include a highly polarized world, meaning the devolution toward darkness was a distinct possibility and we chose to participate in it?

Quan Yin: Yes.

Alison: In order for us to participate in darkness, we have to forget where we come from and who we really are. So feeling separate from Source makes this experience on Earth possible.

Quan Yin: Yes.

Alison: Is the forgetting set up in our DNA?

Quan Yin: Yes, it is. It is encoded.

Alison: So we were born into a body with this handicap, and then we couldn't communicate, feel, or connect with the spiritual realm?

Quan Yin: Well, you have over the years because you have many texts in religion and in stories about other people making those connections. So it's possible to do, but it's not as widely experienced or accepted as it would be, say, in the Arcturian system from the very beginning.

Alison: I see. The handicap is there but it doesn't mean we can't overcome it?

Quan Yin: Yes, it's a very necessary part of the evolution of your consciousness that the soul takes on. It says, "I'll plunge into this reality where I will certainly be forgetting who and what I really am because I can only have this set of experiences while doing that because the soul never forgets who and what it is." The soul is choosing to have the experience through an incarnate human. It is just having the experience without the veil that you have of forgetfulness.

Alison: Our soul is having the experience through us, but without our handicap of amnesia. They know what the game is, but we in the body only see and feel what happens in the physical.

Quan Yin: Yes.

Alison: With amnesia, did we as incarnate humans contribute to how far the pendulum could swing to the darker side, just like the emotions we experience?

Quan Yin: It wasn't the original intention for humans to become this polarized and to go this far down the separation paradigm.

Alison: Ahh, I see. So we carried polarization to more of an extreme?

Quan Yin: You took it further and you developed the ego to such an extent that now you can see how much the ego is running rampant on planet Earth as the dominant force of what controls everything.

Alison: Oh my goodness. I guess we need to see the fallacy of our ego expansion. We need to find our way back to love and light. But it's quite a treacherous path to walk, given how divided we are.

Quan Yin: Yes.

Alison: We not only endure both physical and emotional pains in the Earth classroom, but we also get to make choices between good and evil, and between our heart and our egotistical mind?

Quan Yin: Yes.

Alison: Do we evolve and expand faster this way? We like challenges, and it's rewarding here from that perspective.

Quan Yin: Correct.

The Earth Experiment

If Earth offers a bootcamp experience, so to speak, it must have been by design. As Quan Yin told me many times, there is really nothing random in the Universe. "Earth Experiment" was a term I had come across before. So I asked Quan Yin what made Earth a planet of such captivating diversity but also monstrous extremity.

Alison: How did this special classroom of Earth come into existence? In some channelings, I've seen the reference to Earth as the Earth Experiment. What is the Earth Experiment?

Quan Yin: Well, there is a desire on the part of other life forms to know themselves more as Source. And one of the ways in which they do that is by playing God so to speak, by seeing if they can create a world with life forms on that world and act as the guides to those life forms and see if they can create a balance within the ecosystem where life can thrive with ease on that planet, can raise their consciousnesses, and can devolve and descend.

So that's the real experiment of Earth, which is to have E.T. beings come and terraform the planet and make it a place that the humanoids would be able to evolve and grow and handle all the variety and all the differences that have emerged between the human races.

And the animals and humans getting along has been a long story process in history as well, having animals that you hunt and eat, and having animals that hunt and eat you. It is a big lesson and journey for the consciousness to be able to handle there and grow from. So you have all the different insects and plant life and animal life and sea life, and having to make all that work and be harmonized, that has been the experiment, which really is how you all are going to get along.

Humans all have these different cultures and different races, and are they going to be able to strike a balance with nature, or are they going to go too far with the technology that they are given and cut down too many trees and so on? So you've been getting help from the E.T. beings, you've been getting upgrades from them, and you had your DNA manipulated by them, you interbred with them, all to see where it goes, how the human race would be able to handle all the challenges.

So there was a setup and it was a setup that was established by Lyrans, by Pleiadians, by Sirians, and to some extent, by Andromedans (1), although the Andromedans had not been as involved from the beginning as the Sirians, Lyrans, and Pleiadians were.

Now later on, after humanity had been seeded on Earth, the evolution of the primates had been accelerated with genetic manipulation. After you had established yourself, then other beings started to get interested in planet Earth, beings like the Orions, and they wanted to see how they could capitalize on the presence of this race of beings and all the natural resources there on Earth. So you have that influence as well, that you might call the dark side. So you had to deal with that, and you have to deal with the pain of life on Earth and how you have to experience loss. You don't have one centralized religion, and that would be one belief that all would share. So all these challenges have stretched humanity's creativity. That means they have to be more tolerant, more accepting.

And from the perspective of most of the E.T. races, you're doing remarkably well under the circumstances of your set-up, of not knowing, not having the pure knowing (of your origin), despite the effort of those that have come and tried to teach you that you are Source and Source is never separate from you. But people still have that feeling of intense separation from Source to get over, of wrath, and of fear of death, fear of annihilation.

So all of this means that Earth has essentially been a consciousness experiment, to see what the consciousness would choose, what the consciousness would need in order to evolve there.

Alison: So a special set of circumstances was created for this experiment that were tougher than those on other planets to observe how consciousness could evolve.

Quan Yin: Yes, because on other worlds in this galaxy of the Universe, the evolution of the physical and the spiritual energies was all allowed to happen naturally, organically, whereas on Earth it was accelerated at times and decelerated at other times. You had ice ages to deal with, you had floods that bottlenecked the entire population into a much smaller number. You had to deal with so much there on Earth and that is why there is so much respect for Earth humans throughout the galaxy and Universe because of how hard it is there.

Alison: I remember reading one of Lucy Lee's QHHT case studies (2) in which a subject recalled the seeding of life forms on Earth a long, long time ago. I guess that was the beginning of the Earth Experiment. What was Earth like before?

Quan Yin: Earth was a planet that would be considered more like a moon in that it wasn't a Goldilocks planet, a planet where sentient life forms would want to incarnate. What happened was the E.T.s came and began the terraforming process to give Earth the continents, the oceans, the mountains, the rivers, the valleys, the atmosphere, the planet life, the microbes, the insects, and then the animal life. The human life came last.

(Note: According to NASA, a Goldilocks zone "is the area around a star where it is not too hot and not too cold for liquid water to exist on the surface of surrounding planets." (3))

Alison: As a matter of fact, I am astonished by the role of extraterrestrials in the Earth Experiment. We haven't been exposed to that level of knowledge. So whatever was or is on Earth was first created by E.T.s?

Quan Yin: All of it.

Alison: And the Lyrans, Pleiadians, and Sirians were the three major E.T. races that started the experiment, and then the Andromedans and later on the Orions joined in.

Quan Yin: These are the main three that set it up, and others contributed of course from their species of their planets, the insects and the Antarians, for example. There are really seven big contributors: the Lyrans, the Pleiadians, the Sirians, the Orions, the Arcturians, the Cassiopeians, and the Antarians (4). Those are your seven major contributors throughout the galaxy to this Earth experience, Earth Experiment. I would say those are also the seven root races of humankind.

(Note: The contributions of the seven root races will be discussed in Chapter 9.)

Alison: When did the seeding of Earth's life forms take place?

Quan Yin: About two billion years ago.

Alison: How long did it take before Earth was terraformed?

Quan Yin: 25,000 years.

Alison: And next came trees, plants, and the creation of flora?

Quan Yin: Yes.

Alison: Then it was the development of fauna and animal lifeforms?

Quan Yin: Yes.

Alison: Did humans come later than dinosaurs and animals?

Quan Yin: Yes, much later.

Alison: When did primitive humans first appear on Earth?

Quan Yin: About 12 million years ago.

Alison: Ahh, it was much, much later. Before humans joined the ecosystem, what was Earth used for after its creation?

Quan Yin: Vacation, for E.T.s to take vacation. It was also a place where you could come and just study different life forms, the animals, plants, insects, sea life, and so on. It could be just for an E.T. being who's interested in evolution and the way these beings would mate, get food, build colonies and places to live and so on.

Alison: So the plan was to allow all life forms to evolve naturally so the evolutionary process could be studied?

Quan Yin: Yes, it was until some E.T.s had a different idea for the Neanderthal humans.

Alison: Wow. Sounds like there's a big story there in human evolution?

Quan Yin: Yes, there was.

Alison: What happened?

Quan Yin: It was moving along smoothly on Earth and then the Lyrans came. They were genetic scientists and masters of genetic coding, and they wanted to put their knowledge into practice, and they did.

Alison: This is the acceleration of consciousness that you talked about?

Quan Yin: Correct.

Alison: Okay, we'll have to reserve time to explore that full story.

Quan Yin: Yes.

(Note: We will discuss the Lyrans' genetic work on humans in Chapter 5.)

Alison: Did we make the decision to come to Earth while we were in the fifth dimension?

Quan Yin: No. It was something you started to consider even before you descended into the eighth dimension. So it was more of a ninth-dimensional decision that you made to come to Earth eventually. Yes, that's the level of planning that goes into a soul's journey.

Alison: This is amazing. We should pat ourselves on the back for signing up for the experiment and sticking to it.

Quan Yin: Yes indeed.

Notes

1) Lyrans, Pleiadians, Sirians, and Andromedans are all extra-terrestrials from the star systems of Lyra, Pleiades, Sirius, and Andromeda.

2) Lucy Lee is a Quantum Healing Hypnosis Technique (QHHT) therapist based in Taipei, Taiwan. QHHT, as a healing modality, was founded and created by Dolores Cannon (1931-2014). It takes a subject not only back to past lifetimes under hypnosis, but it is capable of calling forth the person's higher self (referred to as SC or subconsciousness in QHHT) to provide more guidance and input. Lucy Lee has published over 100 QHHT cases (https://soleil3966.pixnet.net/blog/category/list/2256086/1) that she facilitated since 2014, offering a panoramic view of our souls' experiences on Earth and elsewhere in the Universe. All published content is in Chinese.

3) For a simpler explanation, please see "What is the habitable zone or Goldilocks zone?" (https://science.nasa.gov/exoplanets/what-is-the-habitable-zone-or-goldilocks-zone/) by NASA. For more details, please see Fast facts: "What is the Habitable Zone?" (https://science.nasa.gov/exoplanets/habitable-zone/)

4) The Cassiopeians and Antarians are from the star systems of Cassiopeia and Antares. The Orions are beings from the Orion Constellation, and their fifth-dimensional counterparts started the Orion Wars, which we briefly mentioned in Chapter Two.

CHAPTER 4

❧

EXPLORING EARTH IN THE EARLY DAYS

In Chapter 3, we learned that our coming to Earth was a deliberate decision to join the Earth Experiment to greatly advance our growth and expansion as souls. Understanding the challenges involved, I was anticipating dramatic scenarios in our incarnations on Earth that would exemplify the complex struggles we had signed up for. But surprisingly, that's not what we were presented with when we first dipped our toes onto Earth.

I've read from channeled books and spiritual readings that Lemuria (1), a continent believed to have existed in the Pacific Ocean, was the cradle of human civilization. And I assumed that's where many of us started on Earth. But we were nowhere near Lemuria when we made our first physical appearance on this planet. Instead, we had very humble but refreshing beginnings. We were not physical humans yet, and in fact, we were in other forms of existence. This is a precious lesson in understanding the full range of experience a soul could take on in the cosmic journey, and how the soul would make the choice to do so.

In this chapter, we will describe these unexpected and rarely disclosed experiences we've had as incarnate beings. We will also discuss reincarnation, the cycle through which we leave the physical body, bid farewell to a physical lifetime, and then come back to a different body and life when we are ready for the next experience. Our reincarnations really started in the different star systems in the fifth dimension when we first experienced physical birth and death. Reincarnation is the mechanism for us to shift through many experiences of our choice in the physical dimensions. This background knowledge is highly valuable in understanding how we can assemble a portfolio of unique experiences in the Earth Experiment.

Earliest Experiences on Earth

The biggest discovery from inquiring about our early existence on Earth was that for those who chose Earth, it is the planet where we complete our descension journey. This means we not only descend to the third dimension, but we continue on to the second and first dimensions. It is another reason why the Earth's diversity was an important factor in our selection of this planet for descension adventures, and as a launchpad of our ascension back to the nonphysical realm. We have a rich menu to select from for the different experiences in all three lower dimensions.

Alison: Was I part of the original settlers in Lemuria? Was that the beginning of my life on Earth after my time at the Pleiades?

Quan Yin: It was not exactly… You had other experiences of being on Earth. You had been a rock, a plant, and animals on Earth. Through these experiences you completed your descension journey on Earth. Lemuria was just a time when your soul's re-ascension journey took off.

Alison: I didn't know I had been those things! I've always thought of my soul as being in higher-intelligence life forms.

Quan Yin: So as the journey continues and continues, the descension eventually brings you down to the simplest expression, which is that of the rock, the sand, the dirt, the minerals, the being that exists as consciousness but doesn't move, doesn't grow in any way. That's just the baseline of experience. The wind is another experience, and the water is another experience that's first-dimensional. You can exist as fire in the first dimension as well, and you do. You exist in all these different ways to get a lay of the land, to get a sense of what it's like to be physical on Earth.

Alison: Did I go straight from the fourth to the first dimension?

Quan Yin: You descended through the third dimension first before getting to the second and first. So you did have some of those animalistic experiences there on Earth. And then you became a plant, tree, vegetable, fruit in the second, and then the rock and dirt in the first, and you started the ascension from there. You incarnate back in more complex ways as you ascend into human form. You stayed in the third dimension as humans until 2012 when Earth shifted to the fourth dimension.

Alison: What were we trying to experience and learn through a non-human existence?

Quan Yin: You were taking a break from the more complex experiences of the fifth and fourth dimensions you had come from to come to Earth and exist as a badger, a squirrel, a deer and so on, and then as a tree and a rock. After lifetimes of roller-coaster rides, tumultuous experiences, ups and downs, painful emotions, there's simplicity in being a tree to experience the wind and the animals to visit, experiencing growth, delivery of flowers, the sun, the rain. Imagine having a peaceful mind that doesn't get bored. That's the experience of being a tree.

Alison: What about the experience of being a rock?

Quan Yin: With a rock you get to know what it's like to be stable and still know yourself. You were not sending a large portion of your consciousness as a soul to have that experience. It's a smaller fragmented version of yourself to handle some existence that is rather mundane, not filled with a lot of different experiences or excitement. It's like going to a spa in a mud bath with cucumber slices on your eyes, lying there doing nothing. Why would anybody do that? Think of all the reasons you want to do that and realize as a soul, you might want to do that for a hundred years because of the weariness of existence, pain, and instability you experienced in a vulnerable physical body.

Alison: I see. In our rock experience, did it include being a crystal? Are crystals of a higher consciousness?

Quan Yin: Crystals, because of their structure and their physicality, are able to hold more of a consciousness, more energy within them. They have been used as storage devices, transmittal devices, and also amplifiers of energy, and it is because of their physical makeup that they are capable of doing this. And because of that physical makeup, they are also capable of holding higher consciousness than an average rock does. But rocks also do have a consciousness to them, and people have tapped into and have sought to receive wisdom from various rocks, stones, boulders, and so on.

(Note: The potential abilities and uses of crystals will be discussed in more detail in Chapter 5.)

Alison: What do we look to experience as a crystal?

Quan Yin: It's a service-oriented experience for the consciousness. It's a way of relaxing into a life, if you want to call it a life, because there is nothing to do. The crystal doesn't have to do anything to survive. It's an experience of collective consciousness, being a part of the collective consciousness and feeling what it feels like to be connected with other crystals in the same frequency.

Alison: Do crystals have a higher consciousness than trees?

Quan Yin: I would say the trees are higher. But it is very similar. Trees have a very similar relationship with one another as crystals do, but the trees are slightly higher in consciousness.

Alison: Are trees a little more connected with their souls?

Quan Yin: Yes.

Alison: A lot of people are fascinated with crystals and believe crystals have a mystical higher consciousness. If people understand that trees are slightly higher in consciousness...

Quan Yin: Some people have that relationship to trees and Buddha sat under the bodhi tree for a reason.

Alison: Is it also because trees are living and growing organisms?

Quan Yin: Yes.

Alison: In the first and second dimensions, do we have more of that collective consciousness even if we have been individuating more and more while descending?

Quan Yin: Yes, because there is no ego in any of these existences.

Alison: What about the four elements – Air, fire, water, and soil? Are they all first-dimensional existences?

Quan Yin: Yes, they all are.

Alison: So apparently in our journey, we have been elementals?

Quan Yin: Yes, you have.

Alison: Out of the four, it seems that fire is more of an on-and-off and non-continuous experience. Does a tiny fragment of soul energy come and go for the experience?

Quan Yin: You can have a continuous experience as lava to get that fire consciousness.

Alison: Oh, I see. Are the elements similar to rocks in the level of consciousness?

Quan Yin: All the same, all the same level.

Alison: Are mountains the same as soil or rock?

Quan Yin: When you have a mountain, you have a collection then of the soil that creates an expression and experience that is unique and that has a collective consciousness to it, apart from this individuated consciousness that the soil has within it.

Alison: What about oceans or seas, rivers? Are they collectives as well?

Quan Yin: Yes, yes, and yes.

Alison: Are there bigger souls behind rivers, oceans, and mountains? Because in mythology, there is always a goddess or god for a large body of water or a mountain range.

Quan Yin: That's right.

Alison: So the elementals are generally a collective and then there is a larger being in charge. So for the Pacific Ocean, for instance, there is a soul in charge of it. And then other small soul aspects come in as part of the Ocean collective to have that experience. Is this a correct description?

Quan Yin: Yes.

Alison: What are we trying to experience as elementals?

Quan Yin: Creation, support, variety, simplicity. Those are the things you're trying to experience as an elemental.

Alison: What is the creation that the elementals are experiencing?

Quan Yin: Creation of nature, of life within nature, the plant kingdom.

Alison: Much more so for the plant kingdom because of the soil?

Quan Yin: Yes.

Alison: What about support? Is it to give all life forms what they need to sustain themselves, like water and air?

Quan Yin: Yes.

Alison: Then what about the destruction that these elements can bring, such as a blizzard or hurricane or wildfire?

Quan Yin: Well, you know ultimately that they serve a greater and higher good even if it's inconvenient to the humans.

Alison: That means natural disasters are eliminating or cleaning out the energy that needs to be cleaned out?

Quan Yin: And sometimes very physical. Brush is removed in a wildfire, which allows for more growth.

Alison: Then simplicity, I suppose, is referring to the level of consciousness, just like rocks?

Quan Yin: Yes.

Alison: And how is variety experienced?

Quan Yin: The diversity of plant life on your planet.

Alison: Oh, the diversity of plant life they can support.

Quan Yin: And experience.

Alison: But the elementals are not the plants?

Quan Yin: No, but they're so closely intertwined that they sometimes inhabit the plant, the flower, the tree, the grass, the weed.

Alison: Do we have more variety on Earth in terms of the fauna and flora life forms than on many other planets?

Quan Yin: Than most.

Alison: When our souls are embodied in air, fire, water, and soil, how much soul energy is in them?

Quan Yin: It's all viewed with consciousness, which is that consciousness can and is associated with a soul, but that the soul isn't sending a large enough portion of itself to be experienced in the same way that you're experiencing this life, standing in that physical body. So it requires less soul energy, but all consciousness is Source reflecting back on itself, which gives it that awareness. So the wind, the air, every particle of air does have some consciousness, yes.

Alison: There are still many small soul aspects or fragments embodied in the elementals?

Quan Yin: They're still there.

Alison: It's just that I am doing my human incarnation, but others may be experiencing the elementals?

Quan Yin: Yes.

Alison: You spoke about first and second-dimensional existences as having no ego. Do animals have an ego mind?

Quan Yin: The more time they spend around humans, the more they develop it.

Alison: That is very funny. So the ego mind really develops in a human incarnation?

Quan Yin: Yes.

Alison: I assume that we were in the form of animals to have a simpler physical expression in contrast to a human life filled with complex thoughts and emotions?

Quan Yin: Correct.

Alison: Do animals incur karma?

Quan Yin: No.

Alison: Even if animals hunt and kill other animals for food, there is no karma involved?

Quan Yin: Right. It's part of their agreement to be a part of that food chain, which is in nature.

Alison: So they follow their instincts and they don't have bad or conniving intentions?

Quan Yin: Correct. They live in the present.

How Long Has It Been Since We First Arrived on Earth?

We've been many different beings and existences on Earth, animate and inanimate, organic and inorganic. How long has it been since we arrived? Do we always follow a linear order in our reincarnation choices? Well, the answers are in fact not so linear.

Alison: How long had I been on Earth before my human lifetimes began?

Quan Yin: About 150 million years since your first incarnation.

Alison: Wow! That must be the bulk of our time on Earth because you said the primitive "homo" species only appeared 12 million years ago. Is this a common timespan for many, if not most, people living on Earth now?

Quan Yin: Yes.

Alison: One hundred and fifty million years seems like a long time for non-human experiences.

Quan Yin: You didn't spend all that time incarnate. Sometimes you were incarnate, sometimes you're in between lifetimes, just observing, or you're a guide to someone, or you're learning, interacting with your own guides. As I've said, trees, rocks are all aspects of a soul experiencing consciousness. Their journey is different, not creating karma. The times you had to wait for a human body to be available due to ice ages, floods, etc., there were animal bodies, and you took the opportunity.

Alison: And during this long timespan, were we still incarnating in the fourth and fifth dimensions as well?

Quan Yin: That's correct. You were.

Alison: So even if we generally follow a linear order in descension, we do have freedom to jump back and forth between dimensions, say from the fifth or fourth dimension to the third dimension?

Quan Yin: Yes. The key part is that you go home (after physical death in the fourth or fifth dimension) to the seventh dimension, to your soul aspect in the seventh dimension, and from there you can decide to go to the Earth dimension. You can go in at any time point you want to have experiences, and you can jump in between lives as much as you want. It doesn't have to be so linear. You don't have to say I'm a rock now and then 100 years later I'll be a bird, and then 100 years later I'll be an octopus. You don't have to look at it in that way. You can look at it as "I'm going to where and when I want to because time is not linear even if I have a linear experience in my evolution."

(Note: All beings incarnating in the physical realm return to the seventh dimension in between lifetimes. This will be discussed in the next section of this chapter.)

Alison: This is almost like saying I can go to my future and also to my past as I please. This means we don't necessarily experience the dimensions in a completely sequential way, but the experiences are combined in a linear order to reflect our evolution?

Quan Yin: Correct.

Alison: So we can literally move back and forth between the dimensions as we wish. But do we usually want to finish the fifth dimension before starting in the fourth and third dimensions?

Quan Yin: In a descension process, it is really up to you. In the ascension process, you do graduate to get to the higher dimensional plane. But in a descension, you can say, "All right, I feel ready now for this harder part of the journey where I am third dimensional, second dimensional, or first dimensional."

Alison: So we could decide in whichever order we like for the next desired experience?

Quan Yin: Exactly, that's how you can go from being an animal to being a human, from being a human to being an animal.

Alison: Or go from the fifth dimension to Earth and be a rock and rest for a while.

Quan Yin: Yes.

Alison: Does this jumping around happen mainly in the physical dimensions, i.e., we wouldn't normally choose to go from the ninth straight to the fifth dimension?

Quan Yin: Correct. You go from the nonphysical to the physical cycle, and then jump around a little in the physical cycle.

Alison: Linearity helps the human mind to comprehend the descension process, but in actuality, our souls have more freedom in skipping linearity in the physical dimensions during descension.

Quan Yin: You can see yourself as a soul shifting to different dimensions and times, having all the freedom in the world. You get advice, there is a council that helps you, and there are guides that help you. But you are the decider. You are determining ultimately what you want to experience because you are free, you are Source, and you have free will to do whatever you want.

Alison: You talked about the ice age and flooding on Earth that delayed our human incarnations. Did that happen before Lemuria?

Quan Yin: Yes, before Lemuria. You had the dinosaurs as well, for example.

Alison: Oh, right. It would not be fun to be living on Earth when the dinosaurs were roaming around. Were they wiped out by a comet that also caused flooding and an ice age?

Quan Yin: Yes.

Alison: Have I been a dinosaur?

Quan Yin: Yes.

Alison: Wow! That's actually cool. Have most humans gone through this same process of descension and reincarnation?

Quan Yin: A few walk-ins can occur from the higher dimensional plane, and they skip over the typical descension process. But most of you have gone through this descension process. You are a lot of old souls.

(Note: A walk-in is a soul entering the Earth plane not by physical birth but through an energy portal to switch places with another soul in a human body. The previous soul inhabitant leaves the body to go somewhere else. The soul walking into this body will continue living this human's life, sometimes with a different life plan. This change is initiated by an agreement between the two souls.)

Reincarnation Cycle in Physical Dimensions

We appear in different life forms to have different experiences in the physical realm. As Quan Yin said earlier, this happens when our soul projects consciousness into a physical existence such as a rock, a plant, an animal, or a human. We eventually leave a physical form when we have had what we wanted to experience. Then we choose another lifetime or another life form for the next experience.

The projection of soul consciousness to a physical life form is incarnation, and the repeated process is known as reincarnation. We think of reincarnation generally for humans, and only occasionally for animals. The topic of human reincarnations has been covered extensively in publications describing past life regressions in a hypnotic state (2).

What hasn't been discussed to the same extent is how we move in and out of the forms of existence in the first and second dimensions. In these two dimensions, there is often no physical death or a defined lifetime as a human or animal would have. Our journey from the fifth to the first dimension is a long cycle of reincarnations. Knowing the basics of reincarnation for both human and non-human life forms will be beneficial. It will give us a fuller view of the process and mechanics supporting our journey of crisscrossing the physical dimensions.

Alison: When we are an animal or human, the reincarnation endpoints are clear. They are birth and death. What about trees and plants? They seem to have life cycles, too, but trees can live a lot longer than humans. So when we actually reincarnate as a tree, do we usually go through this birth and death cycle?

Quan Yin: You could, because there are trees that die and there are saplings that are born. So it depends again on how you're looking at it. You could say, "Yes, I had an incarnation as an oak, and then I started out as a sapling of a maple for my next tree experience, and that's a different experience." But you're also going to have this type of "walk-in" experience there where you could call it a lifetime or you could call it as "I'm being a tree for now, and I'll withdraw my consciousness and let someone else step in and play the role of this tree so some souls can have that experience." You don't have to wait for a birth and a death.

Alison: I see. And for a first-dimensional existence such as a crystal or rock, that would be the case too?

Quan Yin: Yes.

Alison: I know souls can use "walk-in" to allow a soul to leave a human body and make room for another soul to enter through a portal into the same body. But this is just generally rare and not as common as the birth and death experience for humans?

Quan Yin: Yes, exactly.

Alison: But does that mean that when we're born, when soul consciousness is projected into the new baby, it has to come through this type of portal as well?

Quan Yin: No, the portal is inside the mother.

Alison: Oh, what is that portal like inside the mother?

Quan Yin: Everyone has portals inside of them. It's not just exclusive to a pregnant mother having a portal. You have portals inside of you, and you access energies all the time using those portals. The biggest, most powerful, most often used portal is at the center of the heart.

Alison: Is it through the heart center that we receive energy from our soul and Oversoul?

Quan Yin: Yes.

Alison: Which chakra is usually used for a soul's entry into a pregnant mother?

Quan Yin: The heart.

Alison: Which chakra is used when a soul's energy leaves the body?

Quan Yin: The heart as well.

Alison: I see. Are all our chakras energy portals?

Quan Yin: Yes.

Alison: So most of the time, we use our internal portals for communion with the spiritual realm. We don't really need external portals?

Quan Yin: No, you don't need them for that.

Alison: I know the external portals also exist. Just to make sure I understand this correctly, what would be the definition of a portal?

Quan Yin: A portal is a gateway that allows a being or an energy stream to move through it from one point to another. It can send, transmit, and receive energies.

Alison: And the ability to send and receive energy is true of portals internal to our body or external in nature, such as the one over Sedona?

Quan Yin: Correct.

Alison: So when a walk-in happens, because there's no mother involved, is an external portal used for the exchange of soul energies?

Quan Yin: When the walk-in happens, it is still using the internal portal in the body.

Alison: Oh really? Then when a soul's energy enters life forms in the first and second dimensions using a "walk-in" method, is there a portal inside a tree or plant?

Quan Yin: Yes, the portal is inside the tree or the plant or the rock or the flower.

Alison: Because they also have the ability to open up to the Universe?

Quan Yin: Yes.

Alison: So when a soul's energy enters our dimension for reincarnation, it doesn't really need an external portal for that. But an external portal can be used if E.T.s are coming to Earth, as physical or nonphysical beings.

Quan Yin: Or sending energies from other dimensions, other star systems. That energy comes through the portals as well. But yes, portals can be used to transport beings as well, human beings or orbs or insectoid beings, any type of being.

Alison: When energy is sent from other star systems or dimensions, is it usually a massive energy coming through the portal to be available to everybody?

Quan Yin: Exactly.

Alison: So the large portal in Sedona can be where higher-dimensional energies are pouring in, and some E.T.s may come through it as well?

Quan Yin: Yes.

Alison: Back to reincarnation, does reincarnation happen only in the physical dimensions?

Quan Yin: It does, yes.

Alison: In the old fifth dimension, we still had life and death, so we did have reincarnations in the classical sense?

Quan Yin: Yes.

Alison: Do we have reincarnations in the sixth or seventh dimension?

Quan Yin: Yes, in those dimensions, not all the time.

Alison: We could have physical bodies in the physical realm in those dimensions, but we didn't have death there.

Quan Yin: Right. But you would shift your consciousness out of a different form and into another form, and that would be considered an incarnation.

Alison: I see, just like what we're doing in the first and second dimension when we decided we were ready for a change of experience. But we are dealing with more complex and organic life forms here in the seventh dimension.

Quan Yin: Yes.

Alison: And when you said not all the time, it's because we could be nonphysical in the seventh dimension and there are no reincarnations?

Quan Yin: Correct.

Alison: Is reincarnation in the future fifth dimension different from the past fifth dimension?

Quan Yin: In the future fifth dimension, it will be much more like the sixth and seventh dimensions were previously to you when you were incarnate in those dimensions, yes.

Alison: That means we'll have strong soul connections, and we'll still have a body, but there is no mortality?

Quan Yin: Yes.

Alison: Ascension is exciting.

Quan Yin: Yes.

Home Base in the Seventh Dimension in between Lives

A discussion on reincarnation would not be complete without describing where we go in between lifetimes. Quan Yin already told us that it's the seventh dimension where we would go after we die and before we return for another incarnation. Animals follow a similar process. This makes sense since the seventh dimension spans across the physical and nonphysical.

Below are more answers from Quan Yin about our temporary home base in the seventh dimension while in between physical lives. All these questions and answers, except the last three, were first published in the book A Caregiver's Healing and Awakening: With Quan Yin's Guidance on Ascension.

Alison: Why do souls go to the seventh dimension after leaving Earth?

Quan Yin: It is where your guides are, at the seventh dimension. You go where your guides are, where others are. It's an agreed-upon location where everyone can come together who wants to congregate and review their life and plan the next life and have fun together.

Alison: Why is the seventh dimension chosen?

Quan Yin: To be in the seventh dimension is an experience of being on a break. It's the very edge where a being can no longer be in physical form. It's exciting to have that experience of no longer being physical, but also it affords the person the experience of having a body if they want to have a body. It's a chance to have a transitional period of feeling they can still be physical, and most will eventually choose to exist in a nonphysical expression without a body.

This is where you can feel conscious of yourself as you have known yourself to be, but different enough to give the soul a much different experience. Then, when a soul has more work to do or has more experiences to have in a 3D environment, they reincarnate. If they have had enough, they can choose to reincarnate in a higher dimension.

Alison: The choice to reincarnate in a higher dimension than the third is always there, independent of the current Ascension?

Quan Yin: Yes, it is independent of the Ascension.

Alison: I heard some souls can't make it to the seventh dimension because of the negativity or trauma they are holding. Do they have to work their way to the seventh dimension?

Quan Yin: That portion of their consciousness that would stay back and be like a ghost or thought form (due to trauma or negativity) is a tiny fragment of the overall soul, and the overall soul is going to the seventh dimension regardless of how fragmented it was in the lifetime.

Alison: Will scared or guilt-ridden soul fragments go to a sphere like a purgatory?

Quan Yin: No, there is no such thing as a purgatory. A purgatory implies that you need a certain amount of punishment to cleanse you in order to be worthy of being in a higher dimensional plane, whereas when a soul is fragmented because of guilt, trauma, or some sort of judgment that keeps with them, they are doing it to themselves. There is no force outside of them that's determining they need that experience. In other words, if you forgive yourself, then your fragment comes back, and that part of you also moves to the seventh dimension upon death. There is no purgatory, there is no limbo, there is no hell. You can create an experience that feels like what you are living, but it's not an actual place you go to.

Alison: We go back to the seventh dimension in between our physical lifetimes in the fifth to the third dimensions. In our descension, we also reincarnate into the seventh dimension for the experiences we wanted. So, one soul aspect there would be waiting for us to return to them when we die and leave our physical body. And another soul aspect would be living their lives in the seventh dimension. Are these two different experiences?

Quan Yin: Yes.

Alison: Okay. So the first soul aspect would hold the role of overseeing the incarnations in the physical dimension, especially the fifth, fourth, and third dimensions. Another soul aspect would focus on living the seventh-dimensional experience on their descension path?

Quan Yin: Yes. And of course, they'll swap roles as well.

Alison: Oh, really?

Quan Yin: Yes. They are such multi-dimensional, multi-faceted beings in the seventh dimension that they are not just focused on one thing at the same time.

The Popular Belief of Being Trapped on Earth

Quan Yin's explanation of hell as an experience of our own creation and not an "institution" in our Universe is thought-provoking. There is a similar popular belief about us being trapped on Earth and not allowed to leave. This belief can be found in the lightworker community, and it is most prominent in Buddhist and other Eastern religious teachings about karma. In this view, reincarnations will continue indefinitely until we clear all our karmic debt. Karma as a concept exists in English as well, which can be best represented by the proverb "You reap what you sow."

Quan Yin defines karma as" referring to the completion of a cycle of experiences." It is not a mechanism to meter out rewards and punishments, but a way for us to learn and grow. The interesting question then is how karma can possibly trap us in a dimension or on a planet, as so many have believed.

We just learned that our souls have freedom in shifting up or down the physical dimensions while experiencing different lifetimes. For instance, we can go from a fifth-dimensional planet to the third-dimensional Earth for a lifetime, and then resume our reincarnations in the fifth or fourth dimension. It all depends on what we prefer and what we are ready for. If we are trapped, we can't possibly exercise this freedom. Furthermore, we know we are in a free will Universe, which means souls are free to make their choices. So, is this belief of being trapped another creation and illusion of ours? And if so, what is the purpose of it?

Alison: There is a popular belief that we are all trapped on Earth for a number of reasons including karma or negative forces. The concept is prevalent in some religious teachings and also in parts of the lightworker community. If we are trapped, we have no choice. But we are given free will choices in this Universe. So is this another man-made belief?

Quan Yin: Yes, it's an illusion. Everything is a choice. Your soul always has a choice. You're never trapped, you're never bound by anything. If a soul wants an experience of being trapped, it can give itself an experience like that, but it's still a choice. Now in between lifetimes, you don't look at it that way. In between lifetimes, you always choose to come back. You're not forced to come back because there is some net around your soul or around the Earth.

Alison: So all of us incarnating on Earth actually have a choice to stop our journey anytime, but we have always decided to come back?

Quan Yin: Yes.

Alison: We always gladly come back to this tough third-dimensional classroom?

Quan Yin: Yes. Souls are always choosing what dimensions they're in. They are not in a dimension because they are not evolved enough to be in a higher dimension. It is always by choice for the benefit of the experience. You can go back to Source right now. You don't have to earn your way back to the thirteenth dimension through good acts or anything like that, which you've been told as truth.

Alison: Even if descension and then ascension is a common approach of our cosmic journey, there are no hard and fast rules about having to do it that way.

Quan Yin: Correct.

Alison: Have some souls decided to cut short their journey and go back to the 13th dimension?

Quan Yin: Yes.

Alison: And they just said, "I really don't want to do this anymore. I want to fold back to Source and be immersed in pure love and bliss." And that's okay?

Quan Yin: Yes.

Alison: Is it a very small number of souls?

Quan Yin: Yes.

Alison: This is amazing. It is contrary to the spiritual teaching that says we have to earn our merits for any advancement.

Quan Yin: You chose to be where you are. You are not sent there by some bigger force than you. You are the force that chooses all your experiences.

Alison: Our souls undertake a journey of descension and then ascension because we consider it to be most beneficial and fulfilling for our growth and expansion?

Quan Yin: Correct.

Alison: Why does the idea of being trapped by other forces resonate with people?

Quan Yin: "Being trapped" can be true from a certain perspective that you're holding.

Alison: I see, so it has something to do with experiencing the feeling of being trapped. It has certainly become an ingrained belief in some people's minds. In the QHHT case studies from Lucy Lee (3), a person under hypnosis would talk about the trap or matrix that kept us on Earth, but the same person would also give a self-conflicting statement like "Source will never make any decisions for souls."

Quan Yin: Sometimes you'll have a person who would report, "I chose to come here. It wasn't something that was thrust upon me."

Alison: So were all these statements filtered through the belief system of the subject under hypnosis?

Quan Yin: Yes.

Alison: Since the interpretation of karma as a trap against our free will is not the truth, it must not have been the original teaching in Buddhism or Hinduism. What caused this limiting and distorted view of karma?

Quan Yin: It has everything to do with the feeling of separation, separation from Source, from your soul. You, as human beings, have egos and you have minds, and you have pain, and you have suffering. And the human individual wants to make sense of their pain and their suffering. They do not see the perspective of the soul, they do not hold the perspective of the soul, and some humans would even separate themselves from their soul and think of their soul, or their higher self, whatever they want to call it, as forcing them to live a life against their will. But again, it's only through that experience of separation that someone would feel that way about the choices that their souls have made to have certain experiences on Earth that would be painful.

And so in order to make sense of that, the mind came up with a story. Individuals who have received spiritual teachings do understand that there is reincarnation and there is a life review after physical death. In the life review, people are shown how they could improve in the ways that they are relating to other people and the ways that they're living their lives. In other words, they are shown that they could make some improvements that would better reflect the truth of who they really are as a soul, as an aspect of Source energy.

Now, that can be interpreted by any mind, any ego, to say, "I'm going to keep being sent back here until I get it right. And it will be against my will because I do not feel or know that I am my soul." In every single case since the beginning of time, the soul has consciously chosen to give itself an experience in the physical reality. And the soul has made that choice based on what the soul wants to work on or work through. When the soul feels that it has completed a theme, it has completed a cycle of experiences that are relevant to the theme. Some people, of course, would interpret the experiences from a perspective of karmic causation. But it is really an exploration of a theme, and the soul will go on to explore another theme, and another, and another.

So again, it's all about perspective and how human beings see themselves. If you see yourself as being made to suffer from the life circumstances that you are facing, then yes, it will seem like a trap. It will seem like you have to keep coming back until you get it right. From the soul's perspective, which is what the human being really and truly is, you get to come back and explore this theme, and there is no real cause and effect from one lifetime to another that determines your experience in a certain lifetime. It's all by choice.

Alison: So these very human-centric thoughts seeped into the original teachings of the ascended masters and created a new story of the meaning of karma, like the Wheel of Karma that keeps churning until we pay all our karmic dues.

Quan Yin: In current Western philosophy amongst many New Agers, this idea of karma and the soul trap is perpetuated by the work of Dolores Cannon. And so you will have many more people in the New Age today who believe in it because of her books. Then there are New Agers who believe in it because of Hinduism and Buddhism.

Alison: So the QHHT cases in Dolores Cannon's books could have been filtered through the subject's beliefs about the karmic trap or the evil forces around them to start with?

Quan Yin: Yes.

Alison: I've also read a Chinese book which was created by the author channeling you in a series of conversations. It was published in Taiwan, and it still held the same view of karma as a trap, and the idea of choice was non-existent in the book.

Quan Yin: Yes, but it was also a bit of the channeler's beliefs coming through. How much karma a person takes on in a lifetime is all by choice.

Alison: Ahh, I see. So all in all, we always have our free will choices. Many still believe that we have been trapped on Earth by karma or by evil forces, but we can look at this belief as a creation by ourselves to give us this unique experience of "feeling trapped." Souls can never have this experience because they know they are free. This belief serves us, in a way, in our Earthly journey.

Quan Yin: That's correct. But it is time to stop perpetuating any of those ideas about people being trapped on Earth because of their karma and seeing themselves as victims of a negative force on Earth, very much like the movie "The Matrix" where people want to say, "Oh, it's a simulation, but we're not the ones controlling it. They are." None of it is true.

Alison: Our souls agreed to all these experiences and beliefs about being trapped, but in this time of Ascension, we can see the truth and move on now.

Quan Yin: Yes, it is time to know you are and have always been free. Everything is by choice.

Notes

1) Examples of channeled books about Lemuria include *The Lemurian Way, Remembering Your Essential Nature* by Lauren O. Thyme and Sareya Orion, and *The Submerged Continents of Atlantis and Lemuria* by Rudolf Steiner. The story of Lemuria will be discussed in Chapter Five.
2) Many books have been published on the topic of reincarnation. The most popular ones included *Life after Life* by Raymond Moody, *Many Lives, Many Masters* by Dr. Brian Weiss, and *Journey of Souls* by Dr. Michael Newton.
3) Lucy Lee is a Quantum Healing Hypnosis Technique (QHHT) therapist based in Taipei, Taiwan. Lucy Lee has published over 100 QHHT cases (https://soleil3966.pixnet.net/blog/category/list/2256086/1) that she facilitated since 2014. Please see more details in the Notes section in Chapter Three.

CHAPTER 5

BEGINNING HUMAN INCARNATIONS IN LEMURIA

After manifesting as other forms of physical presence on Earth, we were finally ready to tackle our biggest role of being a sentient human in a physical body. This was going to be the pinnacle of our experience on Earth. Enormous challenges and growth would come with it. Most of us do not have conscious memories of our past lifetimes on this planet, However, we can certainly look at our lives now and the world around us as a microcosm of the challenges we have faced all along across hundreds of lifetimes. That is the Earth experience we committed to eons ago. Even if there have been good times, we all know it hasn't been an easy and smooth journey by any stretch of the imagination.

If we have a chance to review our past, the first question is probably how our human lives began. We all know the human history that's taught in school. There is also myth and folklore, such as Lemuria and Atlantis, two ancient civilizations with little written records or traces of architecture and artifacts. What is the truth of our history? What is the full picture of our existence as Earth humans?

Quan Yin told me that many of us started our human incarnations in Lemuria. In Chapter Three, Quan Yin already clued us in on E.T.s intervening in human evolution. It turns out that this happened in

Lemuria. The emergence of Lemuria coincided with the evolution of humanity from Neanderthals to Homo sapiens.

The evolution was originally designed to occur naturally. We began to incarnate on Earth as humans at this time because the new Lemuria supported a burgeoning stage of human evolution away from its primitive past. But the evolution was later accelerated by E.T.s' genetic experimentation. We achieved higher sentience very quickly, which enabled us to feel more of our emotions, think more thoughts, and experience our reality in a deeper, more meaningful way. Higher sentience was what our souls were reaching for to fully embrace the Earth Experiment. The genetic upgrade dramatically pushed forward the consciousness evolution.

Did we stay in that higher sentience achieved in Lemuria? The answer, unfortunately, was not a positive one. It wasn't all lost, but we did have a major setback. The unfolding of this manipulated evolution was a truly amazing tale, only to be matched by its equally unnatural and shocking ending.

Lemuria and the Idyllic Life

There are many assumptions and imaginings about life in Lemuria in the lightworker community. It has been hailed as our previous fifth-dimensional existence on Earth, where we possessed extra-sensory capabilities and lived a spiritually blessed life. Many spiritual teachers today offer a service to reconnect with our Lemurian spirit and rekindle our zeal for a higher experience. It is not at all clear, however, where and how the Lemurians came into being and then disappeared from the face of the Earth. What is the true story of Lemuria? How did the Lemurians live in those distant ancient times?

Alison: You told me before that many of us who chose to incarnate on Earth started our human incarnations in Lemuria. And it was the beginning of our collective re-ascension journey.

Quan Yin: Ascension started as an individual decided they're going to move up from the first to the second, then to the third dimension. But the bigger collective movement started to happen in Lemuria.

Alison: Did human beings exist as a race before Lemuria?

Quan Yin: Human beings existed before Lemuria but with less sentience. They were basically cave people.

Alison: When did Lemuria exist?

Quan Yin: Lemuria started in 300,000 BC. The continent was millions of years in existence, and the civilization lasted for 1000 years. Souls started to inhabit the body at 300,000 BC.

Alison: What was life in Lemuria like when they started out?

Quan Yin: You can imagine all that ocean in the Pacific between Hawaii and Australia, imagine a giant tropical paradise there that was more like a continent than a series of islands, because usually when you think of tropical paradise, you think of islands or a very small country. But this was a giant continent where people thrived living close to nature, utilizing sunlight, wind, sand, coconuts, crystals, utilizing mud, tree barks, and things of that nature in order to create what they needed to live in harmony with each other and with nature. There wasn't a lot that had to get done. You didn't have to make sure you had protection against the elements. Sure, there were the occasional storms but nothing like what you have today on Earth. It wasn't that level of hurricane or tropical storm that you have today.

So, they lived in harmony with animals, which you knew the Atlanteans were unable to do, because they didn't have a lot of deadly animals roaming around attacking them, causing them to live in fear like other continents had had, like Atlantis, for example. They also knew how to connect with and communicate with the animals to make sure the animals had enough to eat as well. So it was a lifetime for anyone who wanted to have a life living in a resort, a tropical paradise. And there was music created, dance and art of all kinds, sculpting and totem pole building, and carvings of all kinds. There was relationship with the stars, relationship with the night sky, and there was storytelling. A lot of stories were handed down orally from generation to generation.

People had light brown skin, dark hair, and dark eyes. They were able to handle sunlight on their skin very easily, and some fished and some were vegetarians, vegans. All were able to pursue what they wanted to. Of course, they had their disputes, two people falling in love with the same person, or wanting the same tree to harvest from, or land to grow on. There's always going to be disputes, there's going to be times when someone did go off the rails and there was anger, but there were more humane ways to deal with those kinds of things than today with your prisons, death penalties, and so on. They were not having borders, not having pollution, not having people coming to invade the land. Imagine living like that. That's what they had.

Alison: Are there people in our world that look like the Lemurians?

Quan Yin: The original Mayans.

Alison: Oh, I see. That's amazing. Did the Lemurians have a fully physical body?

Quan Yin: Yes.

Alison: Did they get sick or injured?

Quan Yin: Yes and yes.

Alison: And that's how they died because of illness or some sort of accident.

Quan Yin: Well, every soul will end the life they're living in a human body by choice. So yes, they would choose a way to leave their bodies ultimately.

Alison: At the time, did they use energy healing and herbs for treating illness and injuries?

Quan Yin: Yes, all the time.

Alison: What was their lifespan? How long could they live in Earth years?

Quan Yin: The average lifespan of a Lemurian was 225 years.

Alison: Wow. People will be excited reading this because a lot of people are so afraid of death.

Quan Yin: Yes.

Alison: When the Lemurians died, did they have a clear sense that they should be leaving, and so they decided to leave?

Quan Yin: Some did, but no, they weren't all at the same level of spirituality.

Alison: Did they have language or were they telepathic?

Quan Yin: No, they had language.

Alison: Oh, they did. Did they develop a written language too, or just a spoken language?

Quan Yin: No, spoken.

Alison: Okay, but were they ever telepathic?

Quan Yin: No, not in the beginning. But when you ask these questions, remember that there were the Lemurians pre-E.T.s, and Lemurians post-E.T.s. So I'm assuming you're asking pre.

Alison: That's interesting. I guess I've been asking about the pre-E.T. Lemurians. Were they intelligent and capable of collecting information, and organizing and recording knowledge?

Quan Yin: No, they were storytellers and lived tribally, communally.

Alison: Did they have small families or extended families? Did they have a family institution like ours?

Quan Yin: Yes, very similar, but close-knit, large families and larger communities.

Alison: Did they have any knowledge in farming, construction, that sort of thing?

Quan Yin: They didn't really need to. The land provided for them. They were getting the perfect amount of sun and rainfall, having fruits and vegetables and nuts and seeds, and all kinds of vegetation growing all around that you can eat.

Alison: Okay. I assume they could do basic building of houses.

Quan Yin: Yes, they would build huts to live in.

Alison: And they had artistry and craftsmanship as well.

Quan Yin: Yes.

Alison: Did they have any special gifts and capabilities that were spiritual in nature?

Quan Yin: Well, the energy healing. There was always a shaman in every community who could heal and understood how to utilize Earth energies and Sun energies and water energies as well as herbs to help a person heal.

Alison: Other than that, did they have any major capabilities that we don't, such as being psychic or being able to teleport and levitate?

Quan Yin: No, but they were living so close to the animal kingdom, the plant kingdom, the mineral kingdom, and the Earth itself that their abilities in terms of what they were capable of feeling, what they were capable of knowing, were so much stronger by living in harmony, by living in tune. And so it wasn't about necessarily having fancy abilities that would be something that they could show off to other people, but it was about experiencing oneness with everything, experiencing harmony and flow states because of their natural ability.

Alison: So they were already not living like the Neanderthals even before E.T.s arrived?

Quan Yin: No, they had evolved from the Neanderthals.

Alison: At the time, were all the other peoples on Earth much less evolved than the Lemurians?

Quan Yin: Yes.

Alison: What was their governance structure? Was there a ruling class?

Quan Yin: There was a ruling class, but the ruler was always selected. There was not a belief in the bloodline giving you the right to lead, but more an agreement of the elders as to who should lead based on what the elders were observing.

Alison: Lemuria was a large continent. Were the Lemurians concentrated in an area or scattered throughout the continent?

Quan Yin: There were areas that were more inhabitable, that were more appealing to live in, that they chose for themselves. And so there were areas along the water, the waterways where there were densely populated communities, and then there were areas where there were far fewer people choosing to set up residence.

Alison: You said there was a ruling class for the Lemurians. How did they govern this continent? Communication and transportation were difficult in ancient times.

Quan Yin: Well, it was through oral communication, and they would travel at times on horseback to get to different places. And there were times in the year when everyone would come together across the continent and talk about issues that everyone faced.

Alison: That was a big deal to gather together physically in such a large continent with no modern transportation or communication systems. So they must have been unified. They were not separate tribes. They operated more like one big tribe.

Quan Yin: Yes. The tribes were like families.

Alison: So we were seeing an early phase of human civilization developing, and they were the most developed civilization on Earth at the time.

Quan Yin: Yes.

Alison: They didn't have technological development because they lived in a very simple and natural way.

Quan Yin: Correct.

E.T.s' Genetic Manipulation and the Rise of Fully Sentient Humans

Lemurians didn't stay the way they were. Their natural evolution was interfered with when a group of E.T.s landed on their continent. They experienced a dramatic shift in their natural evolution, and they became fully sentient humans later in their civilization.

Alison: You mentioned that the Lemurians did not follow through with a natural evolution to reach full sentience.

Quan Yin: There was E.T. intervention. There was manipulation of the genetic coding that allowed people to expand their consciousness and their mind, more than if they had continued to go along with natural evolution, Darwinian evolution.

Alison: Just out of curiosity, had the primitive human bodies of Neanderthals or even before Neanderthals been used by souls for incarnation?

Quan Yin: Yes.

Alison: Oh, right, we had been animals on Earth too, and there was not a huge difference between animals and early human bodies. But in Lemuria, we began to inhabit bodies of more intelligence, and later we experienced a jump in our consciousness evolution?

Quan Yin: Right. It's the Lyrans and their altering of the human genomes that has been the missing link that your scientists have not been able to find. They just don't know what the missing link is that helps humans become as smart as you are today. They haven't found that in the ape or the Neanderthal man, they haven't found that version of human that would have accounted for the giant leap to Homo sapiens.

(Note: Lyrans are an E.T. race from the Lyra constellation. Quan Yin told us in Chapter Three that the Lyrans are genetic scientists and masters of genetic coding.)

Alison: They need to find the version of human after that genetic recoding?

Quan Yin: That's what they have found. They have not been able to find what came immediately before that would link Homo sapiens to Neanderthals.

Alison: Will they be able to find it eventually?

Quan Yin: They can't because it doesn't exist, because natural evolution was interfered with by the Lyrans.

Alison: I see. The pre-E.T. Lemurians might have offered a clue, the ones that did not have the genetic upgrade?

Quan Yin: Well, they didn't continue to evolve naturally and that whole part of the human race died.

Alison: Right, they all died and then the continent disappeared, so there are no remains.

Quan Yin: Yes, if the scientists want to really go looking, they could go looking at the bottom of the Pacific, but they're not going to do that.

Alison: Wasn't the original plan in the Earth Experiment to allow the human race to naturally evolve to higher intelligence?

Quan Yin: The E.T.s were impatient about the process, so they came in. Lemuria was one where they started tinkering with the humanoids to allow for rapid acceleration of consciousness evolution. Lyrans were coming in their ships and landing and teaching the Lemurians and altering their genetic makeup, giving them upgrades so that they could feel more, understand more.

Alison: Why did the Lyrans want to do that?

Quan Yin: Because they could, because it would be fun to use this knowledge that they had and see what happened.

Alison: Did they have a specific purpose and use for the new humans they created?

Quan Yin: No, they were not trying to create a slave race if that's where you're going.

Alison: Were they simply testing out their technology?

Quan Yin: They were playing God. It was interesting to them to see what happened. It was part of their creative expression.

Alison: I see. What did they want to do with the new humans once they created them?

Quan Yin: Observe, study, and see what they could learn about their sciences, learn about themselves through seeing you all moving into higher and higher levels of consciousness instead of going through a slow evolutionary process that was very natural.

Alison: Were these Lyrans fifth-dimensional beings?

Quan Yin: No, they were third-dimensional.

Alison: That's a surprise. Had they thought about applying the upgrade on themselves?

Quan Yin: No.

Alison: They wanted to try it on another race to see how it worked?

Quan Yin: Yes. They also felt that it was appropriate for them to be where they were in that moment and didn't feel the need to jump or make any sort of quantum leap. They had an understanding that there was value for them in being right where they were, consciousness-wise and evolution-wise.

Alison: So it was just an experiment that they wanted to run with their technology.

Quan Yin: It was also an experiment that they hoped would help humanity.

Alison: What was the type of genetic technology that the Lyrans applied on the Lemurians?

Quan Yin: This was a technology that the Lyrans developed that worked with the physical human body as opposed to a chip or something like that to alter the consciousness of the person.

Alison: Did they have to wait until the next generation was born to see the difference, or were they able to use it on a person and see the change take place?

Quan Yin: The latter. You could evolve through the gene therapy that they had. The technologies that they used to enhance the DNA could be used on a living person, an adult person, or a child.

Alison: How long actually did it take for the Lyrans to see the changes?

Quan Yin: Well, there was some trial and error, of course. And they did get to the place eventually of feeling they were seeing the changes they wanted to see within two months.

Alison: Oh, that's amazingly fast.

Quan Yin: Yes.

Alison: What technology did the Lyrans develop that could perform such miracles?

Quan Yin: Well, they used injections. It was a technology that relied on pulsations of sound to create vibrations in the bodies of the ancient

Lemurians to cause the DNA to change, to upgrade. The sound created new vibrations in the body that had never been experienced before.

Alison: Why did the Lyrans use injections and not put the Lemurians in a sound chamber?

Quan Yin: They hadn't created the sound chamber. In the liquid that was injected, the sound was used to infuse that liquid with the vibration needed. It was the use of sound and water technology. There was some Lyran DNA in the liquid as well.

Alison: Ahh, I see. That's why injections were more appropriate.

Quan Yin: There was light therapy as well. The light was supporting the changes that were going on within the DNA structure that were initiated by the injection. Later on, Lyrans had advanced the technology to using just light, light encoded with frequency and various codes to give an activation to the DNA. So some of it was injections more early on, and then there was a beta testing phase with the light technology, and they then eventually graduated to only using the light technology.

Alison: Wow. And that's a light generated by their own technology?

Quan Yin: Yes, it's an artificial light.

Alison: So, did the Lemurians feel any physical discomfort or mental confusion after receiving the upgrade?

Quan Yin: Yes, it was a bit disorienting, and some experiences for them were ungrounded experiences that they then needed to deal with, but they absolutely were feeling overall that something good was happening.

(Note: An ungrounded experience results from having the upper chakras actively connected to the nonphysical and the lower chakras, especially the root chakra, somewhat dislodged from their connections to Earth.)

Alison: How did the Lyrans persuade the Lemurians to participate in the experiments?

Quan Yin: Because these beings that the Lemurians were standing in front of certainly seemed to them like they were gods and that they had so much to offer. So the Lemurians were absolutely happy to do whatever these beings said was going to make them more like the gods.

Alison: Oh, I see. Did the Lyrans appear to them as humanoid?

Quan Yin: No, they appeared to them as feline humanoid.

Alison: Meaning they had a feline head and a humanoid body?

Quan Yin: Yes.

Alison: Okay, and it didn't bother the Lemurians that they looked so different. Was it because they felt the Lyrans' higher vibration?

Quan Yin: They felt the vibration, and they also felt that the difference in appearance was due to the fact that they were standing in front of gods.

Alison: Wow. How many Lemurians accepted the treatment?

Quan Yin: There were about 20% who did not receive it.

Alison: Because they didn't want to?

Quan Yin: Because they didn't want to. And some were being protected also by the parents. The parents thought this was too risky, it's experimental, and they wouldn't let their children do it. So some parents did it but didn't let their children do it.

Alison: When did the Lyrans come and alter the Lemurian genes?

Quan Yin: The Lyrans came around 800 years into the 1,000-year span.

Alison: So it was much later into the Lemuria civilization.

Quan Yin: Yes.

Lemurians Before and After Genetic Manipulation

We know the Lemurians were more intelligent and fully sentient after the genetic upgrade. How was the higher sentience manifested?

Alison: Many people believed the Lemurians lived in the fifth dimension. Did they ever reach the fifth dimension after the genetic upgrade?

Quan Yin: No, you've never had a 5D civilization there on Earth. Earth has never been able to support fifth-dimensional consciousness.

Alison: If the Lemurians were not in the fifth dimension, were they in the fourth dimension?

Quan Yin: They were third-dimensional. They had attempted to reach the fifth dimension, but they hadn't achieved completion of the cycle to get even to the fourth. Even though they were advanced, it just wasn't time because there wasn't a Universal Shift going on as there is with all of you now. So, you can imagine how you could be third-dimensional there on Earth without so many conflicts, without so much struggle, and you could still be living a very spiritual life and having an experience of life in paradise on Earth. And that's why the Lyrans chose that civilization because they showed such potential for being able to go to higher and higher frequency states. They knew these people would be able to handle being face to face with E.T.s that were of such higher frequency.

Alison: I am still surprised the Lemurians could have such bliss and harmony when they were not that far from Neanderthals.

Quan Yin: Remember, Earth was created to be that, for the E.T. beings to come and have a paradise vacation. The Lemurians didn't achieve it through work. They achieved it through selecting ideal circumstances.

Alison: If the Lemurians already had bliss and harmony, what were the higher states of being that could be achieved through the upgrade?

Quan Yin: You have a type of understanding, when you live in that type of lifestyle, that the wind, the rain, the sun, the moon, the stars, the ocean, the trees, the animals and the Earth, they are all part of you and you're part of them. You want to live in bliss and harmony with it all, but you don't really understand everything. You don't really know where you come from, you don't really have a full understanding of what Source is, what it's like to evolve spiritually, be on a spiritual path, and experience E.T. beings. As soon as the Lyrans landed, that changed the consciousness right away. And it's what's going to happen to you all in the foreseeable future. So the Lyrans landed, and there was automatically a shift in the consciousness to understand, "Oh, there is more than what's just here." And to go beyond that, "Oh, there is a nonphysical reality. That nonphysical reality creates this reality. Oh, we are all one and we are ascending together." So they realized there's a lot more than being in a tropical paradise.

Alison: Okay. So this is what higher sentience leads to. It creates a different reality that we get to experience in higher consciousness.

Quan Yin: Once you become a sentient human, you can begin to contemplate your existence, your relationship to Source, your relationship with time, and who and what you really are, and what it means to be born, what it means to die, where you go after you die.

Alison: How were the Lemurians expressing these changes?

Quan Yin: One of the things they became interested in right away, of course, was E.T.s and the different beings that lived on the different planets and stars and moons. And they became very curious about that. And the Lyrans were able to convince most of them that they weren't gods, and that they were E.T.s, and that there were others like them out there. And so that was a lot of fun for them to consider. They also became much more artistic, much more creative in what they would do with physical objects, but also with music and storytelling, forms of art, self-expression, poetry, those types of things. They became very interested in the relationship between all things, the unity consciousness, and meditation, and attaining a type of enlightenment.

Alison: They became more intellectual and spiritual.

Quan Yin: Yes, but also more emotional and more artistic.

Alison: Right, more artistic, but more emotional too, meaning having access to a larger spectrum of emotions?

Quan Yin: Yes, the range of emotions did increase because of their new awareness, and their new DNA strands were helping them to access different feelings.

(Note: According to Quan Yin, additional DNA strands beyond the pair we have can be activated when we reach higher spirituality and vibration.)

Alison: That's what sentience is about, isn't it? We can think more and feel more. Our experience is richer and has more depth.

Quan Yin: Correct.

Alison: And because of their spirituality, they were not weighed down by the new feelings and emotions they got to experience?

Quan Yin: No.

Alison: Did the Lyrans help the Lemurians change their spiritual beliefs?

Quan Yin: No, their genetic manipulation certainly created a different way that the Lemurians had of thinking of themselves than others. And there was more of a relationship with the nonphysical as a result because their life was so based on what they could see, and all they could see and experience was basically good. So they did not have a need to escape it, or think of heaven, a heavenly realm that they would someday graduate to. After the upgrade, they were able to incorporate more of a relationship with spirit and the nonphysical.

Alison: Overall, were they moving away from the lifestyle they had or were they just expanding it?

Quan Yin: No, they weren't moving away from the lifestyle they had. They were enhancing what they already did with more self-expression, more curiosity, more of an awareness of their place in the Universe. And so it turned paradise into ultimate paradise.

Alison: So they were happy and joyful before. Now they're still happy and joyful, but you can have a deep intellectual and spiritual conversation with them.

Quan Yin: Yes, and they had no fear of death. The one thing that they could have feared prior to the Lyrans coming was not knowing what would happen once they died. But now they had a deeper understanding of who they were, that they were eternal beings. And so without the fear of that, they really could live lives of freedom.

Alison: And did higher consciousness bring higher intelligence?

Quan Yin: Yes.

Alison: Did they finally have a written language?

Quan Yin: They were developing a written language.

Alison: Were they advanced in astronomy, mathematics, physics, those kinds of scientific fields?

Quan Yin: I would say astronomy more so than mathematics and physics, although they would have gotten there pretty quickly had the civilization survived. Lemurians had been advanced in terms of agriculture and working with the energies of the celestial bodies, the sun, the moon, the stars, and Mother Earth.

Alison: It seemed they did develop agriculture later. Did they have good knowledge of soil, water, plants, crops, and also the weather and rainfalls?

Quan Yin: Yes.

Alison: How did they record or pass on the information without a written language?

Quan Yin: A lot of the information was transmitted, transferred into crystals.

Alison: Was information transferred by E.T.s to the crystals?

Quan Yin: No, by the Lemurians who were taught by the E.T.s how to do it.

Alison: Oh, okay. There are a lot of Lemurian crystals in certain regions on Earth. Some would have information and knowledge in it if people know how to access it?

Quan Yin: Some people have been able to, yes.

Alison: Once the Lemurians were genetically tampered with, so to speak, did their bodies change to be less physical?

Quan Yin: Not less physical, but the body was able to handle more energy from the soul.

Alison: And more light?

Quan Yin: Yes.

Alison: Was there ever a war on the continent of Lemuria?

Quan Yin: No.

Alison: And were they still getting sick?

Quan Yin: Yes.

Alison: Okay. So that part didn't change completely. And was their lifespan expanded?

Quan Yin: Yes, but it wasn't that long after the E.T.s came that Lemuria was destroyed. So we actually don't know how long they could have lived for.

Alison: I see. So, 200 years after the genetic manipulation, Lemuria was destroyed.

Quan Yin: Yes, it was.

The Destruction of Lemuria

It was appalling and heartbreaking that a paradise like Lemuria could be destroyed. They were peaceful and joyful beings evolving to a higher plane of consciousness. What could possibly have dictated this fate? What went wrong?

Alison: What happened to Lemuria that caused the destruction?

Quan Yin: Lemuria was destroyed by the Lyrans.

Alison: Why?

Quan Yin: They didn't want their work to be used for evil by those who would use that to take over the galaxy. This was post-Orion Wars. They realized that some beings had the capacity to want to take over the entire galaxy if they had the right tools to do so, to create the armies and so on.

(Note: Please see a short description of Orion Wars in Chapter 2.)

Alison: So they destroyed the entire continent and the people on it?

Quan Yin: Some people survived and that was by design as well. The Lyrans knew that people would scatter. Enough of the evidence of the experiment would be gone, so that they wouldn't be drawing a lot of attention to themselves. The survivors took the information and spread it across the planet so that it became knowledge to all. Well, it wasn't just knowledge but there was crossbreeding that would go on, that would create sort of the hybrid race.

Alison: We are the hybrid race?

Quan Yin: You are more of a watered-down version of the original Lemurians because of the less sentient humans that were still on the planet to mate with for the Lemurian survivors.

Alison: Ahh, so the Lemurians who were genetically re-engineered by the Lyrans were a more sentient version of modern humans?

Quan Yin: Yes.

Alison: But we are catching up now, right?

Quan Yin: Yes, you are.

Alison: The Lemurians were doing so well. You said that the Lyrans were afraid their secret would be misused. Did the Lemurians show any tendency to such misuse?

Quan Yin: No, it had nothing to do with them and everything to do with the technology that was successfully used upon them. If they were discovered, then some other E.T.s would know somebody came in here and made some changes, and these other E.T.s would want to get their hands on that technology. So the Lyrans were afraid they would be found out.

Alison: That humans could be upgraded and misused through this genetic manipulation?

Quan Yin: It could be used not just on humans but in so many other ways. That technology, that knowing that they had, could be used to create all kinds of armies, oppressive weapons, brain control, mind control technologies, and things like that. It went far beyond what others would do to humans. The variety of manipulative uses of the application of that technology would be possible were it to fall into the wrong hands. That was the belief, and Lemurians were simply the evidence of that. The Lemurian civilization should not have evolved as quickly as it did.

Alison: So the technology was used to change human DNA, but it could change the DNA for better or for worse, and its application was not limited to DNA.

Quan Yin: Correct. It's a technology that alters something at its core. A brain cell, crystals, and other physical objects could have been weaponized with the technology.

Alison: I see. But if they could have this level of technology, how could that power be contained or regulated in this Universe?

Quan Yin: Well, think about all of you with your nuclear bombs. It's the same dilemma that you face there on Earth. You have to be able to control your power.

Alison: So that's it. I guess that would be the case for all beings in this Universe. It's light vs darkness. If the technology is used for a negative purpose, it's darkness, only to be offset by the light we can generate. Is that the way to look at it?

Quan Yin: Correct. And anything that may happen, regardless of how it would happen, would always be by agreement at the soul level. It would always be the creation of people or beings who are involved; however, not everyone carries that wisdom inside of them at all times.

Alison: Okay. I understand. We need morality back in our civilization. We need to raise our consciousness if we do not want to learn the hard way.

Quan Yin: Yes.

Alison: The Lyrans didn't intend to use the technology for a bad cause. It's just that the Orion Wars left a shadow of fear in the misuse of technology. The success of the experiment also spelled trouble and danger.

Quan Yin: Yes.

Alison: How did the Lyrans destroy Lemuria? Did they sink the continent with a meteorite or through a massive earthquake?

Quan Yin: They had weapons on their ship for that level of destruction.

Alison: Those were not nuclear weapons, just powerful, destructive weapons?

Quan Yin: Right.

Alison: I understand the reason why the Lyrans felt they had to destroy Lemuria. Maybe they did it for a bigger reason, which was to protect beings in the galaxy. But it felt so unfair to the Lemurians. It was cruel and atrocious.

Quan Yin: It was, and that group of Lyrans met their karmic end as a result of that.

Alison: Ahh. What happened to them?

Quan Yin: They were destroyed while on their ship. They were taken out by Reptilians.

(Note: Reptilians are an E.T. race known for their malicious nature and conduct. This E.T. race will be discussed in Chapter 12.)

Alison: Was it warfare between the two?

Quan Yin: It was more of a pirate type situation.

Alison: The Reptilians were trying to steal the technology from the Lyrans, but there was also a karmic reason for this to happen?

Quan Yin: Yes.

Alison: Karma was served, but this double tragedy was just a very sad chapter in our history.

Quan Yin: Yes.

Alison: I guess the Reptilians didn't get the technology?

Quan Yin: No.

Alison: Did no other E.T. races know what the Lyrans were doing in Lemuria?

Quan Yin: The Pleiadians were in Lemuria.

Alison: That's a surprise. What's their role there?

Quan Yin: The Pleiadians were helping the Lyrans. They were assisting in the experiments and offering their counsel, their healing, and observing, wanting to ensure that things were going well with the Lemurians. They gave teachings that would help the Lemurians with their emerging consciousness.

Alison: Wow. They agreed with the experiment?

Quan Yin: They knew at the time they found out about what the Lyrans were doing, but there was nothing they could do to stop the Lyrans without going to war over it. And so they just thought to assist instead.

Alison: I see. So, were they aware of the plan to destroy Lemuria?

Quan Yin: They became aware of it, and again, they had to accept it.

Alison: So, they just withdrew from it all and let things happen. Did they stay to help with the surviving Lemurians?

Quan Yin: They came back eventually, but they stayed away for a little while.

Alison: How many people actually lived on Lemuria? I know the total number of souls would be smaller because souls reincarnate into multiple bodies and lifetimes.

Quan Yin: Well, there were about 250,000 Lemurians at one time living on the continent. And there were close to 25 million people in total that had lived in Lemuria during those 1000 years.

Alison: I'm still so struck by how some Lemurians were able to achieve a high level of spirituality and consciousness while being third-dimensional.

Quan Yin: It is possible. It is possible to be the most optimized version of yourself while in the third dimension.

Alison: And we lost that optimization.

Quan Yin: Yes, part of the issue with the Lemurian civilization is from the destruction of the continent that caused the traumas, and the traumas affected the DNA of the survivors. A lot of people also mistakenly assumed that E.T.s were gods. So you then have more of a fear of god, gods in the sky, and not gods living amongst us or in the wind, in the flowers.

Alison: And all this was encoded in our DNA through the surviving Lemurians.

Quan Yin: Yes.

Alison: Are Lyrans still around today and working on the genetic technology?

Quan Yin: Yes, they are not the same Lyrans. Those who sank the Lemurian continent did not constitute all the Lyrans.

Alison: They are still the leader in DNA technology?

Quan Yin: Yes, in genetics and hybridization.

Alison: But not involved in anything so ill-conceived with an unmerciful end?

Quan Yin: They learned from that experience.

Purpose of the Lemuria Experience

The dramatic nature of the Lemurian experience befitted a "grand opening" of human incarnations. There was also so much learning, learning about how we could carve out a space in the third dimension where we could live in harmony, purity, and joy. This seemed to be one end of the Earth experience, the pleasant end. The genetic upgrade was a unique E.T. contact experience. It seemed to have removed some of that innocence in Lemurians, but it created the first fully sentient humans on Earth. It was going well for both the Lemurians and Lyrans. Then the pendulum swung, and darkness overshadowed this blissful land. The god-like E.T.s obliterated the continent and most Lemurians on it.

The surviving Lemurians were no doubt left in shock, fear, and disbelief. They were also brutally traumatized. It was paradise lost, even if the Lemurians didn't capitulate to any abominable temptation for this to happen. Is paradise always going to be lost? Do we always have to live in fear and distrust? It is a lot for a human mind to grasp what this all meant. I asked Quan Yin to help us see a higher perspective here.

Alison: For humanity at the collective consciousness level, is there a live-and-learn type of experience here?

Quan Yin: Well, you're learning through the mistakes of the Lyrans, which means that all of humankind would benefit from the trauma and the tragedy of Lemuria because you would know that when you go down this type of path of trying to control and manipulate for your own purposes, there is usually a tragic end. You learned from the Lyrans to be patient because the Lyrans weren't being patient with humanity. You learned through the Lyrans that sometimes using science and technology is not the best way to go about doing something, and even though you can do something, it doesn't mean you should do something.

Alison: What was the purpose of Lemuria for those who experienced it in human form?

Quan Yin: Everything is about Source having as many different possible experiences as Source can. And of course, the souls choosing to participate in it knew that there was value in every single experience that they would have, including the trauma of having their continent ultimately destroyed by those they considered to be gods.

It's also helpful in terms of showing how humanity could come to understand there would be a wrathful God as well, and how the relationship of separation between humans and God, how that was ultimately helped by this experience. Some people may have a hard time understanding the purpose of the need for separation from Source. And remember, part of the Earth experience for humanity has been to explore fear, to explore separation, and to explore separation from both E.T.s and from Source.

And so here you have the ancient Lemurians thinking they were being met by gods at first, and then most of them recognizing that those gods were in fact E.T.s. And in the end, they had reasons to be afraid of both, that which is Divine and that which is extraterrestrial. And so the experience furthered the separation that was always going to be a part of humanity's evolution. You know what you don't want. You know that you don't want to live in fear, and you know that you don't want separation. And you had to experience both before you could come to know that you wanted to experience unity, you wanted to experience yourself as being a part of a galactic community, and experience yourselves as the Divine in the flesh. And so, while it's all unpleasant, unwanted, it is also part of what souls signed up for when they started a series of incarnations on Earth.

Alison: It wasn't that clear to me that there was a separation between them and Source in Lemuria. They seemed connected with everything and every being.

Quan Yin: Correct. The separation happened as a result of the experience of the tragedy. So what I'm saying is that post Lemuria, humanity experienced more of a feeling of separation from E.T.s, from Source, even from one another because of the experience of Lemuria.

Alison: It was in the collective consciousness?

Quan Yin: It was in the collective consciousness, yes, and in those Lemurians that survived and went out and told their stories, and also coupled with the other humans of the different continents that they fled to.

Alison: So the story was passed on to other humans. It was a traumatic and powerful experience. It was the Earth Experiment rolled out in full force.

Quan Yin: Yes.

The Magic of Crystals

Going through the high drama of Lemuria can be an emotional experience. If a surge of emotion follows, it may be our subconscious stirring up feelings of that deep trauma. The trauma is ready to be healed. Releasing it and letting it all go is the best thing to do.

When we are in a peaceful state, let's turn our attention to another topic that's important to the Lemurians. It's the use of crystals. Lemurians were known for their use of crystals, which played a significant part in their blissful life. As Quan Yin said already, crystals could be used for storage and transmission of information. We also know about crystals' healing capabilities. But in a conversation with Quan Yin, I realized that crystals have more magical powers than that. In the next chapter, we will discuss how the Atlanteans used crystals as a natural energy source. Here, in honor of the Lemurians, we will focus on the potential use of crystals in enhancing healing, wellbeing, beauty, spirituality, and just about anything you want.

Alison: There's a lot of discussion about crystals and crystal power today. We know crystal mostly for its healing power. Does it naturally possess healing energy?

Quan Yin: These healing energies are also all around and can be tapped into by those who tune themselves to those higher frequency energies.

Alison: So we can also access the higher frequency energy and store it in the crystal to be released later for a healing purpose?

Quan Yin: Correct.

Alison: So, is crystal mainly a storage device?

Quan Yin: There are many different uses for any crystal, so it's not basically just a storage device, but that's one of its uses. It has a higher level of consciousness.

Alison: Okay. And the other uses would include healing?

Quan Yin: Anything you want. Crystal can do just about anything.

Alison: Wow. Because of the consciousness level it has?

Quan Yin: Yes.

Alison: That's very interesting. People who are spiritually inclined will often come across crystals when they explore spiritual practices. Beyond meditation and healing, what other uses can we get from crystal?

Quan Yin: Yes, it depends on you. So there are giant books about crystals and what each crystal is for, but really it's up to the person what they want to use a crystal for. A person can use a crystal to emit beauty in their room where they're sitting, and every time they look at the crystal, it's easy to appreciate the crystal because of the crystal's beauty, and their vibration is raised. Someone else may want a crystal in their room with them because it helps to put them at peace so that crystal can help them meditate or sleep. Another person may have a crystal because they want that crystal to absorb EMFs, and so they put that crystal by their Wi-Fi modem.

There are so many uses for crystals. There's the fact that crystals can be used to just sit with you and get you to contemplate the Earth. And they come from the Earth, so they're holding that Earth energy, and they can be very grounding just by having them on you or near you. You have an automatic grounding device there. You can create a crystal healing chamber. You can create furniture out of a crystal, and every time you eat on that crystal table, you're getting your food programmed by the crystal with the intention that you have for it to provide healthier meals. So the crystals are very programmable, which is why they have a million uses.

Alison: Are crystals unique to Earth?

Quan Yin: No, other planets have their own crystalline structures within them.

Alison: When the Earth Experiment started, were crystals meant to be a companion to us to help us with just about everything?

Quan Yin: Absolutely. It's the consciousness of Mother Earth in concentrated form.

Alison: Did E.T.s contribute to the creation of crystals?

Quan Yin: Yes. There was great intention placed within the terraforming of Earth, and there was a knowing that the crystals would be needed because Earth would be a place where so many different beings would come, and there would need to be a lot of support from within Mother Earth, from the crystalline structures and the crystalline consciousness.

Alison: I have a Lemurian crystal that I love and use for healing purposes. Now I wonder if it can offer other benefits because it was part of that Lemurian experience?

Quan Yin: Because of the information that is stored in those crystals of Lemuria, they are now helping the humans of today who have unearthed those crystals. Having the history of Lemuria contained in those crystals is helping you now.

Alison: Even if we haven't all had access to the information in the crystal?

Quan Yin: Even if you don't even know how to access it, while it's being held in one of your hands, you're still benefiting from the fact that it's in there.

Alison: This can be for clearing, healing from that trauma, and all the wisdom from the Lemurian experience?

Quan Yin: That's correct.

CHAPTER 6

❧

LOOKING INTO THE MIRROR OF ATLANTIS: THE RISE OF THE CIVILIZATION AND ITS TECHNOLOGY

After Lemuria was destroyed, survivors scattered to both coasts of the Pacific Ocean. Some made their way across Central America and landed on the continent that would birth Atlantis, the second major civilization in human history after Lemuria. Like Lemuria, Atlantis was seen as a myth that vanished with no archeological evidence to date. However, it was amply and specifically described in channeled and past life regression literature (1).

According to Quan Yin, Atlantis was the second attempt by the E.T.s to help speed up human evolution. But this time, the E.T.s' assistance was much less direct or intrusive. They never landed in Atlantis and walked amongst the Atlanteans like the Lyrans did in Lemuria. And unlike Lemuria, technology played a crucial part in the development of the Atlantean civilization. It was the first technologically advanced human

104

civilization on Earth, with its technology matching or even exceeding our technology today. However, the Atlanteans did not master the lesson of using technology with discernment. They did not build a moral and spiritual foundation to guide the development and proper use of science and technology. The tension created by the unfettered use of technology eventually ruptured this thriving civilization.

The preceding account underlies the rise and fall of Atlantis for many people who believed in its existence. However, there are other descriptions of Atlantis that portray people living a very spiritual and high vibrational life (2). As I continued to inquire about Atlantis, I found that Atlantis as a civilization was not entirely dominated by science and technology. It had two different images. One was modern and technological, established in the north, and the other was natural and spiritual, anchored in the south. They coexisted for their history together. Integration of the two cultures could have created a sublime and well-balanced civilization. But unfortunately, they held on to lifestyles and beliefs that were diametrically opposed to each other. Neither was able to influence the other, and they met their fate as one Atlantis.

The story of Atlantis is as engrossing as it is sobering for anyone looking ahead to the future of our civilization. A long time ago, there was a human society that looked and behaved a lot like ours today. We are taught that our civilization did not enter its modern era until after the Industrial Revolution. But it seems that a technology-driven civilization had already come into existence long before that, and it also had a spiritual twin with divergent values and traditions. Atlantis had a split personality. It's a phenomenon present in our time as well. We can see the twin reflections in our own mirror today, even if the spiritual image has shrunk considerably in comparison to Atlantis. What are we repeating here? Are we being given the same storyline and challenge?

Here is part one of the three-part story of Atlantis. In this chapter, we'll trace the development of Atlantis from its early days to a high-tech civilization. We'll focus on their own natural evolution as well as the influence of E.T.s in igniting their technology revolution.

The Rise of Atlantis and Return of E.T.s

We begin the story with the early development of Atlantis and how E.T.s helped the Atlanteans open the door to a future of advanced science and technology.

Alison: Was there any other race in human history that was similar to the Lemurians?

Quan Yin: The ones who would later evolve and become the Atlanteans, but they had help from the Lemurians who made it over to that continent.

Alison: The Lemurians were their ancestors?

Quan Yin: Yes. That was a race that formed from the wisdom of Lemuria and the genetic upgrade of Lemurians. The surviving Lemurians crossbred with the natives, and there was also natural evolution that took place. So they were very close to that level of consciousness of Lemurians because of the natural evolution, and because more E.T. contacts were taking place that were channeled, and people were having their own contact experiences as well.

Alison: When did Atlantis exist?

Quan Yin: Atlantis began around 250,000 BC. The continent was millions of years in existence, and the civilization lasted for 1500 years.

Alison: So they emerged about 50,000 years after the end of Lemuria.

Quan Yin: Yes.

Alison: I guess that's a good period of time they had for natural evolution. Where was Atlantis? Was it a chain of islands or was it actually a continent, because I've seen both descriptions?

Quan Yin: It was a continent and it had islands like Asia, a continent but also with islands. It was in the Atlantic Ocean.

Alison: How far did it stretch in the north and south?

Quan Yin: As far north as Scandinavia, and as far south as the very northern part of South America.

Alison: Did the Atlanteans look like Lemurians?

Quan Yin: There was more of a mixture of the darker skin with the lighter skin because of the crossbreeding that had gone on between humans.

Alison: Did the Atlanteans still have brown eyes, brown hair, and still look more or less like the Mayans?

Quan Yin: The majority had brown hair and brown eyes in Atlantis, just like what you have on the planet now. But there were some green-eyed, blond-haired, blue-eyed, red-haired, and so on people.

Alison: Where did those genes come from? I thought all humans in ancient times were pretty much the same race.

Quan Yin: So the blue eyes and the green eyes, and the red hair and the blond hair, they would sometimes come as a genetic mutation, not because of crossbreeding.

Alison: I see. But it was not the majority of the population?

Quan Yin: No, a very small minority.

Alison: Okay. Therefore, a lot of them looked like Lemurians, but there was a little variety.

Quan Yin: Right, because then you have the brown-haired or the dark-haired and brown-eyed people mating with the blond-haired, blue-eyed people, and the red-haired, green-eyed people and such. So then you have mixtures over time to create what were in between the darker and the lighter, and everything in between.

Alison: What's the lifespan like for the Atlanteans?

Quan Yin: A long life in Atlantis would have been 300 years.

Alison: And did they live that long throughout the 1500 years?

Quan Yin: Some did.

Alison: It's amazing that people in ancient civilizations could live much longer. But they still could die a lot younger because of the vulnerability of a physical body?

Quan Yin: Yes.

Alison: Did they already have spoken and written languages in the early part of their civilization?

Quan Yin: Yes, they did.

Alison: Did the Atlanteans live in a way similar to or different from the Lemurians?

Quan Yin: In the beginning, they were still living very close to nature. And then with more technological advancements being brought forth and being dropped in by different extraterrestrial races, their technology evolution was done in harmony with Mother Earth and not at the expense of it. And so you had the best of both worlds there with less direct interaction, less interference on the part of the E.T.s, but more of the beginning of that time where technology would just be dropped into either the mind of an Atlantean, or an actual gadget, device, or craft would be left behind by the E.T.s for the Atlanteans to work with.

Alison: Did the E.T.s make a new decision to assist humans without outright interference? Were they aware of what the Lyrans did in Lemuria?

Quan Yin: Most of them were aware of what the Lyrans did. Some of them were just curious about what these humans would do with this piece of technology if they dropped it in. Others were seeking to help.

Alison: So they, in a funny way, may have been inspired by the Lyrans and wanted to see if they could make a difference in a better way?

Quan Yin: Yes.

Alison: Since more than one group came, did they coordinate their work?

Quan Yin: They were not working together. There were different factions and different races from different star systems, each with their own agenda. So there wasn't a lot of cooperation going on in which technology should be shared and when and to whom. It did become a little bit chaotic as a result of that, and the Atlanteans did get a little out of control with their use of technology.

Alison: But they didn't manipulate the Atlanteans like the Lyrans did.

Quan Yin: Correct, not as hands-on.

Alison: Who first left the craft for the Atlanteans to work with?

Quan Yin: The Pleiadians.

Alison: Oh, really?

Quan Yin: Yes, they thought they would do a better job than the Lyrans. And they thought that the better way to go about it was to help the Atlanteans develop their own technology.

Alison: Because technology can accelerate human evolution as we have witnessed in our history?

Quan Yin: Yes.

Alison: And you said that there were other E.T.s that followed the Pleiadians.

Quan Yin: Yes. Sirians, Orions, and others.

Alison: Did the E.T.s leave instructions together with the devices or craft they dropped?

Quan Yin: No, the Atlanteans reverse engineered the devices and craft.

Alison: I see. Were the E.T.s assisting humans in other areas as well or just in Atlantis?

Quan Yin: Atlantis really was the hub of the human society at that time. There were just some tribal communities on the outskirts and the other parts of the planet, but there was nothing that interesting going on for E.T.s to get involved with.

Flying Machines and the Technology Revolution in Atlantis

The focus on technology was a major theme of the Atlantean civilization. What was the key discovery that started their technology revolution? Interestingly, aviation was the domain where the advanced E.T. technology was first decoded and applied.

Alison: Were there major stages of development during their 1,500-year civilization, like the pre-Lyran and post-Lyran Lemuria?

Quan Yin: Certainly the creation of flying machines was an important milestone.

Alison: Was that a gift from the E.T. drop-offs?

Quan Yin: Yes, they reverse engineered it.

Alison: So how many years into their civilization did they first receive the E.T. craft and gadgets?

Quan Yin: Around 500 years into the civilization.

Alison: And how long did it take before they were able to understand and apply the E.T. technologies?

Quan Yin: About 200 years later.

Alison: So about 700 years into their civilization, they had a major breakthrough in reverse engineering the E.T. technology and they developed flying machines?

Quan Yin: Yes.

Alison: What were the flying machines like?

Quan Yin: They had really different types of crafts. Yes, they did have crafts that could lift off straight up off the ground, and then they had crafts that could go to the rim of outer space, that could travel quite high in the sky, and they were shaped like orbs. And then they had your more traditional airplanes and helicopters and every imaginable machine you could fly.

Alison: Oh my goodness. Did they use the same aviation technology as we do? They seemed to have something different.

Quan Yin: Well, because they were working from reverse engineering craft material that was left behind by E.T.s, they had more advanced technology, and so they were not working with the same laws of physics and propulsion that say the Wright Brothers were. They had different ways of going about it, different ways of elevating the crafts into the sky, whereas what you've had in recent memory have been spaceships that have evolved over time. They had the more evolved ships and crafts at the same time as the more primitive ones, the helicopters and airplanes, as I mentioned.

Alison: So the more "primitive" ones, such as the early versions of helicopters and airplanes, did they develop them on their own, or was that also inspired by the E.T. technology?

Quan Yin: They developed them on their own.

Alison: Did they do that in the first 500+ years?

Quan Yin: Yes.

Alison: Wow. So they were already strong in technology toward the end of the first 500 years?

Quan Yin: Yes, they were.

Alison: What would be a simple way to describe the technology they reverse engineered from the E.T. craft to create their advanced flying machines?

Quan Yin: It's an understanding of how to use the force that is the gravitational pull and coupling that with the electromagnetic energy that is present all around to reverse that gravitational pull and instead create the opposite of that gravitational pull, which is a polarized effect of it to cause the machine to fly. It wasn't reliant upon a huge amount of fuel being burned out of the jets or the rockets in order to propel them that high into the sky.

Alison: Is that the anti-gravity technology people talk about these days?

Quan Yin: Yes.

Alison: Did they fly their craft in a space voyage or to land on the moon or a different planet?

Quan Yin: No. They would have eventually. They were still developing it.

Alison: I am surprised that the Atlanteans had not launched a spacecraft to land on the moon or another planet. We made it in the 20th century, and they started out with more advanced technology, and they had a few hundred years to do that after E.T.s left the spacecraft for them. Was there a reason why?

Quan Yin: There was no desire. That's why they didn't focus on it. Well, with the Americans and the Russians, there was a desire to control space. And that's why you had the great space race, and the Americans once again proved their might in getting to the moon and controlled outer space. So desire is a huge spark for human ingenuity. The Atlanteans were more concerned about the other earthlings and animals, and other natural catastrophes that they could face, because they had faced those types of things in their recent history to a larger extent. Threats of famine and threats of harsh weather conditions and large animal attacks were much bigger threats to them, which is why they started to rely more on technology to take care of their survival means.

Alison: What large animals did they have in Atlantis?

Quan Yin: The saber-toothed tigers, the wooly mammoths, and the grizzly bears and polar bears that you have today. There were bulls and many more of these animals around.

Alison: Were they deliberately raised or released in Atlantis?

Quan Yin: It was just natural.

Alison: I see. In terms of transportation on the ground, I've read more than once that there was a version of the flying machines that were like cars, but this flying machine hovered a few feet above the ground, and that was their vehicle, a low-flying vessel.

Quan Yin: The original vehicles were on wheels and some people felt safer with the ground travel than with the air travel, and so they still maintained their vehicles on wheels, on two wheels and four wheels and three wheels, just like what you have.

Alison: And the wheeled vehicles were developed by the Atlanteans themselves without needing E.T.'s advanced technology, just like their traditional helicopters and planes?

Quan Yin: Yes.

Reverse Engineering and the Force of Acceleration

Reverse engineering seemed to have generated a wave of pioneering scientific discoveries for the Atlanteans. But primitive humans could not reverse engineer a spacecraft even if they ran into one. Judging by their ability to manufacture traditional vehicles and airplanes, the Atlanteans must have had a strong scientific foundation to engage in reverse engineering. Were they already progressing steadily in science and technology in the first 500 years of their civilization? What else besides the advanced flying machines were they able to reverse engineer?

Alison: And so the E.T.s came and then left the Atlanteans crafts and gadgets to work with, but they didn't necessarily teach them how, for instance, by leaving instructions?

Quan Yin: They did not. They let the Atlanteans use their minds and their imaginations to reverse engineer and create their own flying machines. The Atlanteans were pretty smart already at that point that they were able to reverse engineer.

Alison: It's still inconceivable that the Atlanteans already had scientific knowledge that long ago to reverse engineer very advanced technology that we don't have yet. Did they begin their development with the knowledge in astronomy, mathematics, that type of scientific knowledge?

Quan Yin: That knowledge in astronomy was carried over from Lemuria by certain individuals that had that relationship with E.T.s. So there was an oral tradition of sorts, a passing of information, and the storage of information in crystals that the Lemurians and the Atlanteans both utilized.

Alison: If we think of flying machines and airplanes and cars, we think about mechanical engineering, electrical engineering, aerospace engineering, lots of engineering knowledge. Was there a type of engineering expertise that existed with the Lemurians or Atlanteans?

Quan Yin: With the Atlanteans, yes. So they were much more scientifically advanced. As I said, Lemurians had been advanced in terms of agriculture and working with the energies of the celestial bodies, the sun, the moon, the stars, and Mother Earth, whereas the Atlanteans became quite obsessed with the technology that they found that had been left behind by the Pleiadians.

Alison: What struck me was that the Atlanteans had a certain level of scientific knowledge to reverse engineer.

Quan Yin: They were a naturally developing civilization. They would have developed quite fine on their own without the E.T. technology to reverse engineer.

Alison: So that's why E.T.s chose them to accelerate their development. Before the acceleration, they started as an agrarian society, but they were not just farming. They were developing their scientific knowledge.

Quan Yin: Well, in farming, you developed a certain amount of knowledge of how things work by working with plant technology, earth technology, soil technology, and water technology. You have to grow in your knowledge of how things work. So they were very capable of figuring out how the technology worked, just by observing the function of it and the inner mechanism of it.

Alison: In the first 500 years, they didn't have the downed craft from E.T.s yet, but did they make steady scientific advances since they were able to build cars and planes?

Quan Yin: Yes.

Alison: Did they have any event like our Industrial Revolution to create machines?

Quan Yin: Yes, you could call it an industrial revolution, yes.

Alison: And they achieved it without the assistance from E.T.s?

Quan Yin: No.

Alison: So when did that happen?

Quan Yin: Well, it happened naturally within the 500 years.

Alison: So, was there an equivalent period in our history that would be similar to their first 500 years?

Quan Yin: From 1500 till now, yes.

Alison: So roughly from the latter phase of the Renaissance in the fourteenth century to the twentieth century?

Quan Yin: Yes.

Alison: So, toward the end of those 500 years, they were living in a way more or less like the way we did in the 19th and 20th centuries, and they also had a similar, not identical, but similar knowledge base in science and technology?

Quan Yin: Yes.

Alison: And then E.T.s' downed craft gave them the biggest boost to higher technologies?

Quan Yin: Yes, indeed. They were just able to study it and study it and study it and recognize it had applications and that's it. They could replicate it and make their own, and it went on and on from there.

Alison: I assume the technology for flying machines was not the only technology they reverse engineered?

Quan Yin: Right.

Alison: From the E.T. craft, did they get advanced metals as well? For instance, in the 1947 UFO crash at Roswell, New Mexico, there was a famous discovery of the "shape-memory" metal that could bend but restore its shape. So, was that the type of technology available to the Atlanteans?

Quan Yin: Yes, there was a craft, a very large craft with a lot of that metal on board.

Alison: Did the Atlanteans develop computing technology and artificial intelligence later?

Quan Yin: Yes, they did.

Alison: Wow. Were they ahead of us in terms of what we have today?

Quan Yin: Yes, they had androids, for example, where you could buy an android pretty easily. And their computers were much faster, much more self-learning, and able to do many more computations. It was also able to help people develop their own creations if people wanted to create something, much like with your 3D printers. Your 3D printers now are very primitive examples of what most Atlanteans had in their homes with an ability to create a model for something. And then if a corporation wanted to pick that up and run with it and create it, they would pay the person who created it for their services and their creativity.

Alison: I'm impressed that they were more advanced in computing and artificial intelligence. They didn't have robots, but they had more advanced androids who were able to do more things for humans.

Quan Yin: They weren't self-aware, but they were very good at performing a multitude of tasks, the androids.

Alison: But they didn't have enough consciousness to be themselves?

Quan Yin: Nor to think for themselves outside their programming.

Alison: In 2022, AI went into the mainstream because of ChatGPT, a programmed artificial intelligence that was able to answer our questions based on available knowledge on the Internet and elsewhere. There are advanced versions being developed every day by all the big tech companies and AI startups. Was this what the Atlanteans already had at the time?

Quan Yin: Correct.

Alison: Okay. And did they ever get to a point where they had some issues in terms of takeovers from the AI creations, like what people are concerned about today?

Quan Yin: No. They hadn't gone that far yet.

Alison: I'm also amazed that their computers were more advanced. Did they have quantum computing?

Quan Yin: The Atlanteans, they had their version of it, yes.

Alison: Okay. And so it means that it's not quite the same as ours, but it's fast-speed supercomputing.

Quan Yin: High-speed, yes.

Alison: Okay. And what would be the major difference in quantum computing that they had and that we are developing now?

Quan Yin: Daniel's not technologically advanced enough to be able to give words to that sort of thought.

Alison: Okay. So at what point did they start to have advanced computing and artificial intelligence technologies?

Quan Yin: That would have also been around 200 years after the E.T. technology was left behind, or 700 years into the civilization is when you had the earliest forms of that.

Alison: So it took them a couple of hundred years to reverse engineer and start replicating the major technologies from the E.T. craft, from flying machines to artificial intelligence, maybe not at the same level as E.T.s, but it was the beginning.

Quan Yin: Yes.

Alison: Was there a second wave of technology drop-offs by the E.T.s later?

Quan Yin: No.

Alison: So it was basically that one big round of drop-offs around 500 years in.

Quan Yin: Yes, it was more for them to develop it on their own because the E.T.s wanted to see how far they could go with it without any further help.

Alison: Reverse engineering served to expand their mind and intelligence.

Quan Yin: Yes.

Harnessing Free Natural Energies

Free energy was another key contributor to the Atlanteans' technological advancement. The use of crystal was mentioned often in articles or books about Atlantis. There was also the use of natural electromagnetic energy that Quan Yin spoke about. Natural and free energy requires no mining or drilling into the Earth and prevents pollution and all its health and ecological ramifications. How did the Atlanteans do it?

Alison: Was there any other significant milestone in their technological development?

Quan Yin: The discovery of free energy.

Alison: What were the forms of free energy in Atlantis?

Quan Yin: Many used crystals or free energy, electromagnetic energy that is all around you (3). And they were able to reverse engineer those E.T. technological droppings to figure out how to do that. So there were no fossil fuels.

Alison: What about solar power and other natural energy sources like wind or hydropower?

Quan Yin: Yes, those were also being utilized.

Alison: What did the Atlanteans use to power the traditional airplanes, helicopters, and cars early on? Did they ever have to use fossil fuel?

Quan Yin: No, it wasn't fossil fuel, it wasn't the kind of fuel that you use to power your automobiles and airplanes. They were using solar power that was turned into electric power.

Alison: Did they invent the solar technology without the E.T.s' help? And if so, how did they do it?

Quan Yin: The knowledge of the power of the sun's energy was passed down from Lemuria to the Atlanteans, so they were developing solar power a lot earlier on, whereas when you had fossil fuel, you were less interested in the alternatives because there's less of a need for them.

Alison: Okay, so they had used solar as an energy source early on. How about crystal? I'm curious how the Atlanteans harnessed the crystal energy.

Quan Yin: Well, they had an understanding of the consciousness that was contained within the crystals, and they utilized the sounds that they could generate both from within themselves and using instruments to tap into the right frequency of the crystal to then unlock the power held within it.

Alison: Did the E.T.s help them, or did they just have the knowing because of the Lemurians?

Quan Yin: It was contained, yes, within them because of the Lemurian seed that came over to Atlantis and held some of that knowledge, and then other Atlanteans would bring themselves into a higher vibrational state and be able to receive those downloads.

Alison: How was the crystal energy used by the Atlanteans?

Quan Yin: Crystalline energy was used for communication. It was used to transmit from one person to another, from one computer to another. There's a lot of energy capacity within a crystal that stores and amplifies the electromagnetic energy. As I said before, they're amplifiers. So you could get a lot more energy out of electromagnetic energy because of the use of the crystal, which is a higher consciousness as well.

Alison: So when you spoke about crystal energy, it's really electromagnetic energy within the Earth's electromagnetic field. It's just stored in the crystal which amplifies it?

Quan Yin: Yes, I think your confusion is that when I spoke about using crystals earlier, I did not make clear that the electromagnetic energy was the energy source.

Alison: Okay, so that's what it is. The free energy is electromagnetic energy stored in and amplified by the crystal.

Quan Yin: And transmitted as well, because the crystals have that power, so you don't need wires to power anything. You don't need cords. It's like

Wi-Fi. You don't need to be physically connected because it's just there, you see.

Alison: So crystals can transmit energy over long distances using a series of crystals, and no power lines were needed?

Quan Yin: Correct.

Alison: How would the crystal know to store, amplify, and transmit energy?

Quan Yin: You would use sound to open up the crystal, to program the crystal, to make the crystal into the power converter that it can be, into the transmitter, and the storage device that it can be. And so that's how that was accomplished using sound and using crystals, but the energy stored and transmitted was the energy of the Earth that's all around you.

Alison: So, did crystals act like a form of enhanced batteries? They stored and amplified the energy and then released and transmitted it to be used?

Quan Yin: They could release the energy, or they could project the energy without having it diminished in any way in what they were storing.

Alison: Wow. I'm shocked by that because that means crystals can create self-sustaining, renewable energy once the electromagnetic energy is stored in them.

Quan Yin: Yes, they can.

Alison: In terms of harnessing the electromagnetic energy, did they have that in the first 500 years or more?

Quan Yin: No, not in the first 500.

Alison: So the use of this crystal power coupled with natural electromagnetic energy happened later in their civilization, and was it inspired by the E.T. craft, particularly the harnessing of electromagnetic energy?

Quan Yin: Correct.

Alison: It was also used to propel and power flying crafts later?

Quan Yin: Right.

Alison: We were able to create electromagnetic energy in the 19th century for lighting, but another energy source is required to generate the electricity. While more renewable energies are being adopted, coal and fossil fuels still account for the bulk of energy consumed today. How did the Atlanteans harness natural electromagnetic energy?

Quan Yin: Right, when you are tapping into it, both with the use of consciousness, of intention, of thought, and also to harness it using crystals, you are capable of actualizing more of that energy into your devices, into your vehicles, and so on. But people haven't come across that knowledge to a large enough extent. It's on Earth now for it to be a believable source of energy.

Alison: That is about the electromagnetic energy that naturally exists around us.

Quan Yin: Yes.

Alison: So what we did in the nineteenth century was actually recreating electromagnetic energy and transmitting it through wires without harnessing it naturally using crystals.

Quan Yin: Yes, it's like a synthetic form of it, what you created. It's from a different source.

Alison: I suppose crystals can store other energies that are naturally around us if we program them, such as healing energy.

Quan Yin: Yes.

Alison: This harnessing of crystal and electromagnetic energy feels somewhat like a spiritual technology because of the use of intentions and sounds. Was it used consistently by the Atlanteans?

Quan Yin: Yes, it was used by both the north and south of Atlantis.

Alison: Sounds like there was a difference between the north and south.

Quan Yin: Yes, the north was the technological side of the civilization, and the south remained more spiritual.

Alison: Oh, I didn't know that. But it makes perfect sense now because I've seen both types of descriptions of Atlantis and was a little confused by it. So Atlantis had two cultural personas, and both the north and south used this method of harnessing energy.

Quan Yin: They both used it. But the north used it for more gadgets and flying machines and such, whereas the south would just use it for lighting the home, just like they would use little bits and pieces of technology where they needed it, but they weren't as technologically obsessed as the North.

Alison: So the north was also capable of applying a spiritual method to harness the crystal-electromagnetic energy?

Quan Yin: Well, in the early days, they were able to get to a higher vibration and to be able to have the knowledge of how to use the crystal, how to get the crystal energy.

Alison: I see. They had that spiritual tradition. Did they develop a fully scientific method later to replace the one requiring sound and intentions?

Quan Yin: They were on the way to harnessing it scientifically. They were getting closer and closer to doing so. But they hadn't harnessed it to such an extent that it could be completely understood by the scientists and utilized to the fullest extent by them. They were starting to though.

Alison: So the north still had to have spiritually evolved people to program crystals and harness electromagnetic energy?

Quan Yin: Well, they had the sort of instruction manuals that would help them do that without having to become more evolved spiritually.

Alison: Oh really? They could just focus more without needing to raise their vibration?

Quan Yin: Because they had the instructions of how to do it, they didn't need to change anything inside of themselves in order to utilize their crystals.

Alison: And it still worked and the crystals would respond?

Quan Yin: Yes, the crystals would still work even for those who were not awake yet spiritually.

Alison: It is interesting to know that the north also had a spiritual heritage, and even if they diverged from it, they still made good use of that legacy to garner free energy. They just had more of a utilitarian view of it. They were more charmed by the power of technology.

Quan Yin: That's true.

Notes

1) Examples of this body of literature on Atlantis include the following:
Discover Atlantis: A Guide to Reclaiming the Wisdom of the Ancients by Diana Cooper (2007) gave an overview of Atlantis with many details about the way they lived, traveled, and communicated.
A Hypnotist's Journey to Atlantis by Sarah Bricksman Cosme (2020) was a compilation of Quantum Hypnosis Healing Technique

(QHHT) cases where subjects recalled their lives in Atlantis and in Lemuria.

The Convoluted Universe Book One by Dolores Cannon (2010) described memories of Atlantean lifetimes in QHHT sessions conducted by Dolores Cannon.

Lucy Lee QHHT case reports (please see reference in Chapter 3) included a priestess's memory of the last days of Atlantis and another subject's memory of the genetic experiments in Atlantis.

"The last days of Atlantis" by Bashar, channeled by Darryl Anka (https://bashartv.com/programs/last-days-of-atlantis) gave an account of the destruction of Atlantis and the reason why Atlantis invited this tragic ending.

2) *White Beacons of Atlantis* by Natalie Sian Glasson (2015) recounted a jovial and spiritual life in Atlantis before its fall. Natalie Glasson channeled her past-life self in Atlantis to describe what life was like before the fall of Atlantis.

3) Natural electromagnetic energy is generated by the Earth's electromagnetic field or magnetosphere. According to space. com (https://www.space.com/earths-magnetic-field-explained), "The generation of Earth's magnetic field occurs deep within the Earth's interior, in a layer known as the outer core to be precise. Here the convective energy from the slow-moving molten iron is converted to electrical and magnetic energy, according to the U.S. Geological Survey. The magnetic field then induces electric currents which in turn generate their own magnetic field which induces more electric currents, in a positive feedback loop."

CHAPTER 7

❦

LOOKING INTO THE MIRROR OF ATLANTIS: THE NORTH-SOUTH SPLIT PERSONALITY

As Quan Yin mentioned, Atlantis evolved into two distinct regions and cultures over time. The north went full speed in developing science and technology, while the south continued to honor nature and spirituality. The differences between the two couldn't have been further apart.

In the last chapter, we learned that Atlantis was very advanced in technology. In fact, they were a little ahead of us in computing, AI, clean energy, and aviation. This is such a shock, as we have felt we've been trailblazing these technologies in an unprecedented way. The south, on the other hand, was poised as an oasis against a high-tech backdrop. It shared a kindred spirit with Lemuria. It had more technology at its disposal, except it just chose to remain true to its traditions.

Were they still one civilization? As far as we know, there was only one Atlantis. But life in the north and the south had to be very different, and their political and socioeconomic conditions would vary as well. And how did they interact with each other and keep their peace for 1000 years?

Answers to these questions can begin to help us understand this unusual, bifurcated civilization.

The pursuit of these answers can be significant. The disharmony between technological and spiritual developments can also be found in our society. We do not have a physical manifestation of such a split into neatly defined areas and cultures, but we have these contrasting views embedded in the totality of our society. We have as much, if not more, tension in our civilization.

We can also compare their development with ours and see if we can gain additional insights about ourselves. How far have we been down the path of having technology overpower spirituality? The mirror of Atlantis can give a reflection of our civilization today that is otherwise hidden from our view.

Living in the North and South of Atlantis

We will start by getting a few snapshots of the lives in the north and the south of Atlantis. What was it like living on that continent more than 200,000 years ago?

Alison: In the 1500 years of their civilization, when did the north head down a clear technological path?

Quan Yin: A few hundred years into it.

Alison: Oh, so did it coincide with the time they received the E.T. technologies?

Quan Yin: Yes. Certainly not everyone in Atlantis was going down that path.

Alison: From channeled material, I knew that some Atlanteans lived a very spiritual life (2). And I realize now that they would be living in the south.

Quan Yin: Yes, the spiritual beings were the ones who were living closer to the equator, so in the southern part of Atlantis. And the technological side of Atlantis was in the northern part, where the weather could be harsher in the winter.

Alison: The south had more of the same tropical environment as Lemuria. That may explain at least partially why the south found it easier to be in tune with nature.

Quan Yin: Yes.

Alison: So lifestyle-wise, did people in the north have the same conveniences in daily living, such as cooking, cleaning, and getting around that we have today?

Quan Yin: Yes, they were able to create those machines.

Alison: Did the development of cities occur as well?

Quan Yin: Yes, cities, high-rises, lots of homes, isolation.

Alison: Oh my goodness. Did they have modern medicine?

Quan Yin: A form of it, yes.

Alison: A form similar to our Western medicine?

Quan Yin: Yes, but it hadn't evolved into what you have now with so many pills and so much surgery. But it was well on its way to believing more in the pills and surgery than in the body's natural abilities to heal itself.

Alison: They had an early development of medicine, but they hadn't started doing surgeries yet?

Quan Yin: No, they did. They had some surgeries that they performed and some pills that were being created that were getting further and further away from the natural plants provided by Mother Earth. And so they were definitely going down that same route that you've all gone down.

Alison: It's interesting to know our modern medicine is way more developed than the Atlantean version of it. Since our Western medicine treats a large number of illnesses, I guess the Atlanteans must have been healthier than we are if they could live that long. Was it because Atlantis was less polluted by the use of natural energy?

Quan Yin: Yes.

Alison: Did they have chemical pollution and toxins?

Quan Yin: Yes, they had scientists, and those scientists made chemical solutions that helped in manufacturing, that helped in packaging, that helped them to build their buildings and insulate them because it was colder in the north. And so there were lots of things going on with chemicals in the north.

Alison: Okay, but it wasn't as bad and pervasive as the way we have it now?

Quan Yin: No.

Alison: Did they eat a healthier diet than we do?

Quan Yin: Yes, for the most part. They didn't have as much food available for the most part.

Alison: And in the south, it was even healthier?

Quan Yin: Yes.

Alison: Did they have processed food in the north?

Quan Yin: There was food that was canned and yes, food that was freeze-dried, and it was frozen in a lot of cases because of the weather there. So they utilized more meat and dairy, more of those foods. And in the south, it was more fruits and vegetables and fish.

Alison: So all the changes in lifestyle were not uniform across the entire continent.

Quan Yin: No.

Alison: What you have described so far was mostly the tech-centric and modernized side of Atlantis.

Quan Yin: Correct.

Alison: So life in the south was different and much more spiritual. I have read and heard that priests and priestesses in Atlantis were the spiritual leaders and healers, and that must have been the case in the south.

Quan Yin: Yes. There were priests and priestesses. There were wizards and teachers and shamans and all kinds of things. There was rampant growth amongst the spiritual side when the technological side took off.

Alison: So did the Atlanteans have any spiritual capabilities that people always talked about, like telepathy, levitation, or teleportation?

Quan Yin: That was going on amongst the masters in the southern part.

Alison: So the south did know about Source, and they knew about our Universal origin. That's what the masters would teach about spirituality.

Quan Yin: Yes.

(Note: Please see a discussion about Source in Chapter 1.)

Alison: And they were still third-dimensional in vibration.

Quan Yin: Yes.

Alison: And in terms of healing, were people in the south doing anything different from the Lemurians, which was herbs and energy healing?

Quan Yin: There was more emphasis on sound and the use of water.

Alison: I've heard of the use of higher vibrational sounds in a healing chamber to heal ailments. How was water used?

Quan Yin: Water holds a frequency very well. And when you understand how to program the water, you can use it for healing, and you can use it for raising consciousness. You can also use it for building structures because you use it in the cement to make a strong cement. So there are all kinds of applications to using the programming of water to get the most out of everything.

Alison: Is there a spiritual practice of programming the water where you put yourself in a higher vibration, and then you commune with the water and ask the water to do what you'd like it to do?

Quan Yin: Yes, correct.

Alison: Did people in the north actually have this knowledge as well, as their initial development was closer to nature?

Quan Yin: They weren't as interested. It wasn't as interesting to them.

Alison: Okay, so it's more of a practice in the south?

Quan Yin: Yes, because they were very much more interested in growing their fruits and vegetables and trees and plants, and water was used in all of those practices as well. So there were many ways in which they were seeking to use the natural tendencies of water that were not as interesting to the people of the north.

Alison: It's working with the energy of water at a higher level?

Quan Yin: Yes.

Alison: Were there E.T.s in the south? Did they come to visit and assist the Atlanteans in the south with their spiritual development?

Quan Yin: There were more channels. Yes, some people had visitations, but they weren't visitations that were out in the open, out in the broad daylight.

Alison: I see. It's like people today having E.T. visitations at night. And were there higher-dimensional E.T.s, like the fifth-dimensional E.T.s, giving messages through channels?

Quan Yin: Third-dimensional E.T.s would visit, and yes, fifth or higher would be channeled.

Alison: Okay. And were the E.T.s leaving the crafts behind also third-dimensional as well?

Quan Yin: Yes.

Political and Socioeconomic Structures

It is rare to have two drastically different cultures within the same society, country, or civilization that would go on for 1000 years. We just had a quick overview of their different lifestyles. But how did they structure themselves politically and socioeconomically? How did they manage their relationship with each other, given all their differences?

Alison: Given their modern lifestyle, did Atlantis have a political system closer to a democracy at the time?

Quan Yin: Yes, they developed that.

Alison: Was it very similar to ours or is ours very similar to theirs?

Quan Yin: Yes, in Atlantis, you had representatives that were voted into office, and you had the branches of government. You had all of that.

Alison: Did they have an elected president or premier governing the entire continent?

Quan Yin: What you had, interestingly, is that there were these groups of elders and they weren't elected. It was just by invitation from the elders who were on the council that new ones would be invited to partake, and older ones would, of course, die off. And they were seen more as political leaders as well as wise elders to turn to when there were big decisions to be made about Atlantis. So the politicians who worked as the representatives would often turn to the group of wise elders when they needed help in deciding. They didn't have the political divide that you have now because there weren't political parties. Everyone just was and would be considered an independent now.

Alison: I see. So they didn't have a position equivalent to the president or premier that we have now in the executive branch?

Quan Yin: No. Their view was that no one person could possibly rule over all of everyone else in the population in a fair way. They didn't want a monarchy or emperors and empresses to have a lot of power, and so the power was very evenly distributed.

Alison: Was there one council of elders, or more than one council of elders?

Quan Yin: Just one.

Alison: So would the council of elders just give advice, or would they actually make decisions?

Quan Yin: They would be giving advice to the other representatives who were in charge of making the laws, having the foreign policies, developing armies, and such.

Alison: Okay, so the elected officials were actually like our Congress, but also more than our Congress because they were the sole policy-making and law-making government body, and there was no real executive branch like what we have now?

Quan Yin: No, the wise elders would be the closest thing to that, but they didn't have authority. They were just looked upon as the ones whose thoughts and ideas and opinions should be given the most weight by the others, by those who would consult with them. There was a lot more cooperation in government back then.

Alison: It felt like an honor system. How many elected politicians did they have in Atlantis?

Quan Yin: There were about 300 of them in your equivalent of Congress in Atlantis.

Alison: Did the elected politicians divide up responsibilities and take charge of different government areas such as the military, economy, or infrastructure building?

Quan Yin: No, they were all equally in charge of the different programs and services and such systems. They didn't have one group that was more in control of the military and one group that was more in control of education.

Alison: I see. I guess they could do that because the population was smaller at the time. What was the population of Atlantis at its height?

Quan Yin: It was about 500,000 people.

Alison: It was a small population on a huge landmass.

Quan Yin: Yes.

Alison: And we have since developed a more complex government to manage our complex society and large population. So right now, we have the legislative branch that makes laws and policies, but the executive branch, led by the elected president, would also be making policies in certain areas and issuing executive orders that have the effect of law. It's extremely complicated and often adversarial between the two branches and between the two political parties. The president and his cabinet, as the "administration," also implement federal policies and manage federal affairs in the country. It appears in Atlantis, our executive branch functions were largely merged with the legislative branch. But we now have this division between legislative and executive/administrative branches, both of which have the authority to make decisions, and they don't always coordinate well with each other.

Quan Yin: Yes, you have this division to create the balance that you need there so that no branch goes mad with power and does too much or has too much power over the people, but that wasn't a concern in Atlantis.

Alison: And did they have a central government and local government differentiation as well?

Quan Yin: No, there were no local governments.

Alison: Okay. That also made it simpler. What about the south? Did they have a similar system?

Quan Yin: They had a lot of spiritual leaders, teachers, councils, and the elected representatives in the north would sort of let the south do their own thing. The north Atlanteans didn't feel the need to really enforce the laws of the north on the southerners. They saw them as just being capable of really governing themselves and, of course, not being a threat to the north in any way.

Alison: So the elected politicians had oversight over the south?

Quan Yin: All the politicians were actually elected to be in charge of the entirety of Atlantis, but they just didn't really pay that much attention to the south.

Alison: But shouldn't the south have politicians representing them?

Quan Yin: The elected representatives were for everyone. They were for the north and the south. There was no real political split there. But the southerners didn't really vote. They could vote, but they didn't.

Alison: Oh, they had no real political split. But why did the southerner not want to vote?

Quan Yin: The people of the south were more timid and tame. And they were able to go directly to their councils of elders for advice and not have as much need for representation as a go-between. Remember, the population was much smaller then.

Alison: Did they have different wise elders in the south?

Quan Yin: Yes. They were unrecognized politically. The representatives in the Congress wouldn't go to them, but the people would go to them directly, and no one in the north, like I said, really cared. They didn't say, "Well, that's not the right council of elders." They knew that the southerners would be getting good advice from their elders.

Alison: It sounds like they had several councils of elders in the south?

Quan Yin: Yes, they didn't organize politically in order to come together. They came together organically when they wanted to, but not because they needed to help the politicians make more informed decisions. They were there to help the people.

Alison: So the north and the south loosely shared the same political system, but in reality, the south was given much room for self-governance. Was the south recognized as a separate region?

Quan Yin: No, there were no states, and there was no official line between the north and the south.

Alison: Whose responsibility was it to enforce the laws?

Quan Yin: Yes, there were laws and laws needed to be upheld. So you did have a judicial system and there were still enforcers of the law. The judicial system would determine what to do with these people who didn't want to follow the rules. So yes, you had those aspects of government as well. It just wasn't as corrupt as it is today, so there weren't as many needs for checks and balances as you have today.

Alison: Right. Our judicial system is the court system, and part of the law enforcement actually belongs with the executive branch. And all our laws and policies have become a mosaic that ordinary people don't understand, and even experts would only be experts in a certain area. This muddle was also our creation.

Quan Yin: Well, early on in Atlantis, these people who got into politics or the government were not looking to become rich or famous or go and write a book and sell millions of copies of their books. So they really were public servants because they didn't get paid that well, and they were not power-hungry.

Alison: It's amazing how this early democracy worked with a much cleaner bill of health.

Quan Yin: Well, if you think about your population now, with hundreds of millions of people in that landmass of the United States, of course, there are going to be more bad apples percentage-wise. So you still had those in Atlantis who wanted more for themselves and less for everyone else, and wanted to power over others, but it was a smaller number of people, so you didn't see it as prevalent there.

Alison: Did the north and the south talk to each other in an official capacity?

Quan Yin: Yes, sometimes they would have meetings where they got together and discussed their different issues and interests and policies regarding one another.

Alison: Did they have to coordinate their differences in the implementation of laws or policies?

Quan Yin: Yes. But the north knew they didn't really have to police the south or do anything to ensure the laws were being enforced. They knew they didn't have to. They knew that those weird cousins of theirs down south were only interested in plants and crystals and spirituality, and so they sort of just let them do their thing.

Alison: Atlantis had a very unusual governance structure. It's hard to say if there was just one political system from our perspective.

Quan Yin: It was the fact that the politics of the south were very different from the politics of the north because of the difference in lifestyle and attitude and speaking and such. But they were able to work together, yes, and you could consider it to be one government or two governments.

Alison: This Laissez-faire attitude toward politics is so refreshing. In addition to the political system, did they have similar institutions like ours? I read in Diana Cooper's book about Atlantis that there were hospitals, schools, businesses, the military, media, etc. in Atlantis. I suppose these were the institutions in the north at their height of development?

Quan Yin: Right. And in the south, you had a different form of health care, a different form of education, a different form of media, a different type of economy where people were not as interested, say, in investing or interested in accumulating money or goods. They were fine with trading; they were fine with bartering; and they were fine with having a monetary system. But it wasn't a major point of focus for them with their spirituality.

Alison: Did the north have a modern form of economy and a monetary system, a financial market, a stock market, etc., perhaps not as sophisticated and complex as ours today, but those systems existed?

Quan Yin: Yes.

Alison: So the south just took some aspects of that system, maybe the more basic ones?

Quan Yin: Yes.

Alison: What about the media? Was it like ours?

Quan Yin: Yes, in the south, a different brand of entertainment or media or sharing of stories was still present, but not in the way that it was in the north, whereas in the north it was more like what you have in the modern-day United States.

Alison: So, just on the media side, did the north have something like our mass media, like radio and TV?

Quan Yin: Yes, they did.

Alison: Okay. And did they have Internet and social media?

Quan Yin: Yes, they had internet, and they had ways on the Internet to connect people in that same way that you have now.

Alison: Wow. That's fascinating. If the north was a lot like what we are today, what is the way to describe the south that can give us a concrete idea of how they lived from a socioeconomic point of view?

Quan Yin: If you went to a spiritual retreat center, if you went to a place like Esalen in Big Sur, California, that would represent more of what the life was like in the south, where people were growing a lot of their own food, there was a lot of education in the sense of gatherings and teachers and teachings, but it didn't have to follow a strict curriculum, facts, and figures, which were not as important as spiritual teachings and one's ability to follow those teachings were. There was more of an emphasis on being outside, communing with nature. There wasn't a lot of technology. There wasn't a lot of media being shown in the south, and you wouldn't find that either in Esalen. And you wouldn't find a huge amount of money being exchanged, although there is still exchange going on in a place like that. There's upkeep, and there are people who run their courses and classes there and get paid for them.

Alison: I see. The south was able to have its own system and way of living. In fact, I can see the spirit of the southern Atlantis still alive in different pockets of the modern United States. Esalen is a more concrete and authentic representation of that culture.

Quan Yin: Yes.

Alison: What about the military? The north obviously had military, and the south didn't?

Quan Yin: The south was fine knowing that the north's military was there. The north was not going to let the south be invaded and taken over because then they would be more susceptible to being taken over themselves. The south knew that the north would take care of any sort of attackers that came, and they didn't feel the need to arm themselves because they weren't focused on fear. They weren't focused on their borders or on their vulnerability in terms of being invaded. They just didn't have that focus point, so they would find no need to develop a military.

Alison: Did the north and south speak the same language?

Quan Yin: Yes.

Alison: But their cultures were completely different. The north was officially governing, but the south was also self-governing. It's unusual that they coexisted peacefully. I guess they just focused on their own pursuits. They dwelled on a massive continent, and they were not in each other's way?

Quan Yin: Yes. Now eventually, there would have been a conflict that would have come up if Atlantis had continued on, because the Northerners would have used up a lot of their natural resources up here, such as metals, diamonds, crystals, and other things that could be mined to make bigger and better technological devices. They would have wanted what the southerners had in their enormous landmass, and so they would have come down and wanted to mine there. There would have been quite a bit of conflict, but it never got to that point.

Alison: Ahh, I see. So it was still going to be the north that would have made that move. They were lucky that they only experienced the peace before the storm.

Quan Yin: Yes.

Alison: So, an interesting point you made previously is that Atlantis did have laws and a judicial system, mostly in the north, and the north didn't have to actively enforce the laws in the south. The history textbook would tell us that the Sumerians had the oldest written laws, and then in the Roman Empire, they standardized a lot of the laws to be the template for later generations. So, this is our understanding, but apparently in Atlantis, they already had laws.

Quan Yin: Yes, they did.

Alison: And were they similar to the later laws?

Quan Yin: Yes, it's about thieving and murdering and raping and those sorts of things.

Alison: How about contracts and things of that nature?

Quan Yin: Yes, contracts were held between individuals.

Alison: So they had already developed the laws about people, business, and the code of conduct, or individual rights. In the book *A Hypnotist's Journey to Atlantis*, a QHHT subject described a lifetime as a lawyer and then a judge in Atlantis. And whatever the Romans and others had, they inherited the legacy from the Atlanteans.

Quan Yin: That's true, yes.

Building Pyramids in the South

The pyramids were considered by most people to be the unique creation of ancient Egypt. But the Atlanteans were actually building pyramids hundreds of thousands of years before the Egyptians. They were building them in the south, using spiritual technology that was called forth by priests and masters. This was a largely unknown legacy of the southern Atlanteans, and it was a major contribution to humankind. What purpose did pyramids serve aside from being an architectural marvel?

Alison: Were the Atlanteans the first builders of pyramids on Earth?

Quan Yin: Yes.

Alison: Was that in the south?

Quan Yin: It was.

Alison: The industrial north or the technological north, if I can call them that, was not as interested in pyramids.

Quan Yin: Correct.

Alison: What were the pyramids built for in the south?

Quan Yin: To utilize for purposes of amplifying sound technology and for collecting energy. So, they knew the pyramids would be the most appropriate structure to receive an energy download from above through the pyramid. The energy could then be accessed by anyone entering the pyramid. The energies are also balanced on the planet by the pyramid, so the pyramids themselves were helping the entire Earth, and the beings who helped to co-create the pyramids knew that humanity needed that help.

Alison: Were E.T.s their co-creators?

Quan Yin: Yes.

Alison: The energy accessed by people when entering the pyramid, what purpose would it serve? Was it for healing or good fortune or intelligence?

Quan Yin: They wanted the same things that you wanted. They wanted intelligence. They wanted communication with the E.T.s. They wanted to live longer. They wanted to become younger. They wanted to be able to connect to the spirit realm, the spirit world.

Alison: In terms of balancing the energies on the planet, does that need still exist now? And if so, who is doing that?

Quan Yin: There are many beings all across the planet working with the ley lines and other grids that you have there, and the electromagnetic field. There are many beings who know about the necessity for these energies to be balanced, and they're spread out all across the planet.

(Note: According to Quan Yin, ley lines are energy channels for the Earth and the fundamental grid for the planet's survival. They are the largest and naturally occurring energy grid on Earth.)

Alison: And for the pyramids that were submerged under the water or buried in the soil, do they no longer balance the energies?

Quan Yin: No, they still do.

Alison: They still do. Wow. Did the priests and priestesses in Atlantis also help with balancing the energies?

Quan Yin: Yes. There's more energy present now. There are more people. So you need more help, and the pyramids are still helping. And the monks and high priests and high priestesses and other helpers who are present are also helping to keep the energies on the planet balanced.

Alison: Are there high priests and priestesses today? I thought they existed in Atlantis, Egypt, or other ancient civilizations?

Quan Yin: I'm talking about different cultures where people still identify as a high priest, a high priestess, or a shaman. There are people in the modern era who still identify themselves as a witch and wizard and warlock and medicine man and medicine woman as well. They're just not as well-known or prominent in society as they once were, so everyone would have known who they were previously. But now, as I said, there are so many people on the planet, and there are people in parts of the Amazon, in Africa, and in other tribal areas and tribal island communities where these roles still exist. And certainly, many people who identify as a high priest or high priestess as well are part of your regular society, and they may have given themselves that designation. But they're definitely tapping into something within them that does exist and that has existed perhaps more prominently in society in the past.

Alison: I see. And these people are still serving that role of balancing energies on Earth?

Quan Yin: They realize that part of what they are doing there is balancing energy, yes.

Alison: And then there are other people who are consciously working with energy grids and ley lines?

Quan Yin: Yes. Well, like yourself, you can decide one day, "I'm going to tap into these very real elements of my physical reality and see what I can do."

Alison: Does the energy need balancing because the collective energy radiated by humans is of a lower frequency?

Quan Yin: Yes.

Alison: Okay. So back in the 1940s, or simply the first half of the 20th century, the energy frequencies must have been very low because of the chaos and wars that were going on.

Quan Yin: Yes.

Alison: I remember reading in multiple channelings that many star systems beamed higher frequency light to Earth to keep the axis of the Earth in its place so it wouldn't fly off into space or trigger major catastrophes.

Quan Yin: Yes.

Alison: Back to Atlantis, was the use of sound amplified in the pyramid for healing?

Quan Yin: Yes, sound would be used for healing, but it would be used for other things as well.

Alison: What would be examples of the other uses of sound?

Quan Yin: Creating, creating art, and creating gadgets that they would use, like crystal chambers and such.

Alison: For art creation, was it the inspiration the sound conveyed, or was the sound used to create the artwork?

Quan Yin: It can be used to create artwork.

Alison: Like etching something onto a surface.

Quan Yin: Yes.

Alison: In terms of building structures, what knowledge did the Atlanteans have in building and architecture that we don't have right now?

Quan Yin: Well, they didn't necessarily have more technology in building the buildings in the north. But in the south, as I was saying, they recognized that if you program the water first and then make the cement, you can make a temple or a sacred space, a healing space to be infused with that energy and make it a much more powerful structure.

Alison: Did E.T.s help the Atlanteans to build pyramids through channeling?

Quan Yin: Channeling, yes, and the dropped technologies.

Alison: Was there a specific E.T. group that helped them the most?

Quan Yin: It was more downloads from all the beings in Atlantis who were channeling. So no, not one particular E.T. group helped more.

Alison: What type of dropped technology was applied?

Quan Yin: Well, they were able to learn from data found on the ships in similar ways that the Egyptians discovered telekinesis, of being able to move things with thought and with sound. They were able to learn more about gravity and such as well through what was found on the ships.

Alison: The southerners in Atlantis had that information found on the ships?

Quan Yin: The southerners got the information from data that came from the north, coupled with and validating what they were getting in the channeling experience.

Alison: I see. Okay. So there was more communication there. The north shared data with the south.

Quan Yin: There were times when someone living in the north would decide that they wanted out of the rat race, so to speak, and they would go to live in the south. And at times, they would bring technology with them, or they would bring books or other crystals, something that stored the information that was becoming widespread in the north. And that's how things could get shared to the south. They would sort of migrate down.

Alison: So, did the south also have vehicles or flying machines or other gadgets?

Quan Yin: Yes. They might use them sparingly or out of necessity, but not all the time, not for just pleasure or fun.

Alison: How was the anti-gravity technology used in the building of pyramids?

Quan Yin: It was administered through sound.

Alison: Is telekinesis the same as levitation?

Quan Yin: It is the same principle. In other words, it has to do with the vibration of the body or the vibration of the object. Now, because you're making your own body levitate, it can be easier for you to alter your vibration to change the location of your body to being that of hovering above the ground. But with the object, you are seeking to impose the vibration upon it that would then change its location. It has a lot to do with beliefs. In other words, if you see the object as existing outside of you and separate from you, then you would have to exert a force like gravity or wind over that object to get it to move without being touched. However, when you understand that the object is a part of you and a projection of your consciousness, that it's not in actuality separate from you, then it is easier for you to be in control of it. When you see that there is no separation between you and the object, then your movement can be the movement of the object because it's an extension of your consciousness.

Alison: Did Atlanteans and ancient Egyptians both use telekinesis to move the large stones in building the pyramids? Modern theories could only surmise that such a colossal structure was a product of mass labor over a very long period of time.

Quan Yin: I wouldn't call what was happening in Egypt or Atlantis with the building of the pyramids telekinesis. I would say those objects were able to be moved through the use of thought and the use of sound to lighten the load for the humans who were moving the objects, but true telekinesis involved no pushing of the object or touching of the object at all. There were still people moving the objects with ropes and pulleys. The sound and the thought made it easier to move the objects.

Alison: So human labor was still involved?

Quan Yin: Yes, there was still human labor involved. The practice made it easier for them to believe that they could move the slabs. And also, the sound did have an effect on the movement of the objects in that the sound waves were carrying the object to some extent, like having more force applied to it.

Alison: Did both the priests and the laborers have to keep a focused thought and belief that they could move the slabs?

Quan Yin: Yes, everyone. It was a group effort.

Alison: How did the sound help to lighten the slabs?

Quan Yin: The intent was there in the creating of the sound to negate or cancel some of the forces of gravity, and that intent was carried on the sound wave and went in the minute space between the slab and the surface that it was on to lighten or give the experience of lightening of the object itself. You could say that the sound waves were also applying a vibration to the slabs to make them lighter.

Alison: It's like putting an invisible skateboard under the slab to move it?

Quan Yin: But an intelligent skateboard that knows where the slab is supposed to be going. But you can't just point to one thing and say, "This is what moved them." A lot was involved in this gigantic undertaking, which could not have been done without the teachings that the E.T.s were offering to help the human beings to create the sounds, and also to use the power of their thought, their will, and their intention. And of course, there was hard labor involved as well.

Alison: I know there were slaves in ancient Egypt. How did the Atlanteans manage to find such a huge labor force?

Quan Yin: You could certainly find many Atlanteans in the south who were eager to participate in a monumental project of building a pyramid.

Alison: I see. Even if manual labor was used, the spiritual technology made the building of pyramids possible without modern technology and machines. It's simply amazing to know how spirituality can spark off our innate capabilities and harness natural forces.

Quan Yin: That's true. You're just beginning to understand the power of spirituality.

CHAPTER 8

LOOKING INTO THE MIRROR OF ATLANTIS: THE FALL

When we began the story of Atlantis, a forewarning was already given of its tragic finale. Catastrophe befell the continent, and it sank into the Atlantic Ocean. Even if Atlantis was never acknowledged in our official history, there has been much interest in finding its archaeological sites and relics. There are videos on YouTube featuring the exploration of Atlantis on land and in the undersea world (1). It is eerie that both Lemuria and Atlantis ended up on the bottom of the ocean floor after a cataclysmic destruction. We know the Lemurians could not be blamed for their untimely demise. But Atlantis had a different set of circumstances surrounding its eventual exit.

In most of the literature on Atlantis, it is believed that the Atlanteans were somewhat accountable for the annihilation of their continent and civilization. In the last chapter, we learned about the systems and institutions, and the interactions between the north and the south of Atlantis. Both sides practiced tolerance, if not full acceptance, in treating their differences. This peaceful co-existence was aided by each side focusing on themselves and their interests only. The population was small at the time, and the land was vast. The fall of Atlantis was not precipitated by explicit conflicts and strife between the two sides at the time it happened.

Atlantis was ultimately destroyed by disasters brought on by nature, but the triggering of it had much to do with the intentions and behavior of the northern Atlanteans. As we will see, they had relentlessly pursued science and technology to enhance material benefits at the expense of a higher consciousness. The south, however, was not completely free of accountability, as they were part of this once blossoming civilization.

How did the mighty civilization fall? Here is part three of the story of Atlantis. It was a steady deterioration as the northern Atlanteans became enthralled by their technological prowess and the wealth and power it bestowed upon them. They went down a slippery slope without a countervailing force of ethics or spirituality because they had downplayed that part of their development. This extraordinary set of events and its final ending have profound meaning for all of us who find ourselves in a somewhat familiar scenario in the present development of our civilization.

The Inherent Flaw in the Development of the North

Science and technology generally exert a masculine energy on our planet. It needs balancing from a more spiritual and feminine energy. The north did not control or absorb the south, but it also did not accept any influence from the south. The north had its own traditions, including a spiritual tradition that focused on the power of the mind. But over time, their beliefs became more self-serving as a fixation on technology and prosperity took hold of them.

Alison: The E.T.s selected the Atlanteans to try a new approach in helping the humans develop faster. Did the Atlanteans develop in the way the E.T.s expected?

Quan Yin: Well, not exactly. The technology that the Atlanteans developed was not to grow spiritually as much as to grow technologically. So that's where the Atlanteans went wrong with the use of the technology.

Alison: So E.T.s' dropping of craft and devices was meant to help Atlanteans develop holistically, not just technologically?

Quan Yin: Correct.

Alison: In the first 500 years when the Atlanteans were less developed and living closer to nature, were they in a good place spiritually?

Quan Yin: They were in a good place, and later roughly half the population went down the path of over-reliance on and fascination with technology.

Alison: I know the north didn't start out that way. They lived a simpler life in the beginning and had their beliefs.

Quan Yin: Correct. They had philosophy. They were more mentally focused, whereas the ones in the south who were living closer to nature, closer to the land, had more spiritual beliefs in spirit and afterlife and all of that.

Alison: So what did the people in the north really believe in?

Quan Yin: There was always a type of spirituality in the north. It was less connected to nature, more connected to the mind. They believed in the ability to use the mind, and to use the mind to further the self, to make the self more harmonious, more peaceful, more complete. But they still understood the power of meditation and the use of intuition and imagination to go further with their pursuits, just like in the south. But education in terms of physics and quantum physics and astrophysics and these types of things was more emphasized than believing in say dimensions and spiritual abilities, which were more emphasized in the south.

Alison: This sounds like the spirituality of some of the elites in our society now. So in the north, they were spiritual in their own way. Even if it was a mind-centric spirituality, they had a connection to the spiritual realm through meditating and being intuitive. And then maybe because of what technology was able to bring them, they changed?

Quan Yin: Yes, it's easy to get enamored by that which you are creating when that which you are creating is making your life so much easier.

Alison: You said the technological development in Atlantis became a bit out of control. What was the root cause?

Quan Yin: They were given too much too soon. They developed very quickly. They developed the technology before they developed true spirituality. You see the trick is to be able to develop spiritually while still developing your technology, so you have the ethics and the morals to use the technology appropriately.

Alison: I suppose technology is empowering, and it expands our physical and mental boundaries, but we can get carried away.

Quan Yin: Yes.

Alison: And the same thing has happened to our world since the Industrial Revolution. Science and technology changed our morals and spirituality, and I remember you also said technology made us lazier.

Quan Yin: You don't have to chop wood or carry water anymore, and so you'll lose a certain connection.

Alison: And technology gives us the type of power that we would have needed to focus our mind and heart to generate, such as telekinesis to move large objects.

Quan Yin: Correct.

Alison: So this is really a story about being mesmerized by technology without a good spiritual grounding and how that pointed toward a precarious path forward.

Quan Yin: And that's basically what happened in Atlantis.

Genetic Experiments and Slavery

The uncontained development of technology in Atlantis was indeed accompanied by a moral decline. Ironically, genetic experimentation was again a major culprit, but the Atlanteans were in charge now. Atlantis became a darker place as its science and technology soared to new heights.

Alison: You mentioned that the obsession with technology without a spiritual foundation led to the downfall of Atlantis. How did they go down that slippery road?

Quan Yin: They became power hungry, greedy for more natural resources. They became lazy. They stopped wanting to take the patient path of working with nature, working with the natural evolution of consciousness, and exploring their own connections to the nonphysical. Instead, they began relying too heavily on the technology, needed more natural resources to support that technology, and of course wanted there to be a slave race. There tends to be that desire on the part of humans to have a slave race working for them. Humanoids, I should say, throughout the galaxy have wanted that from time to time and have used whatever means they could to secure that slave labor.

Alison: What type of natural resources were the Atlanteans looking for?

Quan Yin: Gold, silver, platinum, and crystals. They were helping them to create the gadgets that they wanted.

Alison: And did they invade other places for these precious metals? I think the area was in Turkey and Greece. I read about it in a channeled story of Atlantis (2).

Quan Yin: Yes.

Alison: I believe I also read in Dolores Cannon's book (3), and in Lucy Lee's case studies (4) that the Atlanteans had done genetic experiments to create half-human, half-animal type of creatures. Was that the slave race you were referring to?

Quan Yin: Yes.

Alison: Oh my. This was the dark history of Atlantis.

Quan Yin: Yes.

Alison: I assume the creation of a slave race was done in the north. How did it start?

Quan Yin: Because it's more technology-driven in the north, there was more of a use of the technology to map the genome that was used in the co-creation of different hybrids, and that was more common there. It was seen as more acceptable to the average person whereas today when you have someone saying, "Well I want to create using technology this new species that's going to be half rabbit, half wolf," let's say, there would be many more people objecting to that, seeing those experiments as cruel and so on. And so those technologies back then, because they were more widely accepted, were harnessed to a greater extent. They were honed and utilized because more and more Atlanteans found them to be quite acceptable.

Alison: You are talking about the genetic technology that eventually led to the half-human, half-animal experiments.

Quan Yin: Yes, indeed, and creating also humans that would be superior in various ways: superior intellect, superior strength, superior sight, abilities, those types of things, and even beauty. These things were sought out and people were ordering their children based on characteristics that they wanted to have.

Alison: Our genetic science is also heading toward improving our genes for health reasons. Did the Atlanteans have technology at our level or higher?

Quan Yin: It was slightly higher than what you have.

Alison: It's higher. Okay. So were they doing gene editing, cutting, and splicing in an embryo to create these designer babies?

Quan Yin: Yes.

Alison: Were E.T.s involved in passing on genetic technology to them?

Quan Yin: There were files that were in the fallen craft as well as some samples, some cellular samples of beings that had those types of experiments done on them. And we're talking about now single cell organisms, so very low forms of life in your measuring of sentience. And the life forms were studied by the Atlantean scientists, geneticists, and so on. Interested parties would study them and would reverse engineer in that way and figure out how to manipulate the human genome.

Alison: Did they use some of the Lyrans' technology to enhance the baby's intelligence?

Quan Yin: Yes.

Alison: Oh, but were they at the Lyrans' level of mastery?

Quan Yin: The knowledge of the Lyrans did come over to Atlantis in a crude form and had to be interpreted by their scientists in Atlantis. So they did the best they could to replicate it.

Alison: The knowledge came to Atlantis via the surviving Lemurians?

Quan Yin: Yes. A lot of that was encoded in the Lemurian mind and DNA, and when the Lemurians made it to Atlantis and started mixing together with the Atlanteans, it was very easy for the Atlanteans to access those memories.

Alison: Was it also knowledge passed down by oral tradition?

Quan Yin: Yes. It was also written down. There were pieces of it that were stored in crystals that the Atlanteans figured out how to access.

Alison: I guess they did have a long tradition of developing genetics with help from the Lemurians and then finally the E.T.s. Unlike the Lyrans, this technology wasn't used for creating higher consciousness. It was used to create a person who was much smarter, better looking, healthier, stronger, and with all the qualities that were desired and valued by human society.

Quan Yin: Yes, and that's one of the reasons why the technology was able to grow and advance so quickly.

Alison: Oh, because there was strong demand, and they also created many smart scientists?

Quan Yin: Yes, indeed.

Alison: So that was fascinating. That was like another attempt to accelerate human evolution using genetic re-engineering, but this time with only indirect assistance from E.T.s.

Quan Yin: The difference between Lemuria and Atlantis is that the Atlanteans were the ones who got to control it, you as humans. You got to find how to use it, and your level of consciousness determined how you would use it and for what purposes, and how well you would be able to manipulate it.

Alison: Was the genetic manipulation done for all the Atlanteans or only a certain section of the population?

Quan Yin: Not everybody was genetically re-engineered to become super, so just some people. This was more available to the rich in the same way that you have more things available to very wealthy people on Earth today.

Alison: So it was within human control, and it created inequality in society.

Quan Yin: Well, the technology started being elite. The parents were able to afford to do the genetic manipulation that's going to result in a smarter offspring who then could take the technology even further.

Alison: So I guess elitism and inequality became more entrenched. Now, the other experiments to create half-human, half-animal creatures, were they a later development?

Quan Yin: Yes.

Alison: And did they go all the way in creating this slave race and abusing them?

Quan Yin: Yes.

Alison: I believe I read in multiple sources that there was slavery and cruelty in Atlantis, and at the end, these creatures were even forced to fight like the Roman gladiators as entertainment for the Atlanteans.

Quan Yin: Yes, they were.

Alison: Oh my goodness. Was it a painful thing for the being to be in a half-human, half-animal hybrid body?

Quan Yin: Sometimes. Yes, it could be. Whenever there's an experiment like that going on, there's trial and error. And the trial part, the error part, was not pleasant.

Alison: Did they do that in a test tube? Did they create a hybrid embryo in a test tube?

Quan Yin: Yes.

Alison: Okay. Did they also alter live people or animals? Because I believe I read in Lucy Lee's case studies that there was one practice through which they just used the focused intent of a group of Atlanteans to force these changes on a live person or animal.

Quan Yin: Yes, there was that use of technology as well.

Alison: And that was the more painful part?

Quan Yin: Those were the earliest attempts, yes.

Alison: I remember that Dolores Canyon said in her book that from a spiritual perspective, these half-human, half-animal creatures allowed humans to experience what it was like to be in an animal body. Was that a valid account of one motivation for this slave race?

Quan Yin: It's not necessarily the motivation of the human who's conducting the experiment, but it can be the motivation of the spirit to have that experience being born into that body.

(Note: This was different from our souls' incarnations as animals in the third dimension. This was a case where a soul consciousness was in a half-human, half-animal body, and could experience confusion, discomfort, or pain as these hybrids were not created by the law of nature.)

Alison: I see. So it was like a co-creation.

Quan Yin: Everything always serves a greater and higher purpose, no matter how nefarious the intentions are of the person who is initiating the experiment or the movement or whatever it is.

Alison: Did the Atlanteans give up on the slave race once they had the androids?

Quan Yin: Well, there were lots of different uses for the half-human, half-animal creatures. And of course, there were gladiator-type battles, and they were pets and sex slaves in a sense, and servants, and so on. The androids gave people a different feeling than the more natural animal-human hybrids did. So the hybrids weren't phased out. It was just that when the Atlanteans had the androids, there was more variety. Some people liked that the androids were more programmable, and some people preferred the human-animal hybrids because they were less predictable.

Alison: Oh, that's really degenerative. I suppose the androids with less self-awareness and not being living organisms would not experience the pain of being a slave. But the Atlanteans were arrogant and cruel in doing this. I guess that's sort of the test we'll be facing as our genetic science is advancing and our AI technology is booming. The only saving grace is that we do have critics now, and slavery is outlawed.

Quan Yin: Yes.

Alison: When did the genetic experiments start?

Quan Yin: Around 700 years into the civilization. So 200 years after the E.T. technology was left, they had figured it out enough to be able to have some success with the experiments they were doing with it.

Alison: It seemed 200 years was the magical mark for the Atlanteans to reverse engineer and experiment with technologies that they uncovered from the downed craft.

Quan Yin: Yes.

Alison: Would it be fair to say that being drawn to enslaving others and to darkness was a natural evolutionary path for humanity?

Quan Yin: Well, darkness will always be there, and will always be an option for you.

Alison: In our history, there has been a lot of darkness. We didn't always choose it, but we have chosen it many times. So, is that what we expected coming to Earth?

Quan Yin: Well, the darkness has to be explored as well, and being given the opportunity to see what it feels like is a part of the natural choices that each being will make at some point, yes. But what you're seeing in this natural evolution is that more people choose the light, realizing the emptiness of the darkness and of that path.

Alison: When the Atlanteans began to plunge into the dark waters of genetic experimentation, did the E.T.s try to steer them away from that choice?

Quan Yin: No. They could have helped, but they didn't.

Alison: Was the reason that they wanted to let the Atlanteans evolve and make their own decisions?

Quan Yin: By the more benevolent E.T.s, yes, that was the reason. By the ones that didn't care, they were just interested in the same way that you are in seeing how a movie ends.

Alison: It is always a co-creation, I guess.

Quan Yin: Yes.

Wealth, Greed, and Corruption

It was inevitable that the decline in morality in the north would affect its political system and the entirety of Atlantis. Corruption grew in lockstep with wealth and greed, and the once honorable democratic institution was infiltrated by the super-rich.

Alison: Did the political system in Atlantis withstand the moral transgressions of the society?

Quan Yin: The elite class became very influential in politics just like today.

Alison: Who were the elites in Atlantis? Were they the wise elders or the elected representatives?

Quan Yin: No, they were the wealthy.

Alison: Did they exert a negative influence on Atlantis?

Quan Yin: They were the people who wanted more power, more control, control over others, and to have more. It was really greed on the part of those who had the technology, had the natural resources, the money, and the influence to do whatever they wanted to. Think of what's happening in your politics today.

Alison: They were doing what they wanted irrespective of what people would say or what the laws would or would not allow them to do?

Quan Yin: The government knew they couldn't control these individuals. They also didn't foresee the kinds of problems that came about. They didn't have the foreknowledge of what would occur if these super wealthy individuals just did whatever they wanted to with technology and with their desires to control not only people, but also the planet.

Alison: And so they didn't foresee the potential threats these people posed to their society?

Quan Yin: They didn't know what to do with them, and they didn't think they were that big of a problem.

Alison: But then the super-rich became a very big problem?

Quan Yin: They were also developing their plans to go into the south and start mining the resources in the south. So they had a type of cabal. They had their own wealthy elite class gatherings where they would talk about the future of Atlantis and how to get more of what they wanted; where they would develop the strategies for convincing the southerners that what they were doing was actually good for them, good for Atlantis, and good for the planet. So that was all in the works at the time that Atlantis fell.

Alison: So, were the wealthy able to influence both the government and the society to carry out their agenda?

Quan Yin: Yes, both. Through media and through using their wealth to sometimes outright bribe elected officials, not the wise elders, because they wouldn't go for that sort of thing. But the rich would sometimes just give the politicians gifts and vacations and offer them free stays at their luxurious resorts and hotels, and boat rides and rides in the aerial craft that they had. They would go to the limits that they could go to.

Alison: So there was corruption and some of the representatives were involved?

Quan Yin: The politicians, I would say, about a third were bribable.

Alison: So this was not in their early development but it happened later in the civilization?

Quan Yin: It increased every year, yes. The number of people who would bribe, and who would accept a gift and then be influenced by what these elites would say to them increased over time. Sometimes the elites would just go to the resort and meet up with the politician and have dinner with them, and they would use that as an opportunity to sort of brainwash the politician. They would be using their intelligence to dupe the politician into thinking a certain way. They would use "evidence" just like people do today by going on any website and saying, "But look, here's evidence." You can prove anything in your day and age, and so could they, because on their version of the Internet, anyone's thoughts could be seen as facts.

Alison: They had a technology to turn thoughts into facts?

Quan Yin: No, what I'm saying is today what you have on your Internet is opinion and thought, conjecture, ideas. Basically, conspiracies can be presented as facts to people as long as the person presenting them seems legitimate enough, and the same was true in Atlantis. So that would be one way in which an elite member of society would present something to a politician and say, "Look, I think you should be voting this way on this issue, and this is why." And they would present some kind of fabrication, some kind of quote-unquote evidence to prove their point, or they would just be so golden-tongued that they would convince the politician to think like they did and get them to change the laws or make a new law or abolish a law.

Alison: Did average people understand what was really happening?

Quan Yin: It depended on the person because some people were not as interested, and other people knew or heard more. There was just as much speculation as there is today over the influence that the rich have on the politicians.

Alison: So it's sort of exactly the same as what we are witnessing today.

Quan Yin: It is exactly the same. You have the good people working in all branches of government in the United States today, and you have those that are not so good, and the same was true in Atlantis.

Alison: So the rich and the compromised politicians could conspire to bring about specific laws or changes?

Quan Yin: Yes, and the changes favored whatever the rich and powerful wanted so that they could become more rich and powerful.

Alison: You said that in the very beginning, the representatives were not well-paid, and they were real public servants.

Quan Yin: It started out that way, yes. Just like in the United States, you didn't have these issues right away with your first Continental Congress. You didn't have people with massive amounts of wealth to even exert their influence.

Alison: So after the Atlanteans made progress on technology, the social and political dynamics changed?

Quan Yin: And after progress was made in commerce as well, as the people who wanted to make more and have more got better at it over time.

Different Tales of the Fall of Atlantis

Power corrupts. Historically, all great empires eventually fell. However, Atlantis wasn't one of those empires that we know of. A good part of Atlantis was advanced in science and technology, it was democratic, and it had the intelligence and sophistication of a modern civilization. Another part of it was natural and spiritual, upholding a tradition that harkened back to the days of Lemuria.

Atlantis wasn't facing an external enemy that could conquer them, nor was it experiencing revolt and conspiracy from within. This was not a typical scenario where a large entity, political or cultural, would collapse. And this fall was also not a change of regime or a subjugation to another race, but an absolute and utter destruction by a massive force of nature. How did it all end, and why?

Alison: Is there such a thing as the Golden Age of Atlantis? It was referenced so often in the literature about Atlantis.

Quan Yin: The Golden Age refers to that time when the Atlanteans first began really thriving technologically and spiritually, but before all of that started to go into the era of, let's say, manipulation of those energies, and manipulation or overuse and overdependency on that technology.

Alison: I guess even after the north started to slide, the south provided a higher vibration to balance the civilization.

Quan Yin: Correct.

Alison: I know eventually Atlantis was destroyed, and there were many accounts of its destruction. I want to describe three examples because I am curious as to how we should interpret these different accounts.

Quan Yin: All right.

Alison: For example, Bashar told a story of how Atlantis was destroyed by a comet that had been orbiting in the solar system, crossing paths with Earth, and sending meteor showers on Atlantis (5). This went on for two decades and was considered by some Atlanteans to be an ominous sign forecasting a calamity. Some of them heeded the warning and fled the continent, and the comet eventually struck Atlantis and sank the continent. Bashar attributed the tragic destruction of Atlantis to the collective low vibration of its residents: "They put themselves in the vibration that was smack dab in the path of the comet, in that reality, in that connection with the cycle of destruction..."

A second account was offered by Dolores Cannon's book *Convoluted Universe Book One* (3). In this story, Atlantean scientists were drilling down to the molten core of the Earth to access an immense energy source, and it caused an explosion so massive that it blew up the continent.

A third account I've read came from a channeling of Archangel Metatron (2). In the story, an overtaxed master crystal satellite crashed and caused the catastrophe. The huge satellite received and distributed solar energy to power stations and grids in Atlantis. The rampant energy surge was triggered by an overseas warfare waged by the Atlanteans.

Most of the stories I came across showed the greedy, aggressive, and reckless side of the Atlanteans in seeking more power and wealth. But each had a different script leading to the cataclysm. What should we make of these different stories?

Quan Yin: The destruction of Atlantis has been described in a myriad of ways now, and there are a myriad of pasts that exist, that coexist.

Alison: Actually, for both Lemuria and Atlantis, each book or article would tell a slightly or very different story about them. Sometimes the times of their existence were different as well. I assume the stories we have here in this book are the reality from the timeline or group of timelines we've been most closely associated with.

Quan Yin: Correct.

Alison: You have taught me that there is no one reality of our past or future, and there are a multitude of them. I guess that's why we have a variety of accounts of Lemuria and Atlantis. How should we deal with these different accounts?

Quan Yin: Yes, you could actually look at the other stories and you don't have to decide that only one of these stories is the true and only story of Atlantis because there are multiple pasts just as there are multiple futures, and you can choose whichever version of the past that you feel resonates with you the most and even take bits and pieces from each of the stories of Atlantis and piece together the reality that you want to make your past. This is because the past is just as malleable as the future is. You just want to be open-minded to the fact that there are many different timelines and versions of reality.

Alison: And all of us as soul aspects have been on many different timelines and realities.

Quan Yin: Yes.

Alison: Parallel realities and timelines are extremely difficult topics for a human mind to comprehend, at least for me. I know we'll explore them in greater depth in the future, but could you give us some ideas on how parallel and different realities are possible?

Quan Yin: Well, look at it this way. This is a free will Universe. If it's a free will Universe, then every time you're faced with a choice between choice A and choice B, you can see that when you choose choice A, choice B still exists. And that the possibility not only exists, but a portion of your soul's consciousness, another soul aspect, goes ahead and lives as though you made choice B. Then you realize that there's more than one future reality from where you're standing right now, that both possibilities must always exist. And if that's the case, from where you're standing right now, there are multiple futures, and therefore there must be multiple pasts as well.

Alison: Okay. We'll need many more teachings to really understand it. For now, we can assume that there were different scenarios of Atlantis's destruction, and whatever brought down Atlantis was likely caused by the collective vibration, which was a low vibration because of their level of morality. As you said before, the physical plane is always a manifestation of the energetic plane. And so the vibration did them in.

Quan Yin: Right, correct.

Alison: Out of curiosity, was their use of technology and slavery not on all the timelines and realities?

Quan Yin: It was across many timelines. You have a similar trajectory for the Atlanteans from the time that they acquired the more advanced technology.

Alison: I see. I feel sorry for the people in the south because they were spiritual and held higher vibrations, but they could not stop or reverse this fate of theirs.

Quan Yin: Well, they were very judgmental of the beings in the north. They looked down their nose, and they thought the northerners were hedonists and going down the wrong path and not at all spiritual. The northerners had their own form of spirituality, but the southerners were seeing them as separate, seeing them as not being a part of them and therefore not having to concern themselves much with them other than to make their jokes and laugh about them, and judge them and do all those types of things in regards to the northerners. And so they did not act and think in terms of oneness, in terms of the truth of who they all are.

Alison: Wow. That is a surprise. And the southerners harbored this attitude ever since they and the north went down different directions?

Quan Yin: Yes.

Alison: Well, as you have taught me so many times, judgment is against the truth of oneness, of us as one. The people in the south could have chosen to see the northerners as making different choices, and thus accept and hold space for them. Judgment is very low-vibrational and even diligent spiritual practices can't reverse its impact. So the south energetically contributed to their collective destiny, and it wasn't all the doing of the northerners?

Quan Yin: There was a co-creation. They also believed that the people in the north were going to ruin the continent, possibly the planet, with what they were doing. There was a lot left over from Lemuria within everyone, where there was a lot of fear around the fall of the continent, the fall of the civilization, because the stories were handed down by oral tradition. And so when Atlantis was fully developed, there was more of a belief in the fact that when you get bigger and more advanced, then something bad will happen. So it became a self-fulfilling prophecy for them.

Alison: Oh, because they believed it. They believed that was going to happen, and then it did happen. Okay, there is so much that we are learning here. Did the survivors go to both sides of the Atlantic?

Quan Yin: They went to mostly Central America, North America, Africa, the Mediterranean, the UK, and some even made it up to Iceland.

Alison: There's nothing left, correct? Or even if there is, we don't have access to it. I remember that Bashar said the comet hit the continent and tore a hole in the ocean floor, and the entire continent sank into it.

Quan Yin: Right, you don't have access to it. You could find remnants on the ocean floor later on in your deep-sea exploration.

Alison: But we probably couldn't get there, or we couldn't tell what those remnants are.

Quan Yin: Not enough people are looking.

Alison: Ahh, because people don't know Atlantis ever existed.

Quan Yin: Yes, most people think it's a myth.

The Deeper Meaning behind the Fall of Atlantis

Perhaps the consequences of corruption and degeneration are inevitable regardless of the level of civilization achieved. It was the end of a trajectory without a course correction, a trajectory dominated by technology and by lower vibration. However, humans on this planet have committed crimes much worse than the Atlanteans had. Why did Atlantis have to endure such a savage end? Was there a deeper meaning or reason behind its fall?

Alison: So Atlantis fell similarly to how Lemuria did, and their low vibration brought it down. But there had been other cultures or civilizations that had done more wrongs, more evil things. WWII was a good example in recent memory, but it didn't destroy our world. Why did the Atlanteans have to suffer such hideous devastation?

Quan Yin: Atlantis had to fall. It was going to fall one way or another, but it was the consciousness that attracted the large body; whether you want to call it a comet, a meteorite, or an asteroid, it doesn't matter. It was a large mass that came into the Earth's atmosphere.

Alison: Why did Atlantis have to fall one way or another?

Quan Yin: Humanity wasn't ready to go to the next level of consciousness, but the technology that they had was being used to attempt to take humanity to a higher level of creator-hood. And if you have the ability for instant manifestation technologically, you have to be able to keep up with that energetically and spiritually. And the Atlanteans would not have been able to keep up because it wasn't the right time for the Shift of consciousness to occur. So the balance on Earth would have been terribly thrown off if Atlantis had continued down the track it was going. In other words, the E.T.s who were dropping those technological gadgets that were reverse engineered made another mistake. So again, the interference with the natural evolution of consciousness that would have occurred on planet Earth caused a major problem that resulted in the end of an entire civilization.

Alison: So the E.T.s' less intrusive plan to galvanize technology development for faster human evolution was still an interference, and it failed?

Quan Yin: Humanity's shift of consciousness had to coincide with the Universal Shift or Ascension that's happening right now. And so if the Atlanteans were moving faster than they normally and naturally would have, it wouldn't have fit with this agenda for the Universal shifting of consciousness to take place right now. So the lesson is always that the shortcuts that people want to take with technology to skip a natural evolution are always a mistake.

Alison: Because the Atlanteans needed to go up to a higher level of consciousness to use the technology responsibly, but they weren't ready or capable of doing that?

Quan Yin: Correct.

Alison: And it wasn't the right time because the level of consciousness they needed to reach for is planned in the upcoming Ascension, and we are receiving massive help from the higher realms to uplift our consciousness in our present time.

Quan Yin: It would have been fine had they not been given technology that they weren't ready for in terms of their consciousness, because they would have developed those technologies on their own when they were ready spiritually. It would have taken many, many, many years for that civilization to get to that place. In other words, you could still have an Atlantis today if it had not been interfered with.

Alison: They could slowly and naturally evolve to fit into the current Ascension plan, but then the world would be and would have been very different with Atlantis being around.

Quan Yin: Yes.

Alison: I suppose, just like Lemuria, it was an experiment to get us to learn something about natural evolution.

Quan Yin: Right.

Are We Recycling the Atlantis Experience?

"If there was a split in Atlantis, there is the acceleration of the split in your time, our time now. The idea of America itself is the recounting and recycling of the Atlantean times for you to lift yourself up to a different future and different outcome..." - Bashar

Alison: What Bashar said about the idea of America being a recycling of the Atlantean experience but for a better outcome, is it true?

Quan Yin: Yes.

Alison: And is that just America, or is it really the entire Earth and humanity, but the recycling is more noticeable in the U.S.?

Quan Yin: Yes, it's more noticeable in the U.S.

Alison: We've progressed very rapidly in modernizing our lifestyle since the Industrial Revolution. Even if Atlantis had more advanced technology in some areas, we have developed further in the size of population, infrastructure, cities, trade and commerce, food and medicine, and cultural and racial diversity. This development is global, and we have many nation states, and unfortunately, major wars and man-made disasters as well. We have gone further and done more.

Quan Yin: Oh, yes, much more.

Alison: We have evolved and expanded the human civilization and tried more experiments and creations, good or bad.

Quan Yin: Yes.

Alison: We have made some progress in understanding our problems and addressing them, such as slavery, discrimination, injustice, inhumanity, etc. Technology-wise, where we're doing poorly is probably the level of pollution and the amount of toxins we have.

Quan Yin: Morality. The morality of the use of the technology is still something that you're working on getting right this time around. In other words, you still use it to exploit and to try to get more power and so on, and not see it in the spiritual ways that it could be seen. Spiritually, technology is to be used to unite, to be used to connect to higher consciousness, instead of just getting as much natural resources out of Mother Earth as you can, and using it for gain, personal gain or gain of the particular families and so on of those who are in those elite positions now.

That's where this is a turning point for humanity with this spiritual awakening that's occurring and the shifting that's going on. You are going to see people who are able to get much more out of it spiritually because they're wanting more than just all the creature comforts they can possibly have, and more and more people are discovering that there's much more to life than having more and more stuff, and more and more money, and more and more power. And so that's the game changer. That's how this time is different than the time of Atlantis because there's more and more awakenings occurring all the time.

(Note: "Awakening" simply put is a heart-opening experience, a realization that there is more to life than we can see and perceive, and that our existence is meaningful, and we are all connected as One and connected by love.)

Alison: We don't have a clear north-south divide as the Atlanteans, and the spiritually inclined population is of a much smaller percentage in comparison. In fact, religion largely represents spirituality in our times. We seem to have lost the unmediated spiritual connections since Lemuria.

Quan Yin: In Lemuria, there was more of an awakening that happened, not in all periods of Lemuria, but after the great awakening of Lemuria occurred. That's when people started to know spirituality more fully. In Atlantis, it was a choice a lot like it is today on Earth, a choice as to whether you believe or not. For those in Atlantis who believed, there wasn't religion at that time, so you didn't have people believing in the religious dogma that you have there on Earth today about heaven and hell and so on. But there were people who believed more in science, and there were people who believed more in nature and spirituality, and there were people who were not concerned with those types of things at all. But those who were spiritual were not religious in Atlantis.

Alison: I see. The unmediated spiritual tradition did continue in Atlantis because there was no religion at the time. Today, religion is helping many to open a spiritual connection, but a true awakening is not roused by religion itself. It is meant to be a spiritual experience emanating from the heart, not called forth by religious persuasions.

Quan Yin: Correct.

Alison: At the beginning of 2025, U.S. politics became quite chaotic with many unprecedented actions taken by the new administration. Some people are happy, but others are gravely concerned. Is this meant to be part of the Atlantean experience we're recycling?

Quan Yin: It's showing you that this is the system you have. It's not behind closed doors anymore. It's not hush-hush, wink-wink, nudge-nudge. It's right out in the open.

Alison: Is this an important crossroads for us?

Quan Yin: It is. It's necessary for people to understand that this is a part of a cycle, and that what you're facing right now is a government in the United States that is for the few, not the many, and certainly not for all, especially not all across the world. Every government needs to consider how their actions affect other countries across the planet. And when you have E.T.s there, that will be a focal point, a very important teaching that you cannot let borders determine where your caring and compassion ends.

Alison: So in terms of what is happening in this moment in the United States, are we kind of reliving that Atlantean experience of the dominance of rich elites?

Quan Yin: You're re-experiencing what you need to re-experience to give yourselves the opportunity to make a different choice this time.

Alison: Are we facing the Atlantean challenges in both our reactions to technology and to our democracy?

Quan Yin: Yes, both are important to consider when it comes to the future of humanity.

Alison: I suppose we're shown our system is ill, and people will finally say, "This is a crisis, and we need to act."

Quan Yin: You can't really blame the system because if the system were used appropriately by the people who are in the system, then you wouldn't have the problems that you have. And "act" is perhaps a strong word for it because you can't get to where you want to go by simply fighting against what you don't want. What people need is to change within themselves in terms of what they're afraid of, what they're resistant to, in order to see the change politically that they want to see. And so ultimately, it does come down to consciousness.

Alison: It is a calling for all of us to raise our consciousness from division to unity, from hate to love?

Quan Yin: Yes, because the way things are right now, you're not going to have a huge upheaval of the power structure as it is in this moment, and so politically speaking, you have to just ride out what you've got. You have to work on yourselves, work within your communities, and work on helping each other because you're going to see a lot of people in need because of the government that you have in place right now. A lot more people need help from their neighbors, their family members, their friends, and you're all going to have to make it a grassroots movement. You're going to need to see more of that and less of this idea that "We're all isolated and live in our separate homes and have all of our devices that we need to entertain us, so we don't really need to go and talk to someone else." But you will need to do that, and you will need to support one another through this mess that you have co-created there in the United States.

Alison: It's a co-creation because what's out there in our reality is always a projection and reflection of our collective consciousness.

Quan Yin: It is.

Alison: And this higher consciousness we need to lift ourselves to will also guide us in the use and development of technology.

Quan Yin: Correct.

Alison: This is an exciting juncture in our evolution. We are having a repeat of what took place in Atlantis, but we will get it right and have a different experience this time. That's the profundity of learning the story of Atlantis.

Quan Yin: Yes.

Alison: Looking back at Lemuria and Atlantis, both were tales of accelerating human evolution over a slower but natural path, and both came to an ill-fated end. Wasn't one experience enough?

Quan Yin: You need to go through different phases of the evolution of consciousness to understand it better. And so when you get to Atlantis, again, E.T.s and humans were trying to make a quantum leap, trying to jump the natural evolution. And there was a lot of use of science and technology to bring humanity to its next level of evolution, rather than waiting for it to happen naturally through experience, which is how it does happen naturally. You have experiences, and those experiences help you to grow spiritually, and you evolve. So Atlantis gave you a different experience.

Alison: If I can ask a "human" question, Lemuria and Atlantis were significant early reincarnations for us, but why did they have to be so hard?

Quan Yin: In order to get the full Earth experience, you get to know all the different emotions you need to have in order for that experience to be complete. That is why you would have the experience of something like the destruction of the entire civilization and continent. That was only experience to get you to feel certain emotions. And the experience of Lemuria was not identical to that of Atlantis. You needed to create it and had that experience to grow from it.

Alison: Okay. We were tackling the emotions of extreme fear, separation, and trauma, and perhaps there was also a feeling of blame, guilt, or remorse, particularly for the survivors. We did a lot of heavy lifting very early in our reincarnations. We stayed true to our commitment to the Earth Experiment.

Quan Yin: Yes, you did. You've done well. Now you just need to focus on making better choices this time and raising your consciousness to complete your last mission on Earth, which is Ascension.

Notes

1) Examples of YouTube videos on the exploration of Atlantis: "Legend of Atlantis | Drain the Oceans" (https://www.youtube. com/watch?v=ErPsyBUCijM) by National Geographic. The research team searched for evidence of Atlantis using new undersea technology. However, the area of interest was along the coastline of Japan and not anywhere near the Atlantic Ocean.
"Journey to Find the Lost City of Atlantis with James Cameron | Atlantis Rising" (https://www.youtube.com/watch? v=Xs6mbuc4tHQ) by National Geographic. This research team searched for the potential site, structure, and artifacts of Atlantis on land and under the water from the Mediterranean to the middle of the Atlantic Ocean. They used Plato's descriptions of Atlantis as their guidance.

2) *Earth-Keeper Chronicles: METATRON SPEAKS* by James Tyberonn (2009). A chapter in the book is titled "The Fall of Atlantis" and the author channeled Archangel Metatron to give an account of Atlantis in its last 100 years.

3) *The Convoluted Universe Book One* by Dolores Cannon (2010).

4) Lucy Lee QHHT case studies. Please see the reference in Chapter Three.

5) "The last days of Atlantis" by Bashar (A channeled video webinar) https://bashartv.com/programs/last-days-of-atlantis

PART II

E.T.s and the Earth
Experiment

CHAPTER 9

✦

E.T.s and Our
Genetic Heritage:
Ancient Ancestry

Both Lemuria and Atlantis experienced natural as well as unnatural evolution of human consciousness. The accelerated evolution culminated in the same catastrophic setback, even if the reasons were different for these two civilizations. Did the final destruction of Atlantis eliminate all the progress they had made for humanity? Perhaps the answer lies in the genes that we carry today. Do we still have the Lemurian and Atlantean genes in the Earth population?

We can first retrace the movement of the surviving Lemurians. After their continent was sunk, the surviving Lemurians settled into the Americas and a continent in the Atlantic Ocean that would later become Atlantis. Crossbreeding with the natives preserved some of the effects of that genetic acceleration by the Lyrans.

Later, when the continent of Atlantis sank just like Lemuria did, the surviving Atlanteans made their way to Europe and North Africa. Their interbreeding with the locals again passed down and spread around the genes that were inherited directly from the Atlanteans and indirectly from the Lemurians.

It is true that the Lemurians and Atlanteans were ancestors of many races on Earth today, especially in the Americas, Europe, the Middle East, and North Africa, where the survivors ventured to settle. Since then, we have developed extraordinary racial and cultural diversity.

Quan Yin told us that the Lemurians, and in fact most early humans, looked like the Mayans, and that the Atlanteans still bore a resemblance to the Lemurians, even if there were some variations in the skin tones and the eye and hair colors. But today we have many different races and sub-races, and the Earth humans look dramatically different between different races or even within the same race. Corresponding to racial diversity, we also have so many cultures and sub-cultures with different beliefs, traditions, and personality traits. What were the catalysts for this remarkable racial, ethnic, and cultural diversity?

We know there has been extensive crossbreeding between all major races and sub-races, and the merging of different cultures throughout history. But where did the major races and cultures come from in the first place? There is a big gap between the homogenous early humans and the multi-faced modern humans. One can't help but wonder if there were significant infusions of genes from other non-human species to create this grand diversity we have today.

As non-human species, the E.T.s had been in the picture in creating the human race. Quan Yin told us about the original seeding of life forms by E.T.s in the Earth Experiment, and she mentioned the seven E.T. root races for Earth and humanity as well. We also know of the Lyrans' work in Lemuria. All this knowledge helped establish an E.T. origin in the human genome. The Lemurians and Atlanteans already had E.T. ancestry in their genetic makeup. What we need to explore further is whether there was ongoing E.T. involvement in our genetic and consciousness evolution after Atlantis. That involvement may have been the reason why we have had this notable diversity and intelligence to build an intellectually and technologically sophisticated civilization today.

We will try to address this question of humanity's E.T. heritage in this and the next chapter. We will offer a glimpse into that hidden but profound history we have had with E.T.s. They have been in our lives since the inception of our journey on Earth, and it's time to learn about our past together and get to know them not as alien beings from outer space but as our ancestral families.

In this chapter, we will first revisit our ancient ancestry. We'll review the original seeding in the Earth experiment, the evolution of primitive humans, and the roles of the seven E.T. root races in our evolution. We'll connect the human race to our galactic roots and the larger family of beings that we are a part of. And before we finish this chapter, we'll also have a close-up of how the Lemurians and Atlanteans became the ancestors of many peoples on Earth.

Our Genetic Makeup and Physical Constitution: The beginning

We'll start from the very beginning by revisiting what went into the original genome of Earth humans, and how we moved from primate to human.

Alison: From your explanation of the Earth Experiment, everything really started with the E.T.s. Do we owe our physical and genetic makeup to them?

Quan Yin: Well, the Earth itself is a major influence on the current physical form that you have because you did emerge physically from the Earth and were born out of the particles and elements that were there physically to begin with. You can certainly trace your lineage back to the primates that came before you and all the different evolutionary stages of the human, and that played a part in who and what you look like physically today, and how you operate physically.

Alison: So, if our physical form is influenced by the particles and elements of Earth, are the Pleiadians influenced physically by the particles and elements of their specific planets in the Pleiadian system? And this is the case even if we might look similar physically?

Quan Yin: That's correct.

Alison: But E.T.s also had a major influence on our physicality and DNA?

Quan Yin: There are lots of physical influences on you that came from the original seeding of Earth, and the intentions are all infused into the physical body in the DNA. So the intentions for you to experience all the emotions, all the vibrations, peace and violence, harmony and discord, they are all part of the intentions of those who seeded Earth originally. So that was pretty much everyone else in the galaxy participating and lending some of their genetic material, some of the species from their world to the Earth Experiment. Earth is a place where those different beings can be represented in a lot of different ways.

Alison: And it sounds like the E.T.s' seeding not only influenced how we would look and operate physically, but also how we would feel our emotions and what intellect we would develop?

Quan Yin: That's correct, too.

Alison: But how did the original seeding of life forms directly affect humans since humans weren't there yet?

Quan Yin: Well, there was a natural Darwinian type of evolution that took place on the planet. That started from the original seeding of different genetic materials in the ocean that would then form into different life forms and evolve, and eventually come out of the ocean.

Alison: So basically, the intentions and the genetics were seeded energetically and then physically. It began with simple life forms, which would evolve to higher life forms in a Darwinian way. The intentions were carried forward, and the genetic changes were enabled from simple to complex life forms.

Quan Yin: Yes.

Alison: Would the different life forms be brought to Earth and added to the ecosystem along the path of natural evolution?

Quan Yin: There was a proper time to bring the different life forms. There was a correct time to do that, yes. It's based on the readiness for that being to coexist with the other life forms.

Alison: When we say bringing the life forms to Earth, is it about the timing of when a life form would be ready to be born out of the evolutionary process, and E.T.s from the life form's originating planet would facilitate its emergence on Earth?

Quan Yin: Yes.

Alison: You mentioned before that the primitive human appeared on Earth about 12 million years ago. Did they appear completely by way of natural evolution from non-human primates?

Quan Yin: Well, there was help from E.T.s to accelerate it.

Alison: Oh, Okay. So E.T.s took the most advanced primate, probably from the ape family, and accelerated their evolution. Who helped, and what did they do?

Quan Yin: It was Lyrans, Pleiadians, and Sirians using their technology with genetics. They were able to alter the DNA with injections.

Alison: With an injection into a live primate?

Quan Yin: Yes.

Alison: This was similar to the Lyrans' injection to the Lemurians, maybe of a lower grade because they were only creating the first form of humans?

Quan Yin: Yes.

Alison: It is a common belief that the first humans started out in Africa. Is that a valid assumption?

Quan Yin: It depends on what your definition is of the first human.

Alison: If it's just primitive humans, the first homo species but not the homo sapiens, did they start out in Africa?

Quan Yin: It's more accurate to say that life sprang up in multiple places at the same time, but Africa is one of those places where you've found evidence of it.

Alison: I see. Our knowledge is limited by what we can and have found.

Quan Yin: Yes.

Alison: When we were the pre-sentient versions of humans, did we have multiple races at the time?

Quan Yin: No, you had one. You all looked very much like Neanderthals.

Alison: Did the Neanderthals receive any direct infusion of E.T. genes at the time?

Quan Yin: No, they were the last race before the E.T.s began tinkering with human genes.

The Seven E.T. Root Races

Quan Yin mentioned in Chapter Three that there were seven E.T. root races for humans. They are the Lyrans, Pleiadians, Sirians, Orions, Arcturians, Cassiopeians, and Antarians. Now that we have some background on the creation of humans, we can go deeper into the contributions of these seven E.T. races. As Quan Yin's answers would reveal to us, their work actually covered our entire ecosystem on Earth, and a good portion of it was energetic in nature.

Alison: Did the seven E.T. root races do something on a collective level to influence the creation and evolution of the human race?

Quan Yin: A lot of the work was done in the nonphysical, and the groups or nonphysical collectives would get together and decide on what would be a nice tapestry to weave together with the various physical beings from their star systems. And so while Cassiopeians and Antarians or any others of the seven wouldn't seem to be working together to create all this, to co-create it, they were, because they were getting their inspiration from the nonphysical collectives of their star systems that they're connected to.

Alison: So the work of the seven root races was not just for humans, but it's for all the other life forms on Earth as well? And they kind of designed the entire ecosystem we had? Is that a correct understanding?

Quan Yin: Yes.

Alison: Did the seven root races do more than the other races in the original seeding process?

Quan Yin: Yes.

Alison: And was it the genetics, or was it the intentions for how humans would develop, or both, because the two were related?

Quan Yin: Both.

Alison: So they were involved in that original planning and seeding work, and they extended a lot of intentions, and they have stayed involved in our development?

Quan Yin: All star systems in the galaxy were involved in contributing something to the Earth experiment, but many of them then considered their contributions to be done. They didn't then see a need to intervene in any way with what was happening on Earth. But there was a great deal of interest in the Earth experiment and seeing it work out throughout the galaxy, and many different groups and beings really wanted this experiment to work. They started the whole thing, so they felt responsible for ensuring that the evolutionary process would continue without the dominant species being wiped out, because then they would have to start all over again. So, there was a lot of tinkering going on by a lot of different E.T. groups to help along the evolutionary process, the evolution of the life forms on Earth.

Alison: What was the tinkering meant to achieve?

Quan Yin: To speed up the evolution of the life forms and to ensure that you all would survive there.

Alison: And this included the acceleration of the primate-to-human evolution?

Quan Yin: Yes.

Alison: And have the seven root races stayed close to humanity in this process?

Quan Yin: Yes.

Alison: We know a little more about the Lyrans, Pleiadians, and Sirians in their work to speed up the evolution of primates to humans. What about the involvement of the others, for instance, the Cassiopeians and Arcturians, as part of the seven root races?

Quan Yin: Well, some involvement was more energetic or philosophical in terms of trying to determine the direction of the consciousness in all the ways they could influence the consciousness evolution.

Alison: Wow. That's interesting. This goes beyond genetic contributions, and it is influencing evolution at an energetic level. What were the examples of the work by the Arcturians and Cassiopeians?

Quan Yin: Spirituality, love, art, those types of influences.

Alison: Oh, so they were sending us inspirations and guiding us to develop love, art, and spirituality?

Quan Yin: Yes, and the Andromedans also played a role in inspiring art amongst early humans.

Alison: Were they in touch with and influencing humanity across all ages? I mean, it wasn't limited to a specific period or a specific human race?

Quan Yin: Correct.

Alison: Did they ever land on Earth and bring something specific to Earth?

Quan Yin: No, not physically.

Alison: I see. And did the Orions do the same?

Quan Yin: The Orions are more influential in terms of growth through conflict, through creating tension, friction, war with one another, and how culture is spread through invasion. How strange that may seem to the average human, but that has been a part of that desire to expand. The manifest destiny kind of philosophy then creates different cultures and different ethnicities, mixing them up with each other that they wouldn't have otherwise if their nations hadn't gone to war.

Alison: That's amazing, but it does make sense. Our experience shaped our awareness and consciousness. So it's important to have very different experiences, and it sounds like we were guided by the Orions and Arcturians and Cassiopeians in different aspects of our development. Did the other groups like Lyrans, Pleiadians, and Sirians serve a similar role in addition to being physical on Earth?

Quan Yin: No. Well, the Pleiadians, yes. You could say the Pleiadians have done both.

Alison: Were they more about sending energies to heal and to instill peace?

Quan Yin: Healing, yes. Tuning in, channeling, teaching, spirituality. They have also contributed energetically and inspirationally to the creation of music on Earth.

Alison: Wow, music too. That's a major contribution. What about the Antarians?

Quan Yin: Their contribution to the humans was also more energetic. It was more about consciousness and mind, like hive mind and that sort of thing, than it was genetic manipulation or contribution.

Alison: Oh, hive mind, meaning they would influence our inclinations to stick together and form a community or a culture?

Quan Yin: Yes.

Alison: It seems that the contributions from the Lyrans and Sirians were more genetic and physical in nature.

Quan Yin: And some of the contributions are not to the humanoid species on Earth, but the Sirians have brought the canines to Earth, the whales and dolphins, and other aquatic beings like the octopus. The Lyrans have contributed the felines, the Pleiadians added the birds and reptilians, and the Antarians brought the insects to the Earth experience. So some of the contributions are very physical, but not having anything directly to do with the altering of the human genome.

Alison: So when you say canines and felines, that would be the animal life forms of dogs and wolves, and lions and cats, and they are not humanoid.

Quan Yin: Correct.

Alison: I think Diana Cooper wrote a book about the galactic and Universal origins of the animals on Earth (1). The entire animal kingdom is important to the evolution of our consciousness because of our relationship with them. And that's where the connection is in terms of the contributions from the root races.

Quan Yin: Yes.

Earth Humans Are a Race of Humanoids in Our Galaxy

If our genetics are linked with the E.T.s, we don't have an independent origin as Earth humans. Is there a broader category of species that we belong to in this galaxy?

Alison: Did we eventually develop many human races, all patterned after the original Earth humans?

Quan Yin: Well, you were all designed from the humanoid meaning two arms, two legs, a head, and a body, looking more human than reptilian or insectoid or feline or canine. So, yes, you have more of the humanoid energy creating your physical body than you have any other aspect throughout the galaxy, any other being or species. Remember, you were evolving from primates, and so you were bound to be humanoid. Humans were always going to be the dominant species there on Earth.

Now, when you had the help from the Lyrans and the Pleiadians in Lemuria, it was more about skipping over some of the traditional or natural evolutionary processes to get you to be more sentient, more conscious, and more of an appropriate vehicle for the soul's consciousness to be fully embodied.

Alison: So what is the definition of a humanoid?

Quan Yin: They're walking on two feet with two arms, two legs, and a head. And that's the definition.

Alison: But humanoids don't look the same. The heads and faces can look very different. For instance, an Arcturian with big eyes, a small nose and mouth, and a bald head would be a humanoid too.

Quan Yin: Yes. And humanoids can have an animal or a bird's head.

Alison: Wow, as long as they have a body with two arms and two legs, they are humanoids.

Quan Yin: For some reason, there's also a distinction between a humanoid and an insectoid. So an insectoid can still have two arms and two legs, but because they will look more like an insect, even if they can walk on just two legs and be the same size or bigger than a human, they will still be classified as insectoid.

Alison: Just because their head is an insect?

Quan Yin: Yes. Some of them do have more than two arms, but still, for all intents and purposes, they look like a humanoid, but are in an insectoid form.

Alison: What about humanoids that have a bird's head?

Quan Yin: They're not always considered humanoid, but again, two arms, two legs, a head, and a body. It's just that they have those bird-like features and wings, and so are considered to be a different race than humanoids. They're called avians, but you could call them avian humanoids. I'm just giving you the nomenclature that they've been given by all of you.

Alison: Oh, I see. It's our classification of E.T.s. But practically, we can just treat them as different types of humanoids for simplicity, even if they can be called avians or insectoids.

Quan Yin: Yes.

Alison: Are there many humanoids in this galaxy that look like us?

Quan Yin: Yes, slight differences, different skin, different hair, different eyes, different head and features. But yes, most of the beings throughout the galaxy are humanoids.

Alison: Oh, just like the Arcturians we talked about, they are humanoids. And is this just in this galaxy, not in this Universe?

Quan Yin: In this galaxy, correct.

Alison: Wow, we think the typical image of an E.T. looks so odd, but we are more similar than different if we look outside of our galaxy.

Quan Yin: Correct.

Human Ancestry in the Americas, Europe, the Middle East, and North Africa

A genetic ancestry testing today would usually show complex origins from multiple human races. This testing is based on what we know of the different races we have had. Do we have complete knowledge of our ancestries? For one thing, scientists do not know of the E.T. influence in our DNA, and they do not believe that the Lemurians and Atlanteans ever existed. Maybe it is not possible to map out the changes in the human genome over the course of our history because we simply don't know everything, and it is too complicated anyway. But a possible and interesting pursuit is to identify the early genetic influencers in major regions on Earth.

We'll start with our ancestors of human origin, the Lemurians and Atlanteans. We'll focus on the Americas, Europe, the Middle East, and North Africa. These were the regions where the whereabouts of surviving Lemurians and Atlanteans were traced. Some areas were occupied primarily by Lemurian descendants, and other areas were the outposts of Atlantean descendants after the loss of their continent. We'll see if and how much that genetic influence is still visible today.

Alison: You said before that when we became sentient humans in Lemuria, our original version looked like the Mayans. Did the Lemurians have any physical attributes that resembled the Lyrans?

Quan Yin: No, there wasn't crossbreeding going on with the Lyrans. It was through the use of technology that the Lyrans upgraded the original Lemurians.

Alison: So that genetic experimentation was all about upgrading their intelligence and consciousness, and it didn't alter their physical appearance.

Quan Yin: Correct.

Alison: Which regions and races did the surviving Lemurians influence the most?

Quan Yin: The Lemurians spread to North and South America and then eventually to Atlantis. And the natives in North America and South America had genes of the Lemurians. The South American natives look more like the original Lemurians.

Alison: So, for the North and South American natives, was there any other major genetic influence beyond the Lemurians?

Quan Yin: No. They're the Lemurians.

Alison: The Lemurians were influenced by the Lyrans. Was there another E.T. race or races that had contributed to the genetic makeup of the natives in the Americas?

Quan Yin: No, there was more of a help that came along the way, as needed, from a variety of different E.T. races, but there was no additional genetic manipulation. No one star system is more highly represented in the natives within North and South America.

(Note: This "as needed" and small-scale help will be discussed in Chapter 11.)

Alison: Then we had some Spanish influence in Central and South America, so there are people who look more Caucasian.

Quan Yin: That was later on, yes.

Alison: I'm curious whether the surviving Lemurians ever went to Asia since Lemuria was in the Pacific?

Quan Yin: Well, they didn't go to Asia. They went to Australia.

Alison: Okay. So Asians don't have direct Lemurian genes, but the natives in Australia and New Zealand do.

Quan Yin: And Antarctica.

Alison: Oh. Well, it seems like nobody's there right now.

Quan Yin: When there was life on Antarctica.

Alison: So something happened for it to drift to the South Pole?

Quan Yin: Yes, it was earthquakes that caused that splitting off and drifting, yes.

Alison: So Antarctica was adjoined with Australia? That was a big continent in the South Pacific.

Quan Yin: Yes.

Alison: So the natives in Australia and New Zealand look like the Lemurians or the Mayans.

Quan Yin: Yes.

Alison: I know that as descendants of the Lemurians, the Atlanteans had a little bit more variety in physical appearances from natural evolution, and they did not look identical to the Lemurians. From the Atlantic Ocean, the surviving Atlanteans also escaped to different territories, settled there, and intermarried with the locals. Which areas received the most influence from the Atlanteans?

Quan Yin: When Atlantis fell, Atlanteans went to Europe and North Africa. So the early Europeans were the result of, in a lot of ways, the Lemurian and Atlantean civilizations.

Alison: I see. And for the ancient civilizations in the Middle East, such as the Sumerians and Babylonians, who were their ancestors?

Quan Yin: They were the descendants of Atlantis.

Alison: Is this true for North Africa as well in the early days?

Quan Yin: Yes.

(Note: The descendants of Lemuria and Atlantis did not re-create the civilizations that their ancestors had built. According to Quan Yin, this was partly due to the effect of trauma that denigrated their genes and also because of crossbreeding with the locals that produced a "watered-down" version of Lemuria and Atlantean genes.)

Notes

1) *The Archangel Guide to the Animal World* by Diana Cooper (2017). This book details the galactic and Universal origins of animals living on Earth, and it speaks to their purposes of incarnating on Earth. Some are in service to humanity and the planet, while others seek spiritual growth through the Earth experience.

CHAPTER 10

❦

E.T.s AND OUR GENETIC HERITAGE: MAJOR HUMAN RACES

In the last chapter, we recounted our ancient ancestry in relation to E.T.s and explained how the Lemurian and Atlantean genes were not lost by the destruction of their civilizations. We will now shift our focus and trace major and significant E.T. gene infusions into humanity since the bygone era of Atlantis.

As we mentioned previously, the racial, ethnic, and cultural diversity on Earth was a result of extensive crossbreeding and cultural amalgamation through continuous migrations and interactions amongst people for tens or hundreds of thousands of years. And some of these minglings were driven by the aggression of wars and invasions. But if we all looked like the Mayans when we first became homo sapiens, there must have been further genetic input that fostered this impressive diversity. Natural mutations could be a factor in this, but it would not have been sufficient to create our level of diversity, especially considering how distinctive our major races are.

As we will find out, E.T.s continued to play in our gene pool over the past hundreds of thousands of years, and they held a pivotal role in forming our major races and cultures from our early history. The first distinctive races that originated in East Asia, Africa, India, and Europe owed their genetics and predispositions to specific E.T. groups that had landed and lived in those areas. The Earth human history has been intertwined with E.T.s' presence, even if our written history does not offer that perspective at all.

Nordic Pleiadians and Caucasians

One good question to start with is where the Caucasian race came from. As far as we know, neither the primitive humans nor the Lemurians looked anywhere near the Caucasians. Even though a very small number of Atlanteans may have had blue or green eyes and blond or red hair, they still mated with the majority of brown-skinned, brown-haired, and brown-eyed Atlanteans. How had the original Caucasian race developed?

What transpired was that we did have additional genetic contributors from the E.T. world. The Nordic Pleiadians, a species in the family of Pleiadians, have been very involved with humanity's development, and they were the primary and original source of the blue eyes, blond hair, and light skin in the human genome.

Alison: You said the early Europeans were a result of the Lemurian and Atlantean civilizations. The Europeans today are essentially Caucasians. Was there another genetic input there?

Quan Yin: Well, there were the Atlanteans that escaped from Atlantis, and then there was the influx of higher frequency energy and DNA when the Nordic Pleiadeans started to mate with the humans as well. The blond-haired, blue-eyed Pleiadians landed in Finland, Norway, and Sweden and started to crossbreed with the humans there.

Alison: That's fascinating! When did the Nordic Pleiadians land in Scandinavia?

Quan Yin: Right around 30,000 B.C.

Alison: That was relatively recent. Early on, you said the Pleiadians came to Lemuria. Were the Pleiadians that went to Lemuria Nordic Pleiadians or other Pleiadians?

Quan Yin: Just the Nordics.

Alison: So they did come earlier in Lemuria.

Quan Yin: They came earlier, but they weren't breeding with the humans until around 30,000 B.C. in Scandinavia.

Alison: Were the Nordic Pleiadians the only Pleiadians that came to Earth, or were there other Pleiadians?

Quan Yin: There were other Pleiadians coming at the time of the seeding of planet Earth, but it's been mostly humanoid. In Egypt, you had some avian Pleiadians coming. That was after the Nordics came to Scandinavia.

Alison: Within the white or Caucasian race on Earth, there is still much diversity in physical appearances. Many Scandinavians look like Nordic Pleiadians, I suppose, with the pure blonde look. Other Caucasians, however, have different eye colors, hair colors, and facial features, but of course, one consistent characteristic is that they have lighter skin. I understand that after we evolved out of the Neanderthals, we all had brown skin. Even if the light skin has different shades, it is not brown. Was that mostly the influence of the Nordic Pleiadian genes?

Quan Yin: Only the Nordic Pleiadians. They're the whole reason for the Caucasian race in all of its many looks. Blond-haired ones have been crossed with others who had dark hair to begin with, and the light skin remains. Even though they received the dark hair or the brown eyes from the breeding with another race, they can still keep their light skin. The Nordic Pleiadians originally were breeding with Scandinavians, and that is why they all had blond hair, blue eyes, and light skin. Now since then, since the Nordic Pleiadians left, the light-haired, light-eyed, light-skinned people have been breeding with those who have had darker hair, darker eyes, and maybe even much darker skin. And that's why not everyone with light skin has blonde hair and blue eyes.

Alison: So the different Caucasian looks came from continuous crossbreeding?

Quan Yin: Yes.

Alison: But a defining attribute of the race is the lighter skin. These are some strong genes from the Nordics.

Quan Yin: Very strong.

Alison: Why did the Nordics want to come and mate with humans?

Quan Yin: Well, there were a lot of reasons. There was the reason of wanting to help, there was the reason of wanting to see what would happen, and there was the reason of wanting to explore the love type of relationship and the sexual expression within the love relationship with beings who were from another planet.

Alison: Why did they choose Scandinavia? Was it because less sunlight would be easier on fair skin?

Quan Yin: That was part of it, and the other part was the smaller population there. There were fewer people, so they were able to exert their influence faster.

Alison: I see. The Nordics helped create a relatively pure Caucasian race in Scandinavia, and then the Scandinavians helped to create the Caucasian race we have today.

Quan Yin: Yes.

Alison: Were the Nordic Pleiadians third-dimensional beings at the time?

Quan Yin: They were.

Alison: So how long did they stay in Scandinavia?

Quan Yin: Thousands of years.

Alison: Oh, that explains it. That was a long time to transform the native Scandinavians. But I'm still amazed by the gene turnover in favor of the Nordic Pleiadians. There is little trace of the Mayan look.

Quan Yin: Because the Nordic Pleiadians are so beautiful and so advanced spiritually, and they certainly were to the Scandinavians, it became a status to have that white gene in you. It became a level of status for people. They felt more advanced, more beautiful, more special, more connected to these beings that they saw as gods.

Alison: So people wanted to have that bloodline, and the natives took on more and more Nordic genes and looked more and more like Nordic Pleiadians?

Quan Yin: Yes.

Alison: Aside from physical attributes, did they pass on any personality or intellectual traits to the Scandinavians?

Quan Yin: Yes, it was an upgrade.

Alison: How can we characterize those traits?

Quan Yin: Pleiadians are very thoughtful, self-reflective, and introspective. They have made great advances in healing, in teaching, and in technology, and so all of that was passed down. There's also the trait of wanting to spread information, wanting to spread ideas, and wanting to move around what was passed down, and so Europeans have had that expansionist kind of mentality.

Alison: That makes perfect sense. Since the Nordics lived there for so long, did they change the lifestyle of the Scandinavians?

Quan Yin: Yes, they did. They spread their culture, their interest in music and the arts, and their farming techniques. There were lots of things that they were gifting to the Europeans.

Alison: Since the majority of North Americans in the U.S. and Canada were originally from Europe, I assume they inherited a lot of the same traits. Americans in the U.S. may have a more complicated genetic background, which includes different European races and literally races from all over the world.

Quan Yin: That's true.

Alison: So the Nordic Pleiadians were in Scandinavia for thousands of years. Did they all become hybrids subsequently? They would not have been Nordic Pleiadians after two generations.

Quan Yin: Some of them who initially came to say, "spread their seed," would then have left and gone back to the Pleiades before the end of their lifespan.

Alison: Oh, so they would come and mate with the locals, and then they would return home later.

Quan Yin: Right, they didn't hang around for the remainder of that life exactly, no.

Alison: So what does it really mean to say they stayed for thousands of years?

Quan Yin: It means there were some coming and going and others coming and then going, so it wasn't like all of them landed at once or stayed forever.

Alison: I see, so they'd been coming and going for thousands of years, and then they stopped coming, but their descendants or the hybrids would stay?

Quan Yin: Yes, correct.

Alison: I guess that's why the complete changeover was possible because there was a continuous infusion of pure Nordic genes for thousands of years, and later on, the Nordic Pleiadians would have been mating with the hybrids. How many Nordic Pleiadians in total came to Scandinavia over thousands of years?

Quan Yin: It was over 10,000.

Alison: Did both male and female Nordic Pleiadians show up?

Quan Yin: Yes, both showed up.

Alison: And then after the Nordic Pleiadians left, the Scandinavians started to inter-marry with the other races?

Quan Yin: Yes, and moving south into other parts of Europe as well.

Alison: In a prior session, you said that some Nordic Pleiadians are working with us today, sometimes directly in the field of science and technology. Are they a more prominent group doing this than the others?

Quan Yin: Very, yes, much more.

Alison: Why are they interested in doing that?

Quan Yin: They are your progenitors, in the sense that these Pleiadians are a continuation of the same consciousness that helped to seed humanity and has also interfered, intervened in the evolution of consciousness at various times. They have been consistently involved in humanity's evolution.

Alison: So, in summary, the Lyrans and Nordic Pleiadians had the most influence on the Caucasian race, with the genetic upgrade performed on their ancestors by the Lyrans and later the crossbreeding initiated by the Nordic Pleiadians with the Scandinavian natives?

Quan Yin: Yes, with other races on Earth, there were other interventions by other E.T. groups that gave the beings their unique appearance or intelligence level.

Alison: Oh wow.

Zetas and Asians

With Quan Yin's mention of other E.T. groups helping to shape Earth races, my thought naturally went to the Asians, as it is my racial identity in this lifetime. Lemurians and Atlanteans, together with Lyrans and Nordic Pleiadians, held a special place in the lineage in the West. What about Asia, the largest and most populous continent on Earth today?

Alison: Which E.T. group had a significant influence on the Asians? I am Asian in this lifetime, and so I'm curious, do we look more like a specific E.T. species out there?

Quan Yin: You do. Yes, you look more like the Zetas.

Alison: Oh, the Greys.

Quan Yin: Grey is a complicated term that confuses a lot of people, so I wouldn't use the term Grey.

Alison: I see. Where are the Zetas from?

Quan Yin: Zeta Reticuli, and that is its own star cluster that has nothing to do with the beings from the parallel Earth that were also called Zetas, because they look like the beings from Zeta Reticuli, you see. So it's similar to Columbus calling Native Americans Indians.

(Note: The confusion between the Zetas, the Greys, and the beings from a parallel Earth will be explained in detail in Chapter 13.)

Alison: Okay. When did the real Zetas from Zeta Reticuli go to Asia?

Quan Yin: It was during the time of Atlantis that the actual Zetas from Zeta Reticuli started to land in Asia, yes.

Alison: So the Zetas must have known what happened in Lemuria, and they were interested in experimenting with humans. What did they want to achieve?

Quan Yin: Yes, they, just like other E.T. groups, had been interested in Earth and in the possibilities for Earth. And they did see the potential there for experimentation to see how far the intellect could go there on Earth.

Alison: So they were there to help the Asians develop their mind? Did they help accelerate the sentience level of the Asian natives?

Quan Yin: Yes.

Alison: What did the Zetas specifically do to help the Asians?

Quan Yin: It was about infusing them with more of the intelligence and the collective experience of the Zetas, and that's what gave them the upgrades. It was like suddenly they had memories of building technology, building civilizations, having structures, and having farming abilities and things like that. They were infused with more of the collective memories of the Zetas and that's what helped them to evolve. And there were also physical characteristics that came along with that infusion of the Zeta DNA into them.

Alison: Did the Zetas use any genetic technology?

Quan Yin: No, it was mainly by crossbreeding with the Asian natives.

Alison: So, it sounds like it's a smaller jump of consciousness than the Lemurian experiment.

Quan Yin: Yes, and more gradual.

Alison: Did the Zetas also serve in a teaching role, teaching the Asians about the knowledge that surfaced in their memories?

Quan Yin: Yes.

Alison: And then were the people much more intelligent?

Quan Yin: Yes.

Alison: And then what happened?

Quan Yin: The Zetas were satisfied with the work, they learned what they wanted to, and they left.

Alison: How long did the Zetas stay in Asia?

Quan Yin: They stayed for about 500 years.

Alison: Okay. That's a long enough period for crossbreeding to take intended effects.

Quan Yin: Yes.

Alison: How many Zetas came to Asia during that time span?

Quan Yin: Thousands of them.

Alison: I assume the Zetas were helpful and had good relations with Asians during their time there.

Quan Yin: Yes, they did.

Alison: Were Asians able to maintain that level of intelligence and consciousness after the Zetas left?

Quan Yin: There was still natural evolution that needed to take place spiritually, intellectually, emotionally, and so it has been a natural evolution for all of the people of Asia ever since the Zetas left, but they certainly were able to build civilizations and have technology and were far less primitive in their ways.

Alison: There really weren't any records about this, just like Lemuria or Atlantis. We did have bronze artifacts from around 5000 B.C., and written records on oracle bones, at least in China, that gave us some sense of their lives back then. So they had technology to make bronze objects for ceremonial and daily use, and knowledge to build structures and to grow food. It was an evolving human society and civilization, but it wasn't like Atlantis.

Quan Yin: That's correct.

Alison: The Asians didn't build modern high-tech civilizations until the last three decades. But at least they didn't get wiped out like the Atlanteans.

Quan Yin: Right.

Alison: I assume the Zetas approached their work more wisely?

Quan Yin: They did in the long run, yes.

Alison: The crossbreeding must have changed the Asians' physical appearances, but I assume we don't look identical to the Zetas.

Quan Yin: No, you're taller. The original Zetas are very short.

Alison: Oh, like five-feet, four-feet short?

Quan Yin: Three feet. That's why Asians tend to be shorter.

Alison: Oh, I see. So that makes sense. Did they have yellowish or light brown skins, like what many Asians have today?

Quan Yin: Grey.

Alison: Oh, they had grey skin. That was the gene to mix with the brown skin gene. And what kind of facial features did they have?

Quan Yin: Smaller features, dark eyes.

Alison: So, hundreds of thousands of years ago, Asians began to take on the Zetas' genes and alter the Mayan appearance. But judging by the diversity of Asian looks today, we certainly have gotten other genes along the way.

Quan Yin: Right.

Alison: Did Zetas pass on any personality and intellectual traits to the Asians?

Quan Yin: Being more stoic.

Alison: Yes, a related word I was thinking of is conformity. Conformity is a big theme in Asian cultures, and Asians also tend to be less free-spirited and more inward-looking. I don't know if these are traits that they received from the Zetas?

Quan Yin: Yes, these are all traits of the intellect as well.

Alison: So in that sense, the Zetas helped create our sense of what we should be like.

Quan Yin: Well, they weren't concerned about what you should be like. They were interested in what you could be like.

Alison: Okay. But in that process, we actually started to behave more like them?

Quan Yin: Yes, and they were aware that it would be a ramification of infusing their DNA into the Asians.

Alison: Which racial group in Asia looks most like the Zetas?

Quan Yin: The Chinese.

Alison: Oh, really? We're racially mixed in China, and I guess it's just the historical interbreeding of peoples from many racial and ethnic backgrounds within and surrounding China. But the original Han race probably looked most like the Zetas. I am also wondering if the use of herbs and acupuncture in Chinese culture, the more natural ways of healing, and the understanding of Feng Shui and I-Ching had something to do with the Zetas?

Quan Yin: It does not.

Alison: Okay. Then these were pure Chinese creations. Where did the Zetas first land in Asia?

Quan Yin: Well, they started out in China. From there, they spread out to other areas in Asia.

Alison: I see. That's why the Chinese resemble the Zetas the most in both appearance and personality traits.

Quan Yin: Yes.

Sirians and Pleiadians in India

Adjacent to Asia is the Indian subcontinent, home to the country that has the highest population in the world today. Indians have very distinct physical appearances and cultural traditions. Is it possible that they were also visited by a special E.T. race in the past?

Alison: India has become the most populous country in the world with 1.44 billion people in May 2024. What is the genetic heritage of the Indians? Was there any E.T. race that contributed to the look the Indians have and the way they are today?

Quan Yin: Sirians and Pleiadians, different Pleiadians, not Nordic Pleiadians. But Sirians and Pleiadians came together and were very prolific in crossbreeding with the indigenous peoples there.

Alison: When did this happen?

Quan Yin: This was in post-Atlantean times. Right after Atlantis fell, there was a huge need for a repopulation of Earth and a need that the E.T.s could see of a higher infusion of consciousness there as well to get back what was lost with Atlantis and the Atlanteans, most of them perishing in the fall.

Alison: Yes, I have read and heard about this period in Lucy Lee's case studies (1) and in Bashar's channeling (2). It seemed many more people lost their lives in the tsunamis and in the ice age that followed the sinking of Atlantis. And this was not limited to the two coasts of the Atlantic Ocean. The disasters were actually widespread. Bashar also pointed out that these were the same epic floods mentioned in the Bible.

Quan Yin: Yes.

(Note: This post-Atlantean period will be discussed in more detail in Chapter 11.)

Alison: So what did the Sirians that came to India look like?

Quan Yin: They had slightly more bluish skin. And so when they were crossbreeding with the natives, the skin did become darker than the original race.

Alison: And they were obviously humanoid.

Quan Yin: Yes.

Alison: Do they have any facial features that are visible on Indians today?

Quan Yin: Yes, the Indian people do look slightly more Sirian than the average original human looked.

Alison: So the big dark eyes and fuller nose and lips were the influence from the Sirians?

Quan Yin: Yes.

Alison: What about the Pleiadians that were also there in India? What did they look like?

Quan Yin: They were also blue-skinned beings.

Alison: They looked like the Sirians?

Quan Yin: Yes, they did. They looked a lot like the Sirians. They had been with the Sirians and been crossbreeding with the Sirians to the point where they took on some more Sirian appearances.

Alison: And did this happen in Sirius or elsewhere, and not on Earth?

Quan Yin: No, and yes on the ships and in Sirius. The Pleiadians were somewhat like missionaries going to Sirius who then decided to live there and mate with the Sirians.

Alison: And they had dark hair?

Quan Yin: Yes.

Alison: And their intention was to infuse stronger genes into the humans who survived the tsunami and other disasters that had happened at the time. And it was done by crossbreeding. They did not try any genetic manipulation.

Quan Yin: No, they didn't need to.

Alison: How long did the Sirians and Pleiadians stay?

Quan Yin: In India for about 300 years.

Alison: And how many came in total?

Quan Yin: There were more Pleiadians than Sirians, about 7,500 Pleiadians and about 5,000 Sirians.

Alison: Wow. That's a large group. Did they pass on any traits and predispositions?

Quan Yin: Spirituality, desire to connect to spirit and to Source, and to have spiritual practices, to meditate, to do yoga, to channel. These are the things that were passed on in terms of propensity within the Indian people to look to spirit, to seek communion with Source.

Alison: That is totally consistent with the traditions in India. So whatever happened later that established the caste system in India was just the humans' doing.

Quan Yin: Oh yes. The people were very proud of their Sirian, Pleiadian lineage, and they thought the more that they had of that blood, of that DNA, the more entitled they were to having more of the stuff and more of that status as well.

Alison: It seemed like a common phenomenon that human/E.T. hybrids would feel superior to native humans.

Quan Yin: Well, you're still very much working within the third-dimensional consciousness dominated by ego.

Antarians and Africans

Now we turn our attention to the second largest continent and home of pristine nature and a major race on Earth.

Alison: What about people in Africa? Did they also have an Atlantean influence?

Quan Yin: People in North Africa.

Alison: Is there an E.T. group that the people in the rest of Africa resemble the most?

Quan Yin: Well, with the black race, the intervention there was from the Antarians.

Alison: So they look more like the Antarians?

Quan Yin: What the humanoid Antarians naturally look like, yes.

Alison: What did the natives in Africa look like before the Antarians?

Quan Yin: They looked more like the Mayans, the original human look.

Alison: What do these Antarians look like?

Quan Yin: They have very dark skin.

Alison: Are they tall or short?

Quan Yin: They are close to the original human height.

(Note: According to Wikipedia, Neanderthal men stood around 5 feet 5 inches tall and women around 5 feet tall.)

Alison: Okay. There's much diversity in the appearances of Africans today. There are very tall, skinny Africans, and there are Africans with a sturdy build. What kind of physique do the Antarians have?

Quan Yin: Muscular.

Alison: When did the Antarians go to Africa?

Quan Yin: That was over 100,000 years ago.

Alison: Oh, that was still in the post-Atlantis period. Why did the Antarians go to Africa? What was their intention?

Quan Yin: Mining.

Alison: So they didn't have the best intentions then.

Quan Yin: No.

Alison: What were they trying to mine?

Quan Yin: Precious metals and diamonds.

Alison: And was this for their own planet?

Quan Yin: Yes, for the use of their technology. They needed certain metals, and they had mined their worlds completely by that time.

Alison: Did the Antarians use any genetic upgrade or manipulation on the natives?

Quan Yin: No, just crossbreeding.

Alison: Was there any interest at all in helping the Africans evolve?

Quan Yin: No, that wasn't their concern.

Alison: Which ethnic group in Africa now looks most like the Antarian humanoids?

Quan Yin: The people who have the darkest skin.

Alison: But did crossbreeding by nature increase the intelligence of the locals without attempting genetic enhancement?

Quan Yin: The next generation, yes.

Alison: How long did the Antarians stay?

Quan Yin: They left within three years of the landing.

Alison: Oh, that was a very short stay. Did they share any technology with the locals?

Quan Yin: They shared none of their technology.

Alison: Was there any higher level of civilization developed in Africa?

Quan Yin: Egypt.

Alison: Okay. Did Egypt have both the Antarian and Atlantean influences?

Quan Yin: That's where most of the crossbreeding was going on in that region.

Alison: The Egyptian people today look different.

Quan Yin: Well, that is because Egypt is very much closer to Israel and the Middle East and that part of the world, and in fact, you can walk by foot from one to the other, so you can see how the interbreeding between human races went on there to create the Egyptian race.

Alison: I see. It's the subsequent human crossbreeding that gave the Egyptians their current appearances. And I know you've said the ancient Egyptians got additional help from E.T.s later on, more so on their intellect and spirituality. What about the rest of Africa?

Quan Yin: Well, they were tribal civilizations, some of which, of course, still exist, do have the same Antarian influences on them in certain regards, certain customs, practices, fascinations with the stars and such. Those do come from those original visitations.

(Note: E.T.s' work in ancient Egypt to raise the Egyptians' consciousness will be discussed in Chapter 11.)

Alison: The Antarians had an extremely short visitation. So they mined the precious metals, they crossbred with the locals, and then they left without sharing any technology. Even the sharing of their genes was not intended to benefit the locals.

Quan Yin: Correct.

Alison: That was a very different story from the Zetas. The Zetas intended to help and did help.

Quan Yin: Yes, the Zetas were more interested in experimenting on the consciousness there.

Alison: I know of some E.T. races that acted like predators, but I've never heard of the Antarians in Africa. Their short stay limited the potential benefits to Africans, but, perhaps luckily, they didn't cause too much damage either.

Quan Yin: Right.

Alison: Well, all these E.T. races we have talked about look different. So there is a lot of diversity in E.T. humanoids in this galaxy. Are we just a microcosm of that overall diversity?

Quan Yin: Yes.

Alison: Since E.T.s travel around and see each other, unlike us who are a bit isolated, they must be very used to seeing completely different-looking races and beings. I wonder if a fifth-dimensional Arcturian comes and looks at the humans, they would not see what we see.

Quan Yin: They are more, much more interested in what you feel like to them than what you look like.

Alison: Right. So humans tend to have specific views and judgments on looks and appearances. It comes from our cultural and historical background. But these reactions are very much our own, very human-specific, very much tied to the physical reality.

Quan Yin: Reptilians see humans as disgusting to look at. Smooth skin seems so alien to them.

Alison: Oh, really? Oh my God. That's too funny because we feel the same about them. We don't like skin with scales. We think that's extremely unpleasant to look at. So, if very diverse races have been created in our galaxy, all races must be beautiful in their own right.

Quan Yin: That's true.

Alison: When we continuously raise our vibration, will physical appearance, be it skin color, weight, height, or beauty, be perceived simply as an expression, and there won't be any standard or judgment anymore?

Quan Yin: That's correct. You'll evolve out of this phase of your history and into a higher state of consciousness of love, appreciation, and unity with other life forms and extraterrestrial beings.

Notes

1) Lucy Lee's case studies discussed the period after the fall of Atlantis. Please see reference to Lucy Lee's work in Chapter 3.
2) Bashar spoke about the same period that saw the epic floods mentioned in the Bible. Please see reference to Bashar's channeling in Chapter 8.

CHAPTER 11

E.T.s' POST-ATLANTIS PRESENCE AND CONSCIOUSNESS EXPERIMENTS

In the last chapter, we learned about the groups of E.T.s that crossbred with humans and helped shape the prototypes of major human races on Earth. The genetic infusions were reflected in the physical and dispositional attributes of the hybrid humans. These E.T. groups came as early as 250,000 years ago when the Zetas landed in Asia, and as late as 30,000 B.C. when the Nordic Pleiadians alighted in Scandinavia. Unbeknownst to us, many more E.T.s besides the Nordic Pleiadians, Lyrans, Sirians, and Antarians came to Earth after the fall of Atlantis, and they did so for a very long time. It started out as a rescue mission for humanity.

After the destruction of Atlantis, humanity endured numerous severe natural disasters. According to Bashar, the sinking of Atlantis triggered tsunamis in the Atlantic Ocean, breaking the ice shelves in North America and causing epic floods referenced in the Bible. An ice age ensued, and Earth became a harsh living environment. The human population was dwindling, and human consciousness was decelerated to a pre-Atlantis level. Humanity was in dire straits and desperately needed help.

Quan Yin told us that all catastrophes led to the experience of trauma, which in turn left damaging effects on human DNA and thus retarded human sentience. Many E.T.s arrived at this time to help repair human DNA and assist us in repopulating planet Earth. In Lucy Lee's QHHT case studies, her subjects reported that E.T.s from multiple star systems came along to help humans, and many E.T.s interbred and lived with humans in keeping with the early tradition established by the Zetas.

These visitations continued for a very long time, and in certain regions, as explained in the last chapter, significant changes to the Mayan-looking natives occurred, and profiles of major human races emerged. After generations of crossbreeding, descendants of these E.T.s that were human/E.T. hybrids all became part of the human society. Our genetic composition expanded to include many more E.T. races, many of which we have no awareness of or names for. This was a long, continuous threading of E.T. input into our racial and cultural diversity.

So we had a history with E.T.s in our evolution through genetic upgrades, whether it was done in the form of genetic manipulation or crossbreeding. The intent of E.T.s was to accelerate human consciousness in earlier times, and in later days to reinstate human intelligence and physical wellbeing impaired by natural disasters. During the long rehabilitation in the post-Atlantis period, did E.T.s try again to fast forward human consciousness to a higher level?

The answer is they did, and they also brought in a different approach. It was no longer altering DNA or fostering technological advancement, but it was teaching, and specifically teaching about spirituality, many times delivered by master teachers. There were mixed results with this wave of E.T. efforts. The project with the most bells and whistles was the one in ancient Egypt, but a less ambitious endeavor with the Mayans turned into an astounding success. It was a brilliant moment in the history of humanity's consciousness evolution, though it remains largely unknown to the world.

In this chapter, we'll look into continued E.T. involvements with human evolution by filling in some of the blanks during the time after Atlantis fell and before our written history began. We will also describe some of the E.T.s' work with a few ancient civilizations to raise their consciousness levels through the method of teaching.

E.T.s on a Mission to Earth in the Post-Atlantis Era

E.T.s' landing and visiting Earth humans after the fall of Atlantis was not a random set of events. Vivid stories in Lucy Lee's QHHT cases offered an account of E.T.s on assignment to help humans end a detour on their evolutionary path. It was not all flawless, but some of the stories matched popular myths from different cultures. I summarized what I read from Lucy Lee's reports to get Quan Yin's comment.

Alison: It seems that the destruction of Atlantis not only caused flooding but a climate change on Earth. Did the force of the comet make the axis of the Earth shift a little?

Quan Yin: Yes.

Alison: So the continents on both coasts of the Atlantic Ocean were flooded. And according to Bashar, that was the epic flood referenced in the Bible.

Quan Yin: Yes.

Alison: There were a lot more deaths and damages beyond where Atlantis once stood?

Quan Yin: Correct.

Alison: Piecing together the available information, this would have been a long period of time when E.T.s were on Earth to offer assistance, perhaps as long as 200,000 years. Some of them interbred with humans, and some didn't return to their originating star systems. One of Lucy Lee's subjects recalled that there were about thirty E.T. races spread in 12 regions around the globe.

Quan Yin: Correct.

Alison: You mentioned previously that after Lemuria, there were still some genetic experiments, but they were very limited in scale or scope. Did the experiments happen in this period?

Quan Yin: Yes.

Alison: Were there any such projects during this time that made an impact?

Quan Yin: There were a lot of influences, but they were more anecdotal, in the sense of not planning it for an entire region or an entire human race, but rather more individualized upgrades and activations, experiments, and hybridization that's going on but not at the mass level in Lemuria and other civilizations.

Alison: So it was through E.T.s' crossbreeding and very small upgrade projects that human sentience and intelligence were gradually restored to help us get to where we are today.

Quan Yin: Yes, it was.

Alison: I found at least three subjects from Lucy Lee's cases giving a detailed account of their lives as the E.T.s on Earth during this time. They didn't give specific dates for the memories they retrieved, but most sounded prehistoric or before our known history. I wanted to describe these stories here and ask for your comments.

Quan Yin: All right.

Alison: The three stories were Venus in ancient Greece, a queen in ancient Egypt, and the Dragon and the Ox races in ancient China.

Venus in Ancient Greece

One subject described her lifetime as Venus in ancient Greece. According to her, her E.T. race who acted like the Greek gods and goddesses was from Sirius, and their job was to explore the adjustment of human DNA to help humans develop further. Their Sirian ancestors could live hundreds or even thousands of years and had supernatural powers. But in the course of time, the Sirian/human hybrids began to lose some of this power because of their lowered vibration. These hybrids were not returning to Sirius and would instead live on Earth, and this was an intentional plan.

Venus herself was assigned the job of releasing a powerful positive energy to help humans reconnect with Source. However, she also noted that not all of her race on Earth had the intention of helping humans. Some of them enjoyed being worshiped as gods and goddesses and were not interested in elevating human intellect and consciousness. With such intentions, these E.T.s were experiencing a decrease in their vibration and power. This story seemed to have happened tens of thousands of years ago.

(Note: Venus is a Roman goddess and the counterpart of the Greek goddess Aphrodite. The mismatched identity could have been a mental filtering by the subject who didn't differentiate between Venus and Aphrodite.)

A Queen in Ancient Egypt

A second subject was a queen in Ancient Egypt. Her race was the ruler class, and they were half-human and half-god or goddess (i.e., they were hybrids). Their ancestors had also come from Sirius many, many years before. They didn't have all the capabilities that their ancestors possessed, but they were still telepathic, and they were able to influence and control humans by interfering with their brain waves. They could adjust the size of their body and shape-shift into other life forms. They didn't need food to sustain themselves, and they knew how to receive cosmic energy to revive their body. They would go to the bottom of the pyramid, be enclosed in a stone box, and be immersed in cosmic gamma rays to rejuvenate themselves.

Overall, they maintained a higher vibration and consciousness in comparison to a third-dimensional being. According to the subject, their intention was to help the Egyptians develop their intelligence and spiritual connections, and they also protected humans against the dark forces or their own animalistic, savage instincts. However, they could see the descent of dark forces upon Earth as inevitable.

The Dragon and Ox E.T. Races in Ancient China

A third subject described a time tens of thousands of years ago in China. She described her E.T. race as the race of dragons. They could appear as humans or dragons and also had supernatural power. They oversaw the area of many islands from Japan to Taiwan, and the southern and southeastern areas of China. She also described the ox race in northern China along the Yellow River, the lizard race further north in Mongolia, the snake race in the northwestern part of China in Xinjiang province, and the Kirin race, which was a mixture of horse and dragon, in Tibet. These E.T. races all had certain supernatural powers. Some were in closer contact with their home planets than others.

The subject explained the differing governing philosophies between these E.T. groups and that they disagreed on exercising more or less control over the humans. Eventually, wars broke out between them. Some E.T. races had mingled with humans and were disconnected from their originating star systems, while others received weapons and fighters from their home planets in this warfare. The ox race was the ultimate winner. Yellow Emperor, their leader, became the ancestor of the Han in China. This is where the QHHT account and the Chinese mythology converged. The subject is Chinese, so there might have been some filtered influence from the popular mythology in China.

Alison: It seems that the myths and folklore in some cultures were not entirely myths. The stories about China resonated with me because those were the legendary tales of the culture's origin. The story of Venus or Aphrodite and the Greek gods and goddesses is also well-known worldwide.

Quan Yin: Correct. Yes.

Alison: Were the accounts in the QHHT cases a fair representation of what happened between us and E.T.s?

Quan Yin: It's hard to put in a nutshell here because so much had happened and there are so many timelines and realities as well. But it's just good to know that your history is much longer and storied than you had previously thought because it helps you all to realize just how much you have experienced there on Earth, how much experience you have within yourself and your DNA to draw from, and how much varied DNA you have within you as well.

Alison: Okay, I understand. These stories may not have happened in all realities or may not have happened in the same way. They can be seen as examples of an untold phase of our history to give it some texture, and to remind everyone that the Earth Experiment produced a big melting pot for DNAs from all over the galaxy.

Quan Yin: Yes, that's true.

Alison: While most E.T.s' assistance was generally benevolent, there seemed to be some E.T. descendants who abused their spiritual gifts and capabilities. This ran counter to the original mission of their ancestors. They felt they were superior, and they wanted to be rulers.

Quan Yin: Yes.

Alison: It felt like a negative influence, but I guess it was part of our complex and colorful history.

Quan Yin: Correct.

E.T.s' Explicit Attempts to Uplift Human Consciousness After Atlantis

E.T.s' presence following the fall of Atlantis was primarily a recovery effort, and humanity did not return to the eminence of Lemuria or Atlantis during this time. I asked Quan Yin if there had been specific cases where E.T.s focused again on accelerating humanity's consciousness. She told me there were indeed two major efforts: one with the prehistoric Egyptians and the other with the ancient Mayans. There were also two smaller undertakings known as Stonehenge and Easter Island.

In these projects, E.T.s shied away from genetic upgrades and turned to the practice of teaching instead. Out of the four, the Egyptians received the most extensive and visible assistance, but the Mayans turned in the highest achievement. It was a rare and breathtaking event in our evolutionary history. But all the stories are amazing and deserve to be told for the wisdom to be found in these experiences.

Pre-historic Egypt

Alison: Was there any deliberate attempt by the E.T.s since the fall of Atlantis to push forward the evolution of human consciousness?

Quan Yin: In Egypt, you had the third attempt of E.T.s to really help you to grow spiritually, although this time, instead of manipulating your genetics or giving you really advanced technology, they came and gave you teachings. So, it was the attempt to have these spiritual masters come and instruct the Egyptians on the importance of their souls and the eternal nature of their consciousness, and how to work with sound technology, how to live in accordance with nature and the stars, how to utilize the positioning of the pyramids, and how to work with the animals and the Nile River. And there was a lot that the Egyptians were being taught that previous civilizations were not.

And yet they had a major problem in Egypt, which was that they had a ruling class. They had the beings there, the pharaohs, and the families of the pharaohs who thought that by virtue of their bloodline, they were better than everyone else. And so they still had slaves, and they still had this idea that certain people's lives were less valuable than others. The pharaohs and the royal family wanted to keep all that knowledge to themselves and didn't want to share it. It really didn't serve the Egyptians very well, and eventually the E.T.s left, realizing humanity still had a long way to go.

Alison: I see. What were the years of ancient Egypt when the E.T.s were around?

Quan Yin: It went for – depending on when you started it – but let's just say from 20,000 B.C. to 15,000 B.C., so a 5,000-year span.

(Note: According to Wikipedia, ancient Egypt was established in 3,150 B.C. when upper and lower Egypt were unified, and a series of stable kingdoms began to rule the land. Prehistoric Egypt existed between 300,000 B.C. and 3,100 B.C. So, the period of the E.T. visitations would have been in prehistoric Egypt.)

Alison: That was a long time for the E.T.s to stay! Why did the E.T.s choose Egypt? It seemed like the arrogant and selfish ruling class was a barrier.

Quan Yin: Well, they had to start with some civilization, and the Egyptians had a lot of Atlanteans that had made their way over. And of course, the E.T.s were also working with Mayans, Druids, and with others who carried on the Atlantean traditions. But in Egypt, they did it with so much flair. And they left behind the pyramids for everyone to see hundreds and thousands of years later, which get a lot of attention. And there were also the cave drawings, the papyrus writings, and so on, through which Egypt gets a lot of the attention in the same way Yeshua gets a lot of the attention, even though there have been many Yeshua's throughout history who have walked the planet.

Alison: There have been many Yeshua's throughout history?

Quan Yin: Many different spiritual masters like Yeshua, like Jesus. There are many. It's during Egyptian times that there were many of these masters, too.

Alison: Were these masters ascended masters from the twelfth dimension who incarnated on Earth in ancient Egypt?

Quan Yin: No, they were E.T.s. Some were in the fourth and fifth dimensions and lowering their vibration to be able to be experienced by third-dimensional beings. Some were third-dimensional.

Alison: Which E.T. groups were working with the ancient Egyptians?

Quan Yin: In ancient Egyptian culture, you had objects or the pyramid drawings of humanoids with bird heads, humanoids with canine heads, and humanoids with feline heads. Those all represented the Pleiadians, Sirians, and Lyrans.

Alison: They were the three major E.T. groups in Egypt?

Quan Yin: And the Orion's.

Alison: And like you said before, even if they have these animal or bird heads, they're still humanoids.

Quan Yin: Correct. They're humanoids.

Alison: Did the Orions look like humanoids as well?

Quan Yin: They did, but some of them looked more humanoid, and some of them looked more like they had a frog-like appearance.

Alison: Is the broader definition of humanoid a reason why the Atlanteans didn't think there was anything wrong with creating the half-human, half-animal hybrids, because some of them would still look like a humanoid?

Quan Yin: They would, yes. But it was the reason why they were using technology to create them that was problematic.

Alison: Right, right, right. Now we are more familiar with the Sirians, Lyrans, and Pleiadians. Did the group of Orions do anything specific in Egypt?

Quan Yin: Well, they helped with the pyramids, but they had more selfish reasons for doing so than the rest. And the other E.T.s knew the Orion's probably had a more selfish agenda, and so when the Orion's left, there was a great sigh of relief.

Alison: What was their selfish agenda?

Quan Yin: They saw Earth as a place to potentially exploit, but ultimately decided that it was too far and took too many resources to get to in order for it to be completely exploitable.

Alison: So they left.

Quan Yin: Right. They showed up, but they didn't stay.

Alison: I see. Well, five thousand years was a long time that the E.T.s committed to, and there must have been an immense amount of accumulated knowledge. Were the teachings not preserved?

Quan Yin: There was a library in Alexandria that was burned and destroyed, where that knowledge was kept. And of course, the oral traditions eventually became like myths. People don't know whether they're true or not. There's the issue of the telephone game with oral traditions, as you know. When you tell a story, and then you whisper it in someone's ear, and then 10 people down the line, it's a different story.

Alison: So what we have now is mostly a distorted version of what happened and what was taught to the Egyptians?

Quan Yin: Yes, you have distortions and speculations from what people gather from the hieroglyphics and the other artifacts and monuments left behind.

Alison: You said earlier that E.T.s did the work in Egypt with much flair. So there are grand structures and artifacts left for us to see even today. But a contemporary analogy for it would be like spending lots of money on a movie that was a box office failure. I know the pyramids are still serving their functions, but overall, did this work serve a purpose and have a positive influence on mankind?

Quan Yin: Oh, yes. It has definitely had a positive influence. It has made a lot of people think, and it has anchored in a lot of energies there. A lot of people who've visited the pyramids and other sacred sites there are forever changed by the activations and downloads they received by being in that energy.

Ancient Mayan Civilization

Alison: In some of the Ascension writings and channelings, there were Mayans who ascended to the fifth dimension. Is this true?

Quan Yin: Yes.

Alison: Did E.T.s help them?

Quan Yin: Yes.

Alison: How did the E.T.s help them?

Quan Yin: They showed them how to use their consciousness in a much more positive way and how to use their knowledge of mathematics and astronomy in a more positive way so that they could raise their vibration deliberately. And they got them to stop using human sacrifice as a way of connecting to the higher realms.

Alison: What would be an example of using their knowledge or consciousness positively?

Quan Yin: Using their wisdom to align their chakras, for example, to connect with Mother Earth's energy and the energy of Source, using their ability to connect with higher consciousness to channel, using it to create new structures that they could then harness galactic energies through.

(Note: The building of pyramids required the knowledge of mathematics, geometry, and astronomy to align with star positions and movements.)

Alison: And were they taught specific spiritual practices to raise their vibration?

Quan Yin: Yes.

Alison: Okay. And the E.T.s definitely helped just a certain group of Mayans to ascend to the fifth dimension, because we know there were Mayans who didn't ascend.

Quan Yin: They were able to help all Mayans, and some Mayans could ascend to the fifth dimension and others couldn't. And others chose to stay back or were too young to do it, too young to understand the concepts and practice them long enough to make that mass ascension event.

Alison: And when did the ascension happen for the Mayans who were able to do so?

Quan Yin: It happened around 15,000 BC.

Alison: Ahh. It was toward the end of ancient Egypt. How many of them ascended?

Quan Yin: There were around 1,200 who ascended.

Alison: Wow. Would it be correct to say that it was the biggest group of humans who have ascended in human history so far?

Quan Yin: Yes. Ever.

(Note: Historically, individuals were able to ascend to the fifth dimension and beyond when their vibration reached a certain level in the moment of enlightenment. This was recognized in the history of Tibetan Buddhism, and there were accounts of highly evolved monks who ascended, taking their physical bodies with them and leaving behind only the clothes they had been wearing. This usually happened as an individual event. The Mayans' mass ascension was indeed unique in that it was a group event. Our upcoming Ascension is also a group event, but this event is a Universal Ascension, a scheduled and destined occurrence on the Universe's agenda. We still have to transform ourselves into a fifth-dimensional consciousness and vibration, but what's coming up will be the Universal mass Ascension of billions of people on Earth, all moving up to a higher dimension at the same time. Please refer to the Introduction for a discussion on Ascension.)

Alison: Why did the E.T.s choose the Mayans?

Quan Yin: They saw the potential there for giving something that humanity could use in a very positive way. They thought that civilization would be able to thrive and move out in all directions and have a positive influence on the rest of humanity.

Alison: I guess the mass ascension was the peak of their civilization, but the Mayans weren't able to keep the tradition. We don't have records of the Mayans in a mass ascension, of course, and we only have that experience in our collective consciousness.

Quan Yin: Yes.

Alison: E.T.s were their teachers, but the Mayans did it on their own.

Quan Yin: Yes, the Mayans were allowed to ascend. No one interfered with it, and that Mayan group continued to ascend within this galaxy and off of this planet.

Alison: Incredible. Which E.T. groups helped the Mayans?

Quan Yin: It was a group of Nordic Pleiadians.

Alison: Oh, the Nordic Pleiadians. So they didn't crossbreed with the natives, even if other Nordic Pleiadians had chosen to do that in Scandinavia earlier.

Quan Yin: Right.

Alison: They were doing something very similar to what other E.T. s were doing in Egypt, which was to teach and not resort to any genetic upgrade?

Quan Yin: Correct.

Alison: How long did the Nordic Pleiadians stay to teach and influence the Mayans?

Quan Yin: 150 years.

Alison: Wow, that was a relatively short period of time, especially compared with Egypt.

Quan Yin: Yes.

Alison: So they started visiting the Mayans about 150 years before 15,000 B.C when the mass ascension took place. They did it right around the time when the work in Egypt started?

Quan Yin: Yes.

Alison: The Nordic Pleiadians gave the Mayans teachings to help them move from the third to the fourth and then to the fifth dimension. These Nordic Pleiadians must not have been third-dimensional themselves?

Quan Yin: Yes, they were.

Alison: Oh, really? They helped the Mayans to ascend to the fifth dimension, but they didn't ascend themselves?

Quan Yin: They learned through the experience of the Mayans that it was possible for them to do so.

Alison: Oh, so when they went there to raise the Mayans' consciousness, ascension may have been a "stretch goal" in our parlance. It's just that the Mayans fully embraced the teachings and thoroughly transformed themselves to make ascension happen. How were the Nordic Pleiadians able to influence the Mayans so effectively?

Quan Yin: The Mayans treated the Nordic Pleiadians as gods, and so they wanted to appease the gods. They wanted the gods to be happy with them, and so they really applied the teachings. They dedicated themselves to the practices that they were given.

Alison: This didn't seem like a higher-vibrational motive if what they wanted was to please the gods.

Quan Yin: It doesn't matter what the motivation was. The effect was the same from using these tried and tested practices that the Pleiadians brought them.

Alison: And did the Pleiadians actually tell them that they needed to please the gods, or was it their own belief?

Quan Yin: It was their own belief.

Alison: I see. That's fascinating. I guess in those days, the Mayans lived a simple and isolated life, and they were attuned to nature. The Nordic Pleiadians must have made an instant impression on them.

Quan Yin: Yes. Right, because the Mayans had more of a pantheism or multiple gods viewpoint, whereas today when E.T.s come, they're not going to be considered gods, because the God concept today is of a nonphysical being far, far away in the sky. Maybe that God would send one son to represent him, but not entire races of E.T.s. So that is the difference in the way things were versus the way things are.

Alison: So we will need more of an awakening from within on our Ascension path because we won't be feeling the same way as the Mayans were. But the E.T.s can put us in touch with a higher vibration and ready us to open up to more truths.

Quan Yin: Yes.

Alison: Is there any other reason why the E.T.s didn't succeed in ancient Egypt aside from the Egyptian ruling class?

Quan Yin: It was because of the ruling class in Egypt, and it was also not the intent of the E.T.s to get the Egyptians to that place of ascension. It was not part of their overall goal because there was a need for the beings to stay and pass on the knowledge. And the E.T.s understood that they would eventually leave, and the people would need to have the teachings passed on in written form and in oral form. And therefore, they knew that everyone needed to stay, and they couldn't have a large group of people ascending.

Alison: That is a crucial point. The Mayans who ascended took their body, their genes, and their fifth-dimensional consciousness with them. They could have been master teachers, but they were all gone. The ones who stayed behind could have followed the same teachings they had received and kept the spiritual tradition alive. Maybe some did. But it seemed they fell back on their old beliefs, and things seemed to unravel at some point. They resumed human sacrifices later in their history. What happened to the Mayans?

Quan Yin: Well, yes, it is true that they were influenced by other tribes, other groups that then had a greater influence upon them than their past helpers and teachers had. The Pleiadians kept coming back and trying to help them to continue their spiritual evolution, but the ones who left in the mass ascension event were the cream of the crop; they were the highest vibrationally. So the ones that stayed behind weren't ready and were not able to learn as much from that ascension or from the teachings of the Pleiadians.

(Note: Once the Mayans ascended to the fifth dimension, they could no longer be seen on Earth or interact with the remaining Mayans in a physical way. This is because the fifth dimension has a higher vibratory frequency and is not accessible to beings in a lower dimension or vibration.)

Alison: There are a lot of influences on Earth, and third-dimensional humans are not always able to stay within a higher vibrational state. Those Mayans who ascended were exceptions. It is achievable if we have a very focused intent and discipline.

Quan Yin: That's true.

Alison: It sounds like the plan for Egypt was to train the royal family and elite class to achieve higher intelligence and consciousness, who would then pass on the teachings to more Egyptians to evolve their consciousness collectively. And the Egyptian ruling class ruined the plan. The plan for the Mayans might have been similar, but that group of Mayans exceeded expectations, and they ascended. Then, not enough teachers were left to carry the torch.

Quan Yin: Yes.

Alison: That's why you said the people who rise to fifth-dimensional frequencies today are not staying there. They come back down to help the rest of us.

Quan Yin: That's right.

The Druids and Stonehenge

Alison: What about the Druids? I think you once said it was another attempt by E.T.s to help humans advance their consciousness.

Quan Yin: Yes, and it was also the Nordic Pleiadians coming at that time.

Alison: Wow, really! When did the Nordic Pleiadians come to work with the Druids?

Quan Yin: About 5000 B.C.

Alison: Oh, it was much later than ancient Egypt or the Mayan mass ascension. Did the Nordic Pleiadians use the teaching method?

Quan Yin: Yes.

Alison: I remember you said that the Druids went some distance but not all the way in raising their consciousness, but they were able to communicate with E.T.s from other systems.

Quan Yin: They were, and they were able to utilize those structures that they built to create portals and to utilize those portals to access energy and information. Some even traveled to other star systems using the portals that they were shown how to create by the Pleiadians.

Alison: Wow, that's amazing! And were those structures what we call Stonehenge?

Quan Yin: Yes, the Nordic Pleiadians helped them to build it.

Alison: How did the stone structures help the Druids to open portals?

Quan Yin: There's actually a natural portal there, and the structures enhance the portal energy that was already there in the same way that the pyramids are helpful in sending and receiving energy. The structures at Stonehenge help to increase the size, the strength, and the reach of the portal there.

Alison: Is it because of their size, shape, or position?

Quan Yin: Every aspect of it was very calculated to enhance the power of the portals. It would also serve as a place where people would go because of the stones. People would visit the location and know it's an important spot to have a cool experience. If it were something flimsy, like a thatched hut that they built around that area, then it would be gone today.

Alison: This felt like a different approach than the one used with the Mayans.

Quan Yin: Yes, it was a different approach.

Alison: And was the plan to help the Druids enhance the natural portal there and teach them to tap into their spiritual capability and open new portals as well to interact with other intelligent beings in the Universe?

Quan Yin: Yes, they wanted to see what the humans of Earth were capable of in terms of their abilities to apply knowledge, to apply the wisdom that they shared with them. So it was a test of some sort to see where you were all at in terms of your development. And the Druids showed that they had the potential, and humanity had the potential, yes.

Alison: And they didn't go the route that the ascending Mayans took, perhaps because they were not taught to do those things.

Quan Yin: They weren't taught, exactly. They weren't being given the necessary instructions to ascend or to raise their consciousness. It was more about, "Let's see what you can do with your physical environment to access more of the energy and the information that we're going to be sending humanity over the next tens of thousands of years."

Alison: Have the Nordic Pleiadians been sending this energy and information ever since?

Quan Yin: Yes.

Alison: Did the Druids stay third-dimensional?

Quan Yin: They did, yes.

Alison: So in the third dimension, they could open the portals and use the energy to communicate with and travel to other star systems?

Quan Yin: Yes.

Alison: This must have expanded their minds in terms of our existence on Earth and the fact that we had a whole galaxy as our neighborhood. That alone should have shifted their consciousness level.

Quan Yin: That's true.

Alison: And how long did the Nordic Pleiadians stay with them?

Quan Yin: Only 20 years.

Alison: Did they have face-to-face interactions with the Druids to give them the instructions, and not through downloads or channeling?

Quan Yin: Yes.

Alison: Was there a reason why the Druids were selected for this trial?

Quan Yin: They had a good foundation of spiritual practice, of connecting with Mother Earth and Mother Nature, so they were showing the potential that they had for going beyond all of that.

Alison: Were the Druids a culture of Celtic priests? That's what I read.

Quan Yin: Yes.

Alison: So that was not a large group of people.

Quan Yin: No.

Alison: What they were able to do was extraordinary, for themselves and for humanity, but this knowledge seems to have been lost. There are so many speculations about Stonehenge, but no real answers. Did the Druids ever pass down the information and their experience?

Quan Yin: It wasn't something they necessarily wanted other people to know about.

Alison: But did they at least want to give it to their next generation?

Quan Yin: Just orally.

Alison: And eventually, the information disappeared.

Quan Yin: Yes. Well, there aren't modern-day Druids who are the true descendants of the ancient Druids.

Alison: No. Okay, that's why. It was never shared externally, and the secrets died with the last of the original Druids.

Quan Yin: Correct.

Easter Island

Alison: Were there other E.T. projects like the one with Druids?

Quan Yin: There have been more, but they haven't been as noticeable. They haven't had the impact. And you can see Easter Island, for example, that there were visitations there, that there was E.T. involvement there, but you don't have as much of a fascination with those Easter Island statues as you do with the pyramids.

Alison: What was the intention of that E.T. visitation on Easter Island? What were they trying to help the natives achieve?

Quan Yin: There was a type of energetic connection with Mother Earth's core that the statues provided because they are as far-reaching down as they are up. And there was a desire to work with the core of Mother Earth and the grid where those statues were placed to help enhance the consciousness of the humans across the entire planet. So it affected more than just the people who were living there on those islands.

Alison: Was that a desire by the natives, or was it a desire by the E.T.s?

Quan Yin: Both.

Alison: And which E.T. group was there to help?

Quan Yin: It was a group effort between Lyrans, Sirians, and Pleiadians.

Alison: Oh, the trio again! When did this happen?

Quan Yin: This was around 40,000 BC.

Alison: Wow. This was earlier than the other three projects. And who were the natives?

Quan Yin: They were people who made it there from Lemuria.

Alison: Oh, okay. They were Lemurian descendants, and they were chosen because they were already spiritual.

Quan Yin: Well, they also summoned the E.T.s, you see. So it was a two-way street. They summoned them with their desire, and they had stories of the E.T.s coming in the past and helping them in Lemuria.

Alison: I see, and they wanted to contribute more to spirituality on the planet. Did they already know about creating this configuration of statues, or did they just make a general request to do more for human consciousness?

Quan Yin: A general request, yes. They didn't know exactly what or how to do it.

Alison: How did the E.T.s decide to place the statues there?

Quan Yin: The enhancement there with the Easter Island statues has to do with the positioning of the islands themselves and the significance of their positioning relative to the grid, and to their vocation when viewing the stars, and it being a good place for people to go and make contact with the E.T.s. The E.T.s also knew they wouldn't always be around. They wanted to leave some evidence that they were there by creating something that could not have been created by humans at that time.

Alison: So the statues utilized the positioning of the islands to connect with Mother Earth's core and provide energy from the core to the grid, where they stood to be sent worldwide?

Quan Yin: Yes.

Alison: What was the grid? Ley lines?

Quan Yin: Yes.

Alison: How long did the Pleiadians, Lyrans, and Sirians stay?

Quan Yin: Only 30 years.

Alison: Did they accomplish what they wanted to accomplish?

Quan Yin: Yes. They're still affecting people's consciousness today with those statutes.

Alison: Oh, the statues are like the pyramids. That's incredible. So this piece of history was probably passed down orally, and then lost just like what happened with Stonehenge?

Quan Yin: Yes.

Alison: Okay. And this indigenous culture disappeared as well.

Quan Yin: Yes.

Alison: Are there people on the island or elsewhere still working with the statues?

Quan Yin: Of course, yes. There are people who recognize the vortex that is there, the power of the gridlines, and the connection to Mother Earth's core that they can tap into with the help of these giant monolithic statues.

Alison: I see. So, basically, it has been there for over 40,000 years, and it's been doing the same thing, sending positive, high vibrational energy to humanity from Mother Earth's core.

Quan Yin: Yes.

Alison: So whenever the E.T.s and the natives had the same intention, this type of project could have been done a thousand times all over Earth.

Quan Yin: It was done a lot all over the Earth. There are lots of pyramids around, not just in Egypt.

Alison: Oh, okay. They're just not that visible to us?

Quan Yin: Well, yes, they are. They're in Mexico, they're in Bosnia, they're in Machu Picchu, and they're under the surface of the ocean. People have awareness of these structures. If you watch the show "Ancient Aliens", you'll see a lot of them talking about all of these different structures that were built. And they're all harnessing energies, and they're all reflective of the E.T. contact that was going on at the time to help people to realize you're not alone. No matter what area you live in, you'll be able to come and see this, and you won't be able to fathom how the early humans did it without help.

Alison: We have these statues and pyramids that are living proof of E.T.s' past work with us. But there are no written records. Having this knowledge now and going to these sacred sites can help us experience the expansion of consciousness that the ancients experienced.

Quan Yin: Yes indeed.

A Perspective of E.T.s' Involvement in Human Evolution

If we go through the history of E.T.s' involvement in influencing humanity's evolution, there were four ways that they carried out their plans. The first is genetic manipulation, the second is the gifting of spacecraft to be reverse engineered, the third is crossbreeding, and the fourth is teaching. These methods have yielded different results in different cases. They could be highly effective, such as genetic upgrades or leaving technologies, but we know there were tragic consequences as well from those actions. And very often humans worshiped E.T.s as if they were God, and E.T. hybrids felt entitled and superior to native humans.

E.T.'s motivations seemed to be between impatience for natural evolution and a true desire to help. Their involvement contributed to our exceptional racial, ethnic, and cultural diversity on Earth. But have they done the right thing all along? Should they have been more patient? What are we all learning from this history?

Alison: If I think about the ways E.T.s tried to accelerate our evolution, there seemed to be four different methods: 1) genetic manipulation, 2) reverse engineering E.T. technology, 3) crossbreeding, and 4) teaching. Is this a fair way to summarize E.T.'s involvement with us?

Quan Yin: Yes.

Alison: Are all these considered to be interference with natural human evolution?

Quan Yin: Well, it depends on how far it's taken. Obviously, genetic upgrade and crossbreeding are forms of interference, whereas just leaving technologies or offering technologies are interventions, but those are a form of help. And teachings are a good way to help as well. But any time that there has been a manipulation of humans physically, that's interference. Interference means you're interfering with something that could occur very naturally.

Alison: Teaching itself is a form of intervention, but it's inducing a change based on people's acceptance of higher knowledge.

Quan Yin: Yes, it's benevolent intervention.

Alison: I am a little surprised that crossbreeding is considered interference by E.T.s because they could be intending to help.

Quan Yin: Yes, it is interference. A lot of interfering and intervening has been done over the millennia, and the E.T.s have learned from their mistakes. In other words, they know now what not to do based on what has been done and has resulted in the fall of Atlantis, the fall of Lemuria, ice ages, and so on.

Alison: Is crossbreeding a bad idea to them now?

Quan Yin: Yes.

Alison: Oh, because it's a physical interference, it's unnatural?

Quan Yin: It's unnatural in the sense of your doing it with an intent to upgrade the consciousness of the native life form that you're doing it with. If it happens because of love, then that's a little different.

Alison: I see. So the E.T.s think now that they should have followed a more natural and non-interfering path. Doing anything for love would be a natural path, and this is their learning?

Quan Yin: Yes. But even if you do it out of love, if you know there are repercussions, you know that it's going to have an effect on the consciousness evolution of a group or race of humans, then you know you're really interfering. Even though you are not doing that for that purpose, even though it's not your intention, you still know that, and you take that action anyway as an E.T.

Alison: I see. But if they had not done all the crossbreeding, then our racial and ethnic diversity would not be the same as it is today.

Quan Yin: Correct.

Alison: So, what is the right way to look at this?

Quan Yin: It has served a greater purpose, even though it was a mistake.

Alison: To serve the greater purpose of creating diversity on Earth for the true Earth experience?

Quan Yin: It's part of the Divine plan. So you can see that even your mistakes in life are part of a Divine plan.

Alison: So, for the Divine plan, I am also thinking about what you said about the Earth Experiment, that it is really an experiment of consciousness. So these mistakes offered many different scenarios for the human consciousness to accelerate, decelerate, or evolve naturally. That's how this experiment can be more complete, and that's how we all live and learn and evolve.

Quan Yin: That's correct.

Pre-Lemurian Earth Civilizations

We have been discussing our evolution in different periods of human history and civilizations. What we have not mentioned is that there had been earlier civilizations on Earth that were not founded by humans. This information is pertinent to bring up, as these civilizations were sometimes referenced in channeled material or QHHT case reports. In the days before Homo sapiens became the dominant species on Earth, there were E.T.s that had wanted to settle on Earth. It was part of Earth's history, but it wasn't a significant experience for humans. Here we will check on one such example.

Alison: In Lucy Lee's case studies, there were beings that lived in ancient times who had spiritual talents and capabilities, and larger bodies like12-15 feet tall. They seemed to be in a civilization that had some Greek and Egyptian elements in buildings and clothing. Was that a different species?

Quan Yin: It was.

Alison: Were they connected in any way to the Lemurians?

Quan Yin: No, it's pre-Lemurian.

Alison: Oh, I see. Were they highly sentient beings?

Quan Yin: Yes. That race of beings was an E.T. group that was hoping to make Earth their home rather than to allow just the natural evolution to take place. That was the goal, and because Earth was meant for others, they didn't survive. They were wiped out in the Ice Age.

Alison: Were there many ice ages in Earth's history, and this was one of the earlier ones?

Quan Yin: Yes.

Alison: Were there multiple E.T. races like that who took residence on Earth, but they were not meant to survive because they didn't belong here?

Quan Yin: Yes.

Alison: Who were these ancient beings referenced in Lucy Lee's case report?

Quan Yin: Some people call them the ancient builder race.

Alison: So before Lemuria, there were civilizations, but there was no human civilization that existed?

Quan Yin: No, not what you call civilization. They were all cave people.

Alison: So if there were civilizations before Lemuria, those were established by the E.T.s. According to Bashar, Elysium was a pre-Lemurian civilization that existed 500K years ago, and we have no knowledge of it.

Quan Yin: Correct.

Alison: And did these E.T.s contribute to human genetic makeup at all? Did they have close contact with the human race?

Quan Yin: No, there was no interbreeding at the time of the Neanderthals.

Alison: So the primitive Earth humans probably thought of them as gods, too.

Quan Yin: Yes.

Alison: And the primitive humans were not sentient enough to benefit from any interactions with them?

Quan Yin: No, they weren't. Your history of being sentient humans really started in Lemuria.

CHAPTER 12

❧

E.T.s IN AN ADVERSARIAL ROLE

So far, we have learned that E.T.s occupied a prominent position in our genetic, racial, and cultural heritage. The E.T. races we have zeroed in on are the Lyrans, Pleiadians/Nordic Pleiadians, Sirians, Zetas from Zeta Reticuli, and Antarians. We have also learned a little about the Orions, Arcturians, and Cassiopeians in their contributions to our evolution at the energetic level. All of these E.T.s are generally benevolent beings that have taken an active interest in advancing humanity's consciousness evolution. Even if they made mistakes, they had started out with good intentions.

Are E.T.s always benevolent? There are many E.T. races in our galaxy, and the diversity easily means that there will be contrarians. For instance, the group of Antarians that made it to Africa was on the selfish side of the bunch. But that was a relatively quick and random event. In the history of E.T. and human interactions, there are indeed two E.T. races that stood out in their misconduct or downright malice. They are the Anunnaki and the Reptilians.

The Anunnaki and the Reptilians are considered malevolent in the New Age literature and much of the lightworker community. They are often looked at as culprits of many of our woes and miseries. There are many references to them in the videos or writings about E.T.s, but I have not found a reasonably complete and credible account of who they are, where they come from, and why they behaved the way they did or still do. They seem to be our nemesis by posing as the darker forces in our world of polarity. I asked Quan Yin to give us a view into these notorious E.T. beings in how they affected the human race and why it was allowed to happen.

The Anunnaki

For anyone interested in E.T.s and starseeds or following the Ascension discourse, the Anunnaki is a familiar name. The Anunnaki were recorded in ancient Sumerian and Babylonian texts as deities. But they were actually E.T.s that played an unusual role in the devolution of human consciousness in our history.

Alison: The Anunnaki have been accused of creating a slave race on Earth. Is this true?

Quan Yin: Well, Lyrans were helping to give humanity a higher consciousness, and Anunnaki were interested in creating good workers.

Alison: The Anunnaki were working with the same early human bodies but going in a different direction?

Quan Yin: The bodies you have today were the bodies the Anunnaki were working with. They came after the Lyrans.

Alison: When did the Anunnaki come to Earth?

Quan Yin: Ancient Sumerian time, about 4000-2000 B.C.

Alison: That was not that long ago. Why did the Anunnaki go to the Middle East?

Quan Yin: Mining gold.

Alison: Now I remember Bashar said something about that. It was like they needed gold because their planet was damaged. Their atmosphere was damaged.

Quan Yin: Yes. Pollution.

Alison: Pollution. Right. Bashar said they needed gold to reflect back the radiation on their planet. Which planet did they come from?

Quan Yin: Nibiru.

Alison: How did they find Earth?

Quan Yin: The Anunnaki started to pay attention to Earth hundreds of thousands of years ago and planted seeds for this eventual coming during the Sumerian time period. There was a lot of research going on across the galaxy and looking at different planets that could be mined, and different groups of sentient life forms that might be accessible for help with that. That was all being studied by various groups, including the Anunnaki, for a very long time prior to them coming and actually perfecting the approach that they came up with to do just that.

Alison: So there were others that did what Anunnaki did on Earth, but it was on other planets?

Quan Yin: Yes.

Alison: When did the Anunnaki come and create the slave race?

Quan Yin: The slave race was completed and put into action around 4,000 BC.

Alison: How did the Anunnaki create the slave race? Did they use genetic technology?

Quan Yin: They used injections and then followed up with a reinforcement method.

Alison: How did the reinforcement work?

Quan Yin: It would have a lot to do with sound technology and also suggestions, mental suggestions. So that's what the ancient Sumerians were being exposed to after injections.

Alison: It's almost like utilizing psychology or mind control. It's the second part, the mental suggestions, that made me feel that it was a psychologically based method.

Quan Yin: If you remember the movie Clockwork Orange, it's similar to that, that type of "we'll give you lots of visuals and sound, and these will be ways in which we control you first with the mind and then the body starts to reflect the new way the mind is thinking, the new way the mind is being programmed and engineered."

Alison: So, we actually do have that on Earth, right? We have brainwashing and mind control, though we don't have genetic alteration as a first step. The Anunnaki were way more advanced with this merciless methodology?

Quan Yin: Yes.

Alison: Was the effect to make these people less smart and more predisposed to obey?

Quan Yin: Yes, easier to control, and to undo what the Lyrans did. They even infused something into the DNA that would make people afraid of God, then gave them a religion that would cause them to believe in an angry God that you had to please.

Alison: So what religion was that?

Quan Yin: It was Judaism.

Alison: I see. It seems some information on the Internet places the beginning of that religion in the Near East around 2000 B.C. or later.

Quan Yin: I would say that prior to that, there were earlier attempts at establishing a religion that predates what you might consider to be the founding of Judaism. It was very similar in that there's a God and God is out there, and God is in the sky and there's a heaven and there's a hell and there's judgment and there's mercy; and without all of the other bells and whistles and the holidays and traditions and rules and commandments. But what those earliest attempts at forming a religion all had in common was basically a separate God that is all-powerful and that you need to appease in some way, or you will upset that being, and that being will punish you for it.

Alison: Did the Anunnaki help with the establishment of Judaism?

Quan Yin: No, they just planted the seeds. They didn't help them in the sense of "Here's what you need to do. Here's what you should call it." But the people created the religion around the experiences that they had with the Anunnaki.

Alison: The Anunnaki were pretty much acting like they were the gods?

Quan Yin: Yes, they were happy to play that role and happy to be seen in that way, acting on behalf of God, a bigger God that wants you to do the things that they actually want you to do.

Alison: This was a deliberate effort on their part?

Quan Yin: They had deliberate intent, yes, because they wanted to get the gold that they needed quickly, and they were devising plans as to how to get the people of Earth to work and work hard and work fast.

Alison: Wow, that was the ultimate success factor in creating a slave race. Humans had created slaves by using coercion and physical force. But a true slave race believes they are slaves. Not all the Sumerians became slaves, did they?

Quan Yin: No.

Alison: So it was a group of Sumerians that the Anunnaki enslaved. Did the Sumerians acknowledge that this happened?

Quan Yin: Yes.

Alison: Did they agree to it, or did they not have a choice?

Quan Yin: They didn't mind because the lower classes were the ones who were given over as the slave race candidates.

Alison: Oh, that's so sad. I recall reading somewhere that the Anunnaki also took humanoids from other planets to Earth to join the slave labor. Did that happen?

Quan Yin: Yes.

Alison: Did they have to brainwash them as well to make them slaves?

Quan Yin: They didn't have to. They already had more of a slave mentality, so they put them on Earth, too.

Alison: The Sumerians must have gotten some benefits from this exchange. I saw a video of an archaeological exploration that uncovered a Sumerian ceremonial mask that was gold-plated with intricate carvings. I cannot find the video again, but I remember it was said that scientists believed the Sumerians would have needed electricity for the gold plating, and some sort of printing and laser technology for the carving and creation of the mask. So were those technologies from the Anunnaki?

Quan Yin: Yes.

Alison: Did the Anunnaki leave the technologies to the Sumerians?

Quan Yin: No, when the Anunnaki left, they took their technology with them.

Alison: When did the Anunnaki leave?

Quan Yin: Fifty years after they landed.

Alison: So it was just a quick use and abuse.

Quan Yin: Yes.

Alison: Did they ever return?

Quan Yin: No.

Alison: Other than a short-term use of technology, did the Sumerians get anything at all from allowing the Anunnaki to turn lower-class Sumerians into a slave race and permitting the Anunnaki to mine gold in their land?

Quan Yin: There was a type of transmission of energy that occurred for the Sumerians by being in the presence of the Anunnaki, so they did still benefit from being around the Anunnaki.

Alison: A higher consciousness?

Quan Yin: Yes, because of their higher intelligence.

Alison: That's why in ancient Sumerian texts, Anunnaki were described as deities, in addition to the fact that they purposely acted like gods.

Quan Yin: Yes.

Alison: So even if the Anunnaki were creating the slave race, they were still higher in vibration than the Sumerians.

Quan Yin: They were still higher in vibration, exactly.

Alison: This higher vibration will be a benefit to look forward to when the benevolent E.T.s land on Earth in the future.

Quan Yin: Yes.

Alison: Did this ancient slave race cause a downside for humanity?

Quan Yin: Yes, they slowed down your evolution considerably.

Alison: Oh, really?

Quan Yin: Yes.

Alison: We had slavery on Earth for a long time. Was the real harm here in creating humans who had a slave mentality, who were fearful, prone to obey, and were thus reduced to a lower level of sentience?

Quan Yin: Yes.

Alison: These changes were marked on their genes?

Quan Yin: Yes.

Alison: What happened to this slave race?

Quan Yin: It's what you have today.

Alison: Ahh. How did the slave race that was created in the Middle East spread their genes to the rest of the world?

Quan Yin: Well, there was a lot of trading going on there. There were a lot of reasons for travelers to come and partake in not only the trade, but also to have relationships and fall in love, and either bring people back home with them or stay there and begin procreating with people there.

Alison: So the slave race and/or their descendants interbred with the natives and the travelers, and they also moved around with the travelers.

Quan Yin: Yes.

Alison: Was Iraq at that time a central location on the route of trade, commerce, and travelers?

Quan Yin: Yes.

Alison: And that's how crossbreeding eventually sent these genes to the entire human population?

Quan Yin: Yes, it was a much smaller population then also, so a lot easier for something to spread to everyone.

Alison: We are a mix of many different bodies.

Quan Yin: Exactly.

Alison: So we carry these slave genes in all of us. What are the traits? Is there a specific group of people that stands out?

Quan Yin: No. You can see it more in certain people playing it out in their lives than in others. You can see they have the dominant consciousness within them that they are simply going to work the 80 hours per week that they feel they must in order to survive and take care of everyone in their family. There is that mentality within certain people.

Alison: I guess it is a deep-rooted fear and insecurity that many have, and they can't feel safe unless they work excessively. That's one reason why we have so many workaholics. Does it include some of the rich and successful people on Wall Street or in Silicon Valley?

Quan Yin: Yes, somewhat, although there is more of an egoic, narcissistic quality within someone who wants to make much, much more than they need and will possibly ever spend. That's coming more from an emptiness, the disconnection from Source, feeling that they can fill that emptiness with fame or material possessions.

Alison: The Anunnaki really had a ruthless and systematic way to benefit themselves at the expense of others.

Quan Yin: Yes, they did, from a certain point of view. From another point of view, they did exactly what you needed them to do to give you the experiences that as souls you wanted to have.

Alison: So they brought on genetic changes, and they contributed to the creation of a God that is powerful, high in the sky, and separate from us. This became the God in major religions around the world. Is this all part of the Earth experience?

Quan Yin: Yes.

Alison: But some people may still find it hard to accept being wronged. Fear and anger can still surface even if they understand this was part of the soul's journey.

Quan Yin: You can change the way you experience or perceive these E.T. encounters by seeing them all as neutral and relating to them more by asking yourselves if you'd ever do the same thing. "Do we ever go into a part of the world and just look at it as being filled with natural resources, whether it be gold, diamonds, oil, something that we want or need, and take it? Do we ever go into a situation where we're trying to get the best out of someone else and trying to further our own agenda?"

In other words, there are lots of examples you can come up with where you can say, "Well, we're looking at these lab rats or these monkeys that we're experimenting on as being less sentient, less important, lower life forms, and so we can do whatever we want to them because it makes our lives better." And so to the lab rat, of course, the human doesn't look so neutral. It looks like they're just trying to do harm to the lab rat.

And you can relate to these E.T.s by saying, "Oh yes, they're not so different from us. We sometimes do the same things that they've done to us." Then you can forgive them, and you can get past the trauma and the tragedy of it all, and this sets you all up for better E.T. encounters in the future.

Alison: So it is for us to reflect on the behavior of humans as a whole. Maybe as individuals, we did not do some of the damaging things ourselves, but other humans did. Maybe we weren't involved in lab rat experiments, or we didn't partake in plundering resources from other regions of the world. But if we benefited from the results and didn't voice any objections, we acquiesced to these hurtful actions. Plus, we might just have done those things in a different reincarnation. So the moral judgment against E.T.s is against ourselves as well?

Quan Yin: Correct.

Alison: Did the Anunnaki learn and grow from this experience like the Lyrans?

Quan Yin: Yes, they have evolved quite a bit since then. You have to remember they are not the same Anunnaki that they were 6000 years ago.

Alison: Since we started the discussion on the Anunnaki, I have learned that there are different accounts of what the Anunnaki did, either through channeling or by authors researching the Sumerian tablets. A very popular view is that the Anunnaki in tinkering with human genes to create slave workers actually helped humans advance to higher sentience, and some would say becoming Homo sapiens. Many connections were also made with the creation story in the Bible. Is this just a different timeline?

Quan Yin: No, it's just a different perspective on it. In other words, you could say that you're being helped when you're being hindered because you're not being given the chance to evolve naturally. So it really is a question of perspective.

Alison: A lot of these accounts also put the timing of the Anunnaki's fiddling with human genes at hundreds of thousands of years ago. That was much earlier than the Sumerian time.

Quan Yin: Remember I was telling you that after the terraforming and the bringing to Earth of all the different animal species and primates and such, some E.T.s stayed around and worked with the genetics of many species to ensure their survival. The Anunnaki were one of the E.T.s to experiment with primitive humans.

Alison: So did they actually come that long ago and create human slaves working for them?

Quan Yin No, the process started then, but they didn't perfect it until much later, and they applied their technology during the Sumerian time. So it started a long time ago and ended in the time frame that I gave you in around 4000 B.C.

Alison: I see. I guess since the Anunnaki's presence on Earth was not part of our official history, people could read the story simply as a myth, and they could resonate with one account or the other.

Quan Yin: What history a person resonates with will also say a lot about how they feel in this life. If they feel like a victim, if they feel like a slave, they're going to resonate more with a limiting type of historical perspective.

However, if people in this moment of this time feel empowered by knowing who they really are as source energy beings, they're not going to resonate as much with the Anunnaki story that's being put out there by so many who very much feel like victims in one way or another in their lives.

Alison: You've told me more than once while working on this book not to worry about getting everything right or getting the details right. The accuracy and precision we put so much emphasis on in our world are not always relevant to our journey in the physical realm. There is much malleability built into the realities we experience just to support our journey.

Quan Yin: What people really need to understand is themselves in this moment and not exactly what happened tens of thousands of years ago. And so, if anything helps people understand certain tendencies that they have, the evolution of their consciousness, the ways that E.T.s have helped, and the ways that E.T.s have hindered the progress of humanity, it is helpful. It's all being orchestrated because of this desire on the part of every soul who's ever incarnated on Earth to have a particular and unique experience.

And so that's the big picture. Those are the broad strokes that people need to understand and they don't need to get hung up on dates and exact details of what happened and why and how, and all of those things that get them caught up too much in the mind, trying to make sense of everything as if they're trying to make sense of their life in the present moment and why it is the way it is. The big picture here is also that Source or God works in mysterious ways, beyond your level of comprehension.

Alison: Meaning we shouldn't insist on using our linear, rational human mind to understand or validate everything. Resonance is a better approach, and we should also ask ourselves why we resonate with something that appears to be negative in tone.

Quan Yin: Correct.

The Famously Infamous Reptilians

The Reptilians have been identified as the unequivocal villains by many people writing or giving opinions on E.T.s. They have been linked to wars, the cabal, the deep state, human trafficking, the pedophilia rings, the cult of human sacrifice, and other heinous crimes against humanity. They are often referred to as the enemy that needs to be defeated. Unlike the Anunnaki, the Reptilians did not pay a few visits and then decide to leave. They have been around for a very long time.

Their continuous existence has brought out deep fear and hopelessness, the human emotions with the lowest vibrations. But we know we all have a fight-or-flight reptilian brain, and thus we share a genetic connection to them. The Reptilians are alleged to have occupied a dark corner of our world throughout our history, embodying darkness on our planet. However, our relationship with the Reptilians may be a complicated one. We, the Earth humans, have our own darkness and have been challenged to choose between light and darkness. I asked Quan Yin to help us understand the origin and history of this E.T. race, and the role they have played for themselves and for us.

Alison: We often hear about our fight-or-flight reptilian brain. How did the Reptilian DNA get into our genes?

Quan Yin: You had Reptilian DNA within the Pleiadeans, as well as the Avians and the Nordic Pleiadians.

Alison: That means Reptilian genes were in our original seeders?

Quan Yin: Yes. Reptilian DNA has served humanity quite well. You need that instinct to survive in order to keep the species going. So that Reptilian brain, that fight-or-flight instinct, is actually quite helpful in terms of keeping the Earth Experiment going.

Alison: So it's not necessarily a bad thing. People seem to think of it as a completely negative trait.

Quan Yin: You don't really need it now. You've outgrown it. But if you still operate with fight or flight, then yes, it's moot at this point. It represents the survival, fight-or-flight portion of the human brain that is meant to be integrated, that humans are meant to utilize at times and make peace with, but not go into with the idea that you're supposed to live as a fight-or-flight type of being.

Alison: The Reptilians are frowned upon in the lightworker community and blamed by conspiracy theorists for their association with the Illuminati and crimes of all kinds. Do the Reptilians deserve this reputation?

Quan Yin: They're very much self-interested beings.

Alison: What's their origin? Where do they come from?

Quan Yin: The Pleiadian star system.

Alison: Wow. They are Pleiadians. That's why we got the Reptilian DNA.

Quan Yin: They are Pleiadians. However, they went out from the Pleiades in the third dimension to conquer other worlds. So even though they're from the Pleiades, they don't return home to the Pleiadian system. They left to conquer other worlds like locusts to wipe out and take everything they can from a planet, enslave and rape and pillage and then move on. And they built their vast fleet of ships from the natural resources that they could obtain from those systems.

Alison: So they've been to multiple star systems?

Quan Yin: They've moved around quite a bit, yes.

Alison: And they are third-dimensional beings?

Quan Yin: Well, they're fourth-dimensional now. They've shifted as well. They are evolving, just like humans are evolving.

Alison: Are they in our galaxy or the entire Universe?

Quan Yin: In the galaxy, all over the galaxy.

Alison: When did they first come to Earth?

Quan Yin: They first came to Earth before the dinosaurs millions and millions of years ago. The Reptilians came to Earth and tried to create a dominant species of Reptilians on Earth. So they were the first ones to do genetic experimentation there.

Alison: On humans?

Quan Yin: No, on the dinosaurs that were Reptilian.

Alison: Oh, they created dinosaurs.

Quan Yin: Yes.

Alison: What was their purpose?

Quan Yin: Well, they wanted to be gods, they wanted to play God, and so they created a race that they thought they could be in control of, and they were interested also in observing and learning from the behaviors of the dinosaurs.

Alison: I thought dinosaurs were just animals that preyed on other animals because that was their instinct. Did they have more negative traits?

Quan Yin: Most of them would hunt for fun.

Alison: Oh, I see. So that was a little different than most of the animals on Earth because most of them just hunt because of hunger.

Quan Yin: Yes.

Alison: Were dinosaurs destroyed by a comet?

Quan Yin: That's right.

Alison: Okay. Was it also that their savagery and vileness brought out a low vibration that invited a path to destruction?

Quan Yin: Yes.

Alison: Okay. Have the Reptilians continued to stay on Earth?

Quan Yin: Yes, but they went away for a while to focus on other worlds and other star systems. They didn't hang around after the comet hit.

Alison: And then when did they return to Earth?

Quan Yin: The Reptilians came back during the time of Lemuria and were observing what was going on there. And they were the ones that the Lyrans were afraid of getting that technology that they had honed with the human beings on Lemuria. So they were trying to keep that from getting into the hands of the Reptilians.

Alison: Right. You said that those Lyrans were eliminated by a group of Reptilians in a pirate-style raid.

Quan Yin: Yes.

Alison: Are the Reptilians still with us today?

Quan Yin: Well, look at your crocodiles and alligators. Yes, they've stayed with you. They survived in extinction events.

Alison: Are anacondas in that category?

Quan Yin: Yes.

Alison: What about the Reptilians who are the shapeshifters and can look like humans? Are they the real culprit of many bad things on Earth?

Quan Yin: That's correct.

Alison: Are the shapeshifters born on Earth, or do they kind of just walk in?

Quan Yin: Those are beings who came through portals.

Alison: Were there significant events or entries into Earth by the Reptilians that mattered in humanity's history?

Quan Yin: No.

Alison: Okay, so they've been just dropping in on us all the time. And they have been with us since Lemuria hundreds of thousands of years ago.

Quan Yin: Right.

Alison: I think Lucy Lee has lots of QHHT cases where the subjects recalled how evil beings came from nowhere and infiltrated into the human society to cause trouble, i.e., wars, murders, thefts, crimes, power struggles, you name it. They had a dark underground network, and they could shapeshift. There were lots of gory details, and most recounted stories that happened in Europe and some in the U.S. and Asia. A few other subjects also recalled being fifth-dimensional beings living in the center of Earth who came up to the surface to fight with these evil beings. They were doing this to balance the light and darkness quotient on Earth when things got out of hand. I assume these were stories about the Reptilians?

Quan Yin: Yes.

Alison: And there have been accusations that some of the richest families and political leaders have been Reptilians.

Quan Yin: Well, what I would say is that they get close to those families and influence those families.

Alison: I see. These shapeshifters did and still do so.

Quan Yin: But they can't procreate with other humans.

Alison: Oh, Thank Goodness. But why is that the case?

Quan Yin: Genetically speaking, it doesn't match up.

Alison: Oh, so the E.T.s who stayed and interbred with humans were the ones who had a genetic match with humans. It wasn't just any E.T.s.

Quan Yin: Not all E.T.s can do it. Some are compatible and some aren't.

Alison: This is because the Reptilians are not humanoid.

Quan Yin: Right, just like two different species there on Earth can't naturally mate, such as humans and animals.

Alison: Now I realize how hideous it was for Atlanteans to use genetics and create animal-human hybrids against nature.

Quan Yin: Yes.

Alison: After all these years, we are dealing with ill-intentioned Reptilian shapeshifters and their wrongdoings?

Quan Yin: There are some who eventually become enamored by the human race and shift into a positive type of agenda because they cannot help but have their hearts opened by humanity's struggle and humanity's beauty and creativity.

Alison: I see. But many are still behaving badly. It's very sad that we still have them around after all the pain and trouble they have caused.

Quan Yin: It's not all sad. There is an antagonist in any good story.

Alison: Oh, I see. I suppose they are a valid player in the Earth story. But when I read Lucy Lee's QHHT cases about this piece of dark history, I was a little taken aback by the amount of violence and cruelty in them. I know these were candid accounts from subjects under hypnosis. I only wonder how these horrid experiences would serve us, how knowing them would serve us.

Quan Yin: Sometimes creation is messy, and it's all right to acknowledge that humans have been through a lot and that a lot of the traumas you all experience right now are based in something very ancient within the human consciousness, so people understand more why things are the way they are today. It's not just because of the flaws of the current human collective, but because you are coming forth from a lot of death and destruction, chaos and abuse, and so on, that has made the journey where you are right now difficult. So that can be helpful for people to know.

Alison: So we have had a long history living with darkness, but we don't need to believe or be afraid that we are controlled by it, even if some humans did choose to work with the Reptilians.

Quan Yin: Well, if all you're ever doing is being helped, then where's the challenge?

Alison: I see. It's growing pains, growing and learning the hard way. The Orions had sent energetic influences to push us to wars and conflicts, but the Reptilians were hands-on instigators and perpetrators in the physical. It is amazing how much E.T. influence we have had in our heritage, for better or worse.

Quan Yin: It is. People need to understand why the races on planet Earth are different, and that you are bringing together a lot of different galactic energies there, and it is what makes life on Earth even more challenging because you have all of these different energies from different star systems.

Alison: Are there any good Reptilians?

Quan Yin: Yes.

Alison: And who are they?

Quan Yin: Well, they're Reptilians in higher dimensions.

Alison: Oh. So they're not the ones that are roaming around on Earth.

Quan Yin: There are also Reptilians within the fourth-dimensional Reptilian race that are good, yes.

Alison: Are they on Earth?

Quan Yin: Some of them, yes.

Alison: Okay. And are they trying to help?

Quan Yin: Yes.

Alison: Now the ones that are good and the ones that are not so good, are they all ascending?

Quan Yin: Yes, whether they know it or not.

Alison: Would the transformational experience be much more dramatic for the ill-behaved Reptilians when the Ascension journey begins for them?

Quan Yin: Yes, it will be harder for them to handle the energies of Ascension.

Alison: And they may take longer to complete the journey?

Quan Yin: Yes. So another way to address this feeling toward the Reptilians is to remember that everyone in the whole Universe is evolving and ascending. So when you're looking back at tens of thousands or hundreds of thousands of years ago at what E.T.s had done in the past, remember all of them have evolved since then. You are all evolving.

Alison: You have said to me more than once that focusing on shifting our own consciousness and raising our vibration is much more important than tracking whether the Illuminati have been arrested and put in jail, because higher consciousness and vibration have that magical power to dissolve and light up darkness.

Quan Yin: Exactly. It's your higher consciousness level that will truly change everything.

CHAPTER 13

∞

E.T.s AND HUMANITY
SINCE THE 20TH CENTURY:
THE UFO CRASHES AND
PARALLEL EARTH HUMANS

We know that E.T.s were instrumental in setting off a technology revolution in Atlantis. They crashed craft for the Atlanteans to reverse engineer and provided genetic files and samples. The Atlanteans developed a technologically advanced civilization using their minds and without E.T.s working alongside them. This was what the E.T.s intended. The sinking of Atlantis, however, took with it all the advanced science and technology. The surviving Atlanteans retained some of the knowledge, but the cutting-edge know-how and the upper echelon of scientists were gone.

What Atlantis achieved technologically was not replicated until now in the 21st Century. I started to ask Quan Yin what our developmental path had been like, dating from our earliest records thousands of years ago. What I learned was that after the tragic loss of Atlantis, E.T.s stopped intentionally leaving craft for humanity to work with. Of course, humanity still had some scientific knowledge that E.T.s had shared early on. E.T.s also remained helpful in sending ideas to Earth telepathically to be picked up by scientists who were tuning in.

So for a very long time, the development of science and technology followed the route of natural evolution without explicit E.T. assistance. Our own efforts culminated in the scientific discoveries and the Industrial Revolution that laid the building blocks of our modern civilization. Then, in the mid-twentieth century, as Quan Yin would tell us, E.T.s became actively involved with our development again. Crashed crafts were again spotted on Earth, ushering in a technology rush still going strong today.

Below is a series of conversations with Quan Yin to track down the reappearance of downed E.T. craft and their impact. This history remains a mystery except for the famous UFO crash in Roswell, New Mexico, in 1947. We'll look at how it all happened and what choices we have made in regards to this new source of scientific knowledge. Bashar has said that we are recycling the Atlantean experience, so the fast-tracking of science and technology in our time is not surprising. But we are given a concomitant challenge of steering our development wisely and balancing it with a revival of spirituality. How have we been doing? What is the role of the E.T.s in all of this since the mid-twentieth century?

Scientific and Technological Development Since Atlantis

Before we go into the twentieth century, let's first get a sense of what natural evolution was like during the thousands of years of our recorded history.

Alison: I am curious about the development of science and technology in our history. I did some research, and it seems that during the thousands of years before our modern age, people had continued to study astronomy, mathematics, anatomy, medicine, alchemy, etc. There was inherited knowledge from ancient civilizations, and people built on that base to develop new bodies of knowledge. The speed of progress varied in different eras, and during the Renaissance, a rebirth of scientific studies began (1).

I've also watched a video called "The Universe in a Nutshell" by Dr. Michio Kaku (2), in which he gave an overview of the development of modern science and physics. He explained that the new astronomy by Copernicus and Galileo during the Renaissance led to the discovery by Isaac Newton of gravity and the force of planetary movements. And Newton's equation that force equals mass times acceleration, powered the Industrial Revolution because it was the foundation of the mechanics of force and energy in creating machines. And then, we invented electricity and light bulbs. All these and other inventions gave us a vastly improved modern life beginning in the 20th century. For this long transition from an agrarian to an industrial society, did E.T.s ever intentionally crash any craft to give us clues like what they did for the Atlanteans?

Quan Yin: No.

Alison: Did we have more of a natural progression of scientific discoveries?

Quan Yin: Yes, exactly.

Alison: Did we have a good knowledge base that we received from E.T.s in ancient times?

Quan Yin: Well, you have the fall of Lemuria, and you have the fall of Atlantis, and when some E.T.s like the Anunnaki left, they took their technology with them. So a lot of things have been lost over time. The Library of Alexandria in Egypt, where manuscripts of such information and E.T. visitations were kept, was burned to the ground by the early Christians. So you've lost a lot of knowledge, a lot of information, a lot of technology over time, and you've gotten it back, of course.

Alison: We've gotten most of the knowledge and technologies back at this point?

Quan Yin: Yes.

Alison: During our natural evolution, was there still the dropping of ideas into people's minds from higher realms or E.T. beings?

Quan Yin: Yes, for farming practices and irrigation practices and so on, sometimes from physical E.T.s, sometimes from nonphysical helpers, which you all have and always have had.

Alison: So, going into the 17th century, when Isaac Newton looked at the apple falling from the tree and went on to discover gravity and the basis of mechanics, was there a dropping of ideas to Earth that were picked up by scientists like him?

Quan Yin: Yes.

Alison: Okay. So throughout our history, there were always many ideas that were dropped to humanity from our physical or nonphysical helpers?

Quan Yin: Yes, it's the more natural way, it's the better way, it's the slower and surer way than having a piece of technology that you reverse engineer, that you may or may not be ready for.

Alison: Did the E.T.s participate in our rapid technological development after the Industrial Revolution?

Quan Yin: No, not in an active way. It wasn't until the 1940s with the development of the atomic bomb. That was when the E.T.s really started to offer more help.

Alison: Wow.

The Return of Crashed Craft and Rise of Nuclear and Quantum Technology

As Quan Yin said, the return of the E.T. craft in the twentieth century led to the advent of the atomic bomb. This is a wild and stunning association. The question is why. Was it because E.T.s were trying to give us weapons to end the war, or did they simply have a plan to supercharge our science and technology? Or alternatively, was it something else, such as an accident?

Alison: Did E.T.s start to offer help by dropping ideas of the atomic bomb into people's minds in the 1940s?

Quan Yin: That too, as well as crafts that were crashed.

Alison: Was that the UFO crash in Roswell, New Mexico, in 1947? But that was after the war ended.

Quan Yin: That was one incident, yes.

Alison: Oh, so there were others that we don't know about?

Quan Yin: Yes, and not just in the U.S. There were other places as well where there were downed crafts.

Alison: What were the other crashes?

Quan Yin: There were crashes in Russia and China as well as Germany, Italy, Japan, and India.

Alison: Wow. Was this before the war or during the war?

Quan Yin: This was before.

(Note: An E.T. crash in Italy was identified to have taken place in 1933. Please see note (3).)

Alison: Who got hold of the crafts?

Quan Yin: Well, the German and the U.S. scientists were able to do something with it, you see.

Alison: Oh, so we have no knowledge of what actually happened.

Quan Yin: Yes, that's correct. No government has released all that they know about extraterrestrials and extraterrestrial technology. Not a single government has.

(Note: In the U.S., there have been two congressional hearings on Unidentified Anomalous Phenomena (UAP) or Unidentified Flying Objects (UFO) in 2023 and 2024 (4), but no official statements on E.T.s or UAP/UFO have been given by the U.S. government.)

Alison: So humans were given the knowledge to create the atomic bomb?

Quan Yin: You were given knowledge and you used it to create the atomic bomb.

Alison: What specific knowledge was that?

Quan Yin: To help you explore the power that lies within each atom, within each molecule, each subatomic particle.

Alison: So the key knowledge was understanding the atoms, subatomic particles, and the power within them that can be released. That was the basis of not just the atomic bombs but nuclear technology in general?

Quan Yin: Yes.

Alison: Was it known at the time that humans would develop atomic bombs?

Quan Yin: It was known that it was a possibility that you would use that technology for that purpose.

Alison: I guess the U.S. won the race in creating atomic bombs. Otherwise, the war might have ended differently.

Quan Yin: Yes.

Alison: How did the scientists understand atomic power by just looking at the craft that the E.T.s left behind?

Quan Yin: Because this is like a sonology of nothing you can see. It's beyond what a non-scientific mind can grasp. But in the same way that you can understand how looking at cells under a microscope could help someone to become a master geneticist, you can see how looking at a craft and how its propulsion system works could help a scientist who already has that natural inclination towards understanding these types of things to draw those conclusions. That's what reverse engineering is.

(Note: According to Wikipedia, "In medicine, the term sonology is used in the field of imaging to describe the practice of medical ultrasonography.")

Alison: I see. So a scientist's trained eyes and mind could pick up things that would not make any sense to ordinary people. Was there anything on the ship that offered direct clues to the development of atomic bombs?

Quan Yin: There was research in the computers on board that the scientists were able to figure out because math is sort of a universal language.

Alison: That's amazing. Was the math in the research written and presented using similar symbols that we use?

Quan Yin: The symbols were different, but they were able to be interpreted. Scientists would say, "Okay, this one means multiply, this one means divide," and so on and so forth.

Alison: And the numbers were represented differently as well, and not in Arabic numerals?

Quan Yin: Yes, correct.

Alison: Okay. So our scientists were able to look at all this and figure out the mathematical symbols, the numbers, and the equations.

Quan Yin: Yes, they were able to reverse engineer the math as well.

Alison: Wow, that is really smart. They were geniuses. And there were computers on the ship, and this was in the early 1940s or even the 1930s. That must have been where we first got the idea of computers.

Quan Yin: Yes.

Alison: We had already been developing quantum physics before the 1940s. So scientists had a basis of knowledge to take advantage of the E.T. research.

Quan Yin: Correct.

Alison: So, the E.T. crashes from the 1940s and perhaps in the 1930s as well represented a renewal of E.T. assistance in humanity's technology development. Was there anything in genetics that was passed on to us?

Quan Yin: No.

Alison: We are advanced in genetic technology today, maybe not as advanced as the Atlanteans yet, but it's hard to comprehend how we achieved that without any prompting from E.T.s.

Quan Yin: Normal, fine exploration and study with microscopes and so on. You figured it out. In other words, you didn't need something to reverse engineer. You're reverse engineering your own cells.

Alison: I see. Okay. I assume the knowledge transfer from the crashed craft also benefited the study of quantum physics and energy and matter. The ideas of the Big Bang, black hole, wormhole, dark energy, and dark matter were all ideas to understand the Universe better. Even if these pursuits are scientific and not spiritual in nature, they began to unveil the truth of the Universe and to expand our minds in a potent way.

Quan Yin: Yes.

Alison: I also understand from Dr. Kaku and others that the theoretical physicists are very interested in quantum computing (5) because they needed to test string theory, and they couldn't do it with the processing capacity of digital computers. They needed to go to quantum computing to go beyond the limitations of digital computing. And quantum computing promises not only to unlock more secrets of stars and galaxies, but also to develop cures for cancer, Alzheimer's, and all those supposedly incurable illnesses. There is a race in quantum computing between countries to come up with the first successful model. Is this something that E.T.s will help us with, and if so, how are they going to help this time?

Quan Yin: When you're standing in the face of an extraterrestrial being, the type of activations you get include activations of the mind, and that will be all that a person needs to fully harness quantum computing. It won't be like E.T. will have to sit down next to the scientist or mathematician with instructions on what formulas to plug in here, how to create using programming to do this. It will just be an automatic type of experience where the codes and the DNA get activated within the person who is standing in front of the E.T.

Alison: Wow. So you're talking about E.T.s showing up in person here and having an effect on us with their higher vibration.

Quan Yin: Yes.

Alison: So that means we never really have to develop quantum computers the way we're going about it?

Quan Yin: But you will. You will develop it. No, what I'm saying is that what's activated within the smart person will then help them complete the quantum computing issues that they're facing.

Alison: So this activation is different than receiving a message into their mind, an idea dropped into their mind?

Quan Yin: Correct. But sometimes they will get an idea as a result of that activation, you see.

Alison: Okay. So it's possible that scientists who are open-minded and rise to a higher frequency could just tap into these ideas that are sent to our realm instead of encountering a physical E.T., and they'll figure everything out?

Quan Yin: Yes, that's true.

Alison: This activation effect is interesting, though. It must have happened to the ancients when they met with E.T.s, and that's why they instantly liked or even worshipped the E.T.s.

Quan Yin: Yes.

The Mysterious Beings That First Crashed the Craft

It was natural to assume that the spacecrafts were crashed by our old E.T. friends deliberately to help us, just like the old times, the old Atlantean times. I was completely surprised to hear that it wasn't them. It wasn't even a typical E.T. race. As the saying goes, the plot thickens.

Alison: Which E.T. race or races actually crashed the craft in the 1930s-1940s?

Quan Yin: The Zetas.

Alison: Oh, the Zetas, and not our usual friends like the Pleiadians and Sirians.

Quan Yin: No.

Alison: That's interesting because I think you said the latter crashed the craft in Atlantis.

Quan Yin: They have been with you for a long time, but the Zetas are relatively new.

Alison: And are these the real Zetas from Zeta Reticuli?

Quan Yin: No, these are the Zetas from the parallel Earth.

Alison: Oh, I see. You did mention before that the ones from the parallel Earth are not the real Zetas. What's the real name for them?

Quan Yin: Other Earthlings. They don't really have a real name. They're just other humans from another Earth. You think they're E.T.s from another planet, another system, the Zeta Reticuli system, but they're not, no.

Alison: Oh, these are humans. When you say a parallel Earth, is that Earth on another timeline, a parallel reality?

Quan Yin: Yes, it's another timeline.

Alison: So these Earthlings must have come from an Earth that is so much more advanced.

Quan Yin: Technologically, yes.

Alison: Were they of a higher vibration?

Quan Yin: No.

Alison: Oh, so even if they had similar vibrations to ours, they were much more advanced technologically?

Quan Yin: Yes, because that's where they chose to place their focus.

Alison: Why were they so technologically advanced like other E.T.s if they were just third-dimensional humans?

Quan Yin: Just a different timeline with a different event in their past. So if you had a different past, you'd be more advanced technologically. Their Atlantis did not fall.

Alison: Ahh, I see. That's amazing. You did mention before that Atlantis didn't fall on some timelines, and I assumed those were higher timelines where better choices were made.

Quan Yin: No, those were not necessarily higher timelines.

Alison: I guess they were just continuously high-tech but not high-vibrational. And so how did their Atlantis affect their development since it didn't fall?

Quan Yin: It affected their development by speeding it up because they didn't have Atlantis falling, and they didn't have to start over again technologically. So they were able to go further technologically in the same number of years as you've had on Earth. So they were building cities and manufacturing many things. They wanted to create more technological gadgets, and ships and aerial craft. Then they wanted to reach space, and they did. And they wanted to tunnel through dimensions and universes, and they did. And all of that took a lot of technological know-how and experimentation and building devices and more devices, and they really didn't care about the toxic waste that was being created or the mining that was required. And mining itself can be very hard on the planet and has a lot of toxic residues. They just weren't caring about nature and what pollution they were creating because they were so obsessed with getting to the next technological advancement. And then eventually that piled up on them, and they had toxic air, water, and soil.

As you know, humans, not even corporations, but just humans with the garbage that you create on your Earth, it creates a huge impact on the ocean, and the landfills are seeping toxins into waterways and seeping underground and causing radiation. And so, even though you're not as technologically advanced as the Atlantean civilization, which had so much longer to develop their technology and passed it down to the parallel Earth humans who continued to develop it, you still create quite a bit of toxicity and pollution just with what you buy at the supermarket and the hardware store and then wind up throwing away.

Alison: Did this pollution wreak havoc on the parallel Earth humans on their planet?

Quan Yin: Yes. They eventually abandoned their planet.

Alison: Oh my goodness. I was thinking how they could have let this happen, being so highly intelligent. But then you pointed out that's what we are actually doing as well.

Quan Yin: Yes. You don't care about something if you're not thinking about it. If you don't think it matters, then you're not applying that intelligence to it. They were a highly intellectual civilization, but by the time the parallel Earth humans realized they had a problem and tried to fix it using their intellect and their technology, they were just too late.

Alison: Did they look like us at all?

Quan Yin: No, they mutated into the Grey form that you've seen them depicted as, because they polluted their world and because they so emphasized thought and the mind, their brains grew larger and their heads actually got bigger. And they were so not interested in physical activity that their arms, legs, and body got smaller. They atrophied because they allowed technology to do so much for them. They didn't care about exercising or getting outside and being in the sun, going for a bike ride or a run, so they developed bigger eyes because they were looking at screens so much.

Alison: Did they hide underground and get that grey skin?

Quan Yin: Yes, they hid underground, and some of the greyness, too, came from the toxins. So the toxins that got into the body did also alter the appearance of the body and the height that people would reach. They became shorter and shorter.

Alison: How long did they hide underground?

Quan Yin: About 250 years.

Alison: So, the crashes in the 1940s, including the 1947 Roswell crash, were done by these mutated humans from a parallel Earth?

Quan Yin: Yes.

Alison: And the deceased being from the Roswell crash was drawn or illustrated to look like a Grey just as you've described them, but this race was not the real Greys.

Quan Yin: Correct.

Alison: So this race of mutated humans has been called Zetas or Greys but they were not them.

Quan Yin: Some people refer to any grey E.T. as a Grey and don't differentiate between the Zetas of Zeta Reticuli, the real Greys that were AI beings formed by Reptilians, and these parallel Earth humans. So that lumping together of all three of those groups because they all have a similar physical appearance is the unfortunate use of the term Grey. People don't think of them as different because they're not looking beyond the appearance or knowing the history, the back story of each one of them.

Alison: We know a little about the Zetas of Zeta Reticuli because they came to Asia eons ago. What is this group of Greys created by the Reptilians? Are they sentient androids?

Quan Yin: No, these ones created by the Reptilians are not self-aware enough to become soul beings now. It's a slave race.

Alison: I see. Not a surprise, as they are the creations of the Reptilians. Are they in this galaxy?

Quan Yin: Yes.

Alison: Are they on Earth?

Quan Yin: No.

Alison: How did humans get to know them if they're not here on Earth?

Quan Yin: There have been times, of course, when you've been visited by Reptilians, and these beings have been on the ships.

Alison: I see. Okay, so back to the mutated humans from a parallel Earth. The toxins contributed to the mutation of their physical form. Did it cause health problems, too?

Quan Yin: The pollution made their bodies more frail and more likely to get sick.

Alison: Oh, okay. They were advanced in technology and in intellect, but now they were having major health issues.

Quan Yin: Yes.

Alison: What was their intention in coming to our Earth? Were they trying to help us?

Quan Yin: No. They wanted to help themselves. Their intention was to get your eggs and sperm and other genetic material that they would need to create test tube babies with you, so that they could then continue to live on as a race and have children.

Alison: That sounds like the hybrid that Bashar talked about.

Quan Yin: That's the hybrid.

Alison: Oh my goodness. So what had happened to them since they left their Earth?

Quan Yin: Now when you talk about the 1940s, that's when they came over to this Universe. So they abandoned their planet a long time ago. They were dying off, and they needed to perpetuate their species in some way, and they found you and they said, "Well, this is just us in our pre-mutated form, so we definitely can reproduce with this race." And so they did. But the ones that came over all had a date at which they were going to die one way or the other. The only question was whether they'd live on through their children. And they did.

Alison: They knew they were going to die?

Quan Yin: Everyone dies.

Alison: Yes, everyone dies, and also their whole generation, the whole race was sick.

Quan Yin: Not sick in the sense that they would be given a diagnosis with something, but they weren't healthy and having the same type of potential and function with the physical body that you do now in your reality. So this is pre the ability to ascend. That's why I said everybody dies because they weren't at that place where they could live forever. They had an average lifespan just like you do. So if the average age, let's say, was 35 of the parallel Earth humans who came over, they knew they would be expiring within 50 years. Most of them would just die of natural causes within that time frame, just like a human on your Earth would. So you see, they knew they had to somehow create children in order to continue living as a species.

Alison: Oh, they couldn't reproduce.

Quan Yin: They couldn't. No, not really, not naturally.

Alison: I should have figured it out when you said they needed our genetic material to make test tube babies. I thought they wanted to improve the health of their race, but the bigger issue was their infertility and survival as a race. So, afterwards, that generation or that parallel Earth human race all died?

Quan Yin: Yes, they're all gone, and their children are hybrids.

Alison: At the time they came to Earth, were they living on spaceships?

Quan Yin: Yes, they were.

Alison: Oh, so that's a lot of ships they had then.

Quan Yin: Very large ones too, yes.

Alison: I've heard that a large E.T. ship can accommodate hundreds of thousands of beings living on it.

Quan Yin: Yes.

Alison: And these hybrid children live on the ships now?

Quan Yin: Yes.

(Note: The topic of hybrids will be discussed in Chapter 15.)

Alison: Why did they crash their ships?

Quan Yin: They hadn't perfected their traveling into your parallel reality yet. Eventually, they perfected it, and they were able to exist in your atmosphere in their ships and to get what they needed to create a hybrid race.

Alison: So the crashes only happened because they hadn't mastered the space technology yet at the time.

Quan Yin: They hadn't mastered the navigation from their parallel reality to yours. So technology was fine, but they were running into some challenges in the transition.

Alison: That's why we had a series of crashes in the 1940s?

Quan Yin: That's why.

Alison: It was never meant to be a knowledge transfer?

Quan Yin: No.

Alison: But from these unintentional crashes, our scientists developed nuclear technology and a new phase of quantum physics and quantum mechanics through reverse engineering.

Quan Yin: Through downloads as well.

Alison: Who gave us the downloads?

Quan Yin: They're just out there. Scientists could tap into it.

Alison: Right, right. Have we on Earth figured out about these crashes?

Quan Yin: They had no idea what was happening. No idea what these E.T.s were up to.

Alison: Who were "they"?

Quan Yin: The U.S. government or any of the governments where the parallel Earth humans crashed their ships. It's not like they were able to go on board and say, "Oh, look what they're planning to do." It wasn't evident from what they could see. They just knew that these were E.T.s and they were probably going to be experimenting on humans. Because they had spaceships, of course, the natural assumption would be that they came from a far, far off place in your solar system and galaxy.

Alison: Are there other human species who exist on other parallel Earths?

Quan Yin: Everything that you can imagine is out there.

Alison: The infinity of the Universe is beyond belief.

Quan Yin: Beyond your ability to comprehend.

Alison: Right, beyond our ability, exactly. Earth is a small planet within the solar system, and the solar system is pretty small within our galaxy, and there are many, many galaxies in this Universe. So if the same principle applies across all planets, systems, and galaxies, it definitely is not something we can comprehend. It's a feeling of awe and insanity at the same time, at least to a human mind.

Quan Yin: Yes.

More Crafts, Gadgets, and Technologies from E.T. Friends

The accidental crashes by the parallel Earth humans felt like a wondrous mistake that inadvertently propelled our science and technology to a new height. But these parallel Earth humans weren't really the E.T.s that have had a long history with us. It is difficult to believe that we got to where we are today without any involvement of our old friends. I asked Quan Yin specifically about this.

Alison: In addition to the series of crashes by the parallel Earth humans, was there any other intentional E.T. assistance?

Quan Yin: Yes, there have still been advancements made technologically because of different pieces of technology that have been left behind purposely and "accidentally." And I put the accidentally in quotes because nothing is really an accident from a higher perspective.

Alison: So there were other crashes too by E.T.s?

Quan Yin: Yes, and deliberate drop-offs.

Alison: What kind of drop-offs?

Quan Yin: Gadgets and devices.

Alison: What are the examples of gadgets they left us?

Quan Yin: Fax machines, cell phones, 3D printers.

Alison: Did they actually drop these devices to us?

Quan Yin: A form of them, yes, not what you hold in your hands, but their rendition of that was able to be reverse engineered.

Alison: And again, we don't have full knowledge of how these technologies were developed.

Quan Yin: Right.

Alison: Were these all done by other E.T.s?

Quan Yin: Some by the humans from the parallel Earth, of course, and some by Pleiadians, Sirians, Lyrans, Andromedans, and others.

Alison: Who are the others?

Quan Yin: Well, there are so many E.T. races that you don't even know about, that you don't even have names for. Sometimes they are really E.T.s that are just curious about Earth, and they're coming down, and they're exploring. They might land, and they might leave a piece of technology by accident or on purpose. But there are so many races. The E.T.s out there are doing all kinds of things.

Alison: I see, but some of our old friends returned. So the crashes or drop-offs by the real E.T.s were all intentional.

Quan Yin: Some, yes.

Alison: Oh, really, some were not? Even for Pleiadians and Sirians, the crashes were not always intentional?

Quan Yin: Correct.

Alison: So if it was not intentional, what were they trying to do?

Quan Yin: Well, when you're from another star system and you're having to navigate through a different atmosphere and not everything is familiar to you, there's the potential for something to go wrong with the navigational system or with the pilot error. Those types of things can happen, and of course, these mistakes are only mistakes on that level of consciousness that is egoic, but in the larger scheme of things, it was very intentional for the crashes to take place to plant certain seeds within the consciousness of humanity.

Alison: Meaning to help us understand we are not alone here, or to get a piece of technology for our advancement?

Quan Yin: Yes.

Alison: That's what you meant when you said there's really nothing accidental, not in the larger scheme of things. The "accidental crashes" by the parallel Earth humans or even by E.T.s served the purpose of getting us to a higher level of technology and civilization.

Quan Yin: Correct.

Alison: Was there a long period after Atlantis that the Sirians, Pleiadians, Lyrans, Andromedans, and others didn't travel to Earth in their ships? Or have they always been doing that?

Quan Yin: They've been doing it for a very long time, yes.

Alison: But they didn't drop gadgets or deliberately crash craft in the earlier history?

Quan Yin: Well, it's not as noticeable for the technological advancements that you've made, but they've still been helping, dropping helpful clues from the ships.

Alison: I see. So, even during a natural evolution, the E.T.s would still drop ideas or even physical clues to us?

Quan Yin: Yes, always.

Alison: So they traveled here to check on us, and occasionally they would crash their crafts or drop gadgets intentionally or unintentionally. But in the past, it may have been in a location that nobody could get to, so there wasn't as much effect in terms of humans seeing or harnessing what was left on the ground.

Quan Yin: The crashed crafts were only able to be reverse engineered when humans reached a certain level of knowledge of technology. In other words, by the time you get to the 1940s, you've evolved quite a bit there in terms of your technological know-how, your understanding of the Universe and how it works. And so the scientists were just smarter than people in more primitive times who might come across the fallen spacecraft and have no idea what to make of it.

Alison: So there were crashes by E.T.s and parallel Earth humans in the twentieth century, and there were crashes by E.T.s before that. No matter what the original motivations were, the crashes were all meant from a higher level to give us something and move us forward.

Quan Yin: Yes.

Alison: When and where were the other E.T. crashes in the twentieth century?

Quan Yin: Well, the times, the dates, the places are not important.

Alison: Okay. Did the crashes happen continuously in the decades following the 40's?

Quan Yin: Well, I wouldn't say continuously. These are rare things that will happen, you see. There'd be large gaps in between.

Alison: I see. Were there a few more crashes in the 20th century after the 1930s and 1940s?

Quan Yin: Yes.

Alison: And these additional crashes, did they happen in the U.S. and the more developed countries?

Quan Yin: Yes.

Alison: They were not in the remote, undeveloped areas that nobody could get to?

Quan Yin: Or cover up.

Alison: Oh, so there were cover-ups in developed countries?

Quan Yin: It's covered up, yes.

Notes

1) Please check the topics of "History of Science" and "Science in the Renaissance" on Wikipedia

2) "The Universe in a Nutshell" (https://www.youtube.com/watch?v=0NbBjNiw4tk) by Dr. Michio Kaku, on YouTube.

3) According to David Grusch, a former U.S. government official and UFO whistleblower, a crashed E.T. craft was found in Italy in 1933, and Italy invited Germany to inspect the craft, and eventually the U.S. arranged to have the craft shipped to the U.S around 1944-45, toward the end of WWII. Grusch explained that this was the earliest crash that he was permitted to talk about, and the total number of such crashes in the twentieth century was in the double digits.
Sources:
"Whistleblower David Grusch on Early UFO Recoveries" (https://www.youtube.com/watch?v=6WMX41AqIdk) by PowerfulJRE on YouTube.
"David Grusch Opening Statement at Unidentified Anomalous Phenomena (UAP) Hearing" (https://www.youtube.com/watch?v=lcrCMLVk614) 2023, C-SPAN on YouTube.

4) U.S. Congressional hearings on UAP/UFO:
"House holds hearings on UFOs, government transparency 2023" (https://www.youtube.com/watch?v=SNgoul4vyDM) on YouTube.
"House Hearing on UFO Sightings 2024" (https://www.youtube.com/watch?v=4zT_cQoBdwk) on YouTube.

5) Brief introduction to Quantum computing:
According to Google AI, in simple words, "Quantum computing uses quantum mechanics to solve problems faster and more efficiently than classical computers. It's a multidisciplinary field that combines physics, computer science, and mathematics."
Two short articles on quantum computing:
"The Future Unleashed: AI Meets Quantum Computing" by Ahmed M. Al-Ghamdi, www.linkedin.com
"It's Time to Plan For An AI And Quantum Future" by Alan Baratz, www.forbes.com

CHAPTER 14

❦

E.T.s AND HUMANITY SINCE THE 20ᵀᴴ CENTURY: OUR CHOICES AND E.T.s' STEWARDSHIP

The downed E.T. craft in the twentieth century did not first show up because of an intention to help us accelerate technologically, but the effect was the same. We were given advanced technologies that adorned the fallen craft. We also embarked on reverse engineering that the Atlanteans went through to unlock these technology secrets. What technologies did we get our hands on? And how have we been able to harvest what we have found? Have the E.T.s beings worked with us since the twentieth century?

Here is part II of the story, where we began to make a quantum leap in our technology development, but also faced difficult choices in how to apply them. We'll find that we have received E.T.s' help on the technology front since the 1940s. Surprisingly, we have seen an influx of E.T. teachings as well since the 1980s through channeling and energy transmissions. Humanity is still treading the revived path of Atlantis, and E.T.s are extending their love and service in a crucial juncture of our history, and for our future.

Harnessing the Technologies

It is always tempting to compare the technologies developed between us and the Atlanteans, given that both had a slew of downed crafts to ignite the technology revolution. The comparisons brought out interesting differences. In conversations with Quan Yin, there are two specific technologies in the downed crafts that the Atlanteans had decoded and utilized, but we decided to place them on the back burner for reasons specific to our society at its stage of development. These were significant decisions. How should we make sense of them?

Alison: Overall, did all those crashes in the twentieth century give us more than nuclear science, quantum physics, computing, and the jazzy devices we received?

Quan Yin: Space travel, yes.

Alison: What was the specific technology or knowledge to reverse engineer for space travel?

Quan Yin: Well, it's how to work with the atmospheric changes that come about when you're moving through something like the Van Allen belts or entering back into Earth's atmosphere. It has to do with propulsion, which is about the way that you have been traditionally getting your vessels out into outer space through your space programs (1), and the next-generation antigravitational technology (2).

Alison: So getting through the atmosphere safely would mean there was material science?

Quan Yin: Yes, material science.

Alison: So this gave us the ability to develop a space program so we could do more explorations in outer space. Was all this knowledge or technology also given to the Atlanteans?

Quan Yin: Yes.

Alison: So let's see. I know you've said that the Atlanteans didn't develop the same space program as ours because that was not their priority. But they did have advanced flying machine technology. In the Atlantis chapters, you talked about how we have been burning a lot of fuel to lift rockets and spaceships into space. So we must not have really gotten the antigravity technology and the use of electromagnetic energy that the Atlanteans received. Did we not get the same craft in the 1940s?

Quan Yin: Well, you're assuming now that people who got that technology would have just shared it with everyone else. (3)

Alison: Oh, so they might have gotten it, but they didn't share.

Quan Yin: They didn't say, "Okay, now we can get off fossil fuels because we have this new technology."

Alison: So the U.S. space program still used a more traditional technology of burning fuels to create a thrust of force over the gravitational pull.

Quan Yin: They had to.

Alison: And burning fossil fuels has also been the primary method to power vehicles, aircraft, and vessels.

Quan Yin: That's true.

Alison: So way back when, they didn't want to show that they knew of a new technology. They made a decision not to share it.

Quan Yin: Well, yes, it was a policy not to let everyone know and say, "Hey, we have this new technology. It's taken us hundreds of years into the future in terms of what we can do. And here's how we got it. And we're going to make it available to everyone so that everyone can have cleaner-burning fuel."

Alison: Did they get this in the 1940s?

Quan Yin: Well, yes, but they didn't necessarily unlock all the power of the fallen crafts in the '40s. It wasn't until the '50s and much later that they started to understand it more and be able to utilize it more.

Alison: Given that it took the Atlanteans about 200 years to reverse engineer the craft they'd gotten, did it take a long time, like decades, before we could reverse engineer the antigravity technology?

Quan Yin: Yes.

Alison: Do they have the antigravity technology now?

Quan Yin: They do. They have it. They're not using it openly.

Alison: Some of the latest fighter planes are doing these vertical landings and short takeoffs. And the stealth bombers have laser weapons. Are we harnessing the UFO technology now?

Quan Yin: Yes, they're starting to show more and more of the technology that they've had.

Alison: Can we say we've got the antigravity technology, and we can match the capability of the E.T.'s craft?

Quan Yin: Different crafts are powered by different forces. In some cases, the E.T. pilot might be very evolved and can use their consciousness to navigate the ship, and the ship might also be alive in some cases, meaning it is sentient.

Alison: Ahh, I see. I remember now reading somewhere that an E.T. pilot could merge their consciousness with the ship's. So what we have is an advanced technology, but E.T.s can be far more advanced because they are more evolved, having a higher consciousness and capability.

Quan Yin: Correct.

Alison: Can our antigravity technology be used on cars?

Quan Yin: You do have it. You're just not using it in mass-produced vehicles, but there are those vehicles that do exist.

Alison: Oh, so first, the government knew about what this technology could do, but they couldn't reverse engineer it as of yet. Then they did reverse engineer it, but they couldn't announce this technology, not even the idea of it, because there would be too many questions to answer and too many ramifications on the economy if the use of fossil fuels were to stop.

Quan Yin: It's complicated. Yes, exactly, it's just complicated. It's not that they wanted to use the old technology. It's just that they couldn't just introduce this new technology without saying where it came from, without disrupting all of these major corporations and the ways that they had of earning money and employing people who worked for them, and all of these things that would have been a huge disruption to the socioeconomic order that you have, even though it would have been better for the environment, you see.

Alison: Now I am thinking of another technology that the Atlanteans had, and it was their very advanced 3D printers. You mentioned that this technology was one that the Atlanteans got from the downed craft. So I'm wondering if there was another major technology behind their 3D printers?

Quan Yin: Well, it was a re-atomizing technology. It was a technology to take matter and move the particles around so that it could become something else. They could transmute matter using technology that was re-atomizing the matter into something else, something that they would want more so than, say, the rock or the wood or whatever substance they would put into the machine.

Alison: And was that not something that we received and have in our possession now?

Quan Yin: Certain elements within the highest levels of the governments, the major governments, their militaries, and scientists have this technology, yes.

Alison: Does the public have any inkling of this technology, this miracle machine?

Quan Yin: You've already seen it in Star Trek movies. It was called a replicator. (4)

Alison: And that's part of what we got from the crafts because we received a lot of knowledge about atoms and quantum mechanics. It came from the same source?

Quan Yin: Yes.

Alison: This means we could manufacture some products at home?

Quan Yin: Yes.

Alison: The information about these two new technologies was withheld for fear of potentially destabilizing the existing socioeconomic order, but they would have had a major impact on the environment and the way we live. Now I am wondering if this information would be considered to be adding fuel to the conspiracy theory that's popular in many circles.

Quan Yin: Well, no, it's fine to talk about it as it is because it is true. This is how the average person gets to decide what they do with certain information because it would be naive for people to assume that things are exactly as they are told by their government, and we also don't want to promote that idea that everything that you're being told is 100% true all the time. When a person realizes that some things are being held back, some things are being suppressed, they could choose not to go down that rabbit hole of mistrust and thinking then everything is false, that everything you're being told is a lie. Rather, they can see how there is actually a legitimate reason for why these things are being held back. In other words, national security.

You don't want other countries to know or have the same technology and then use it against you. There's the problem with the re-atomizers of these things that could take away all kinds of jobs and manufacturing, and that could be a huge blow to the economy if there wasn't as much industry because you suddenly had a re-atomizer in every home. Same thing with the antigravity technology. So there are some good reasons as well why things are being held back from people, including not wanting to have widespread panic because of the existence of E.T.s. So people don't have to look at the reasons for things being held back as only because there are those who have nefarious agendas or who are power hungry or anything like that.

Alison: Yes. This is really helpful. We need a balanced perspective.

Quan Yin: Yes. The only problem is, of course, they started the lie of "Oh that wasn't a flying saucer, it was a weather balloon" back in the 40's, and of course, people also had hidden from them the fact that there were E.T.s found as well in the ship. Once you start lying, you sort of have to keep telling lies to cover up the initial lie.

Alison: And it's getting harder and harder because there are so many sightings, and everybody has a cell phone. There are constant UFO videos posted on social media.

Quan Yin: Yes.

Alison: If other countries had crashed crafts as well, they're likely catching up on the technologies. It can't remain a secret forever.

Quan Yin: Right.

Alison: And going back to how we used the knowledge to develop the technologies, did the Atlanteans have enough knowledge to develop quantum physics as well?

Quan Yin: Yes, they had their crude understandings of quantum physics. Absolutely.

Alison: And do we have a more advanced understanding?

Quan Yin: Yes, you do.

Alison: Okay. And so for that matter, did they develop nuclear technology?

Quan Yin: No, they did not.

Alison: Oh, I guess it's because they didn't have to develop it. They had free energy available to them.

Quan Yin: Yes, they had free energy, and they simply weren't making the connection between what they had been able to discover and that particular application of it. In other words, necessity is the mother of all invention. And they didn't have a need. Even though there were wars in Atlantean times, it simply wasn't the time for humanity to undergo that kind of trauma to help to shift your consciousness in a new direction as the 1940s were at that time.

Alison: Are you speaking about the trauma of the detonation of atomic bombs?

Quan Yin: Yes.

Alison: So, a lot of things happened for a reason at the higher level. The Atlanteans had their challenges, and we have ours. But fundamentally, we need to find our spiritual compass just like the Atlanteans needed to find theirs. We've come a long way. It is time for more truth to come out so we can deal with our challenges more wisely in our reality.

Quan Yin: Yes.

E.T.s' Active Involvement to Date

E.T.s scaled up their involvement with us in the 1940s, and they have stayed close to us in the physical and nonphysical ever since. They have helped our scientists in making breakthrough discoveries. Higher-dimensional E.T.s have been sharing spiritual guidance and teachings through channelers. Many spaceships have been visiting us all over the world. We have been surrounded by E.T.'s company with or without our conscious knowledge of it.

Alison: Have E.T.s been more active than leaving us crafts or sending us ideas?

Quan Yin: Well, there have been E.T.s who have been working with scientists directly as well. So now you have an acceleration of helpers and ways of helping. So you have some Nordic Pleiadians, for example, blending into society to infiltrate certain aspects of government and the military to help people who are on the leading edge and on the verge of a breakthrough.

Alison: So E.T.s like Nordic Pleiadians are actually walking on Earth right now and working with our scientists? I have also read in channeled material and even in mainstream media (5) that there have been undisclosed meetings between the government and E.T.s. So when did that direct involvement start?

Quan Yin: It really did start in the '40s.

Alison: And it has continued to date.

Quan Yin: Yes.

Alison: Is the existence of E.T.s common knowledge in the government?

Quan Yin: Not everyone in the military or the government knows this, but in certain branches, yes, there's knowledge.

Alison: Okay, still a top secret?

Quan Yin: Yes.

(Note: There have been whistleblowers who provided information on the U.S. government's UAP/UFO projects and programs (6).)

Alison: So, how would the Nordic Pleiadians come in and help us? What is their way of entry?

Quan Yin: They'd just be dropped off. They just show up in a ship or through a portal.

Alison: They can prove they are a legitimate citizen somehow and have all the paperwork and records?

Quan Yin: Yes.

Alison: Are they in Western countries?

Quan Yin: They go all over.

Alison: Do they have IDs created for them? Like, all of a sudden, they have a history here.

Quan Yin: Yes, they needed those types of things. So, they developed them on ships. It was just automatically updated for them.

Alison: So automatically, the government has this person's birth record, IDs, and all the other necessary records?

Quan Yin: Yes.

Alison: This is so sci-fi, but I guess it is happening in our reality. And so they appear just as Scandinavian-looking people in different spots of the world?

Quan Yin: Yes.

Alison: Is there any suspicion of who they are?

Quan Yin: No, there's no suspicion amongst most humans.

Alison: So they would be fourth-dimensional Nordic Pleiadians?

Quan Yin: That's right.

Alison: Who are the other E.T.s that are helping with science and technology?

Quan Yin: There are Arcturians and Sirians and Lyrans, and mantid beings. There are E.T.s that are in aquatic form who are helping. There are orbs, spheres. There are all kinds of beings helping that are extraterrestrial in nature and from places you don't have names for.

Alison: I haven't heard about the mantid beings.

Quan Yin: They're called insectoid, but they have two arms, two legs, a head, and a body.

Alison: Are they on Earth in physical form?

Quan Yin: They are not on Earth, but they are physical.

Alison: Are they helping our scientists?

Quan Yin: Yes, all of them that I mentioned and more. They're helping with the science and technology end of the human experience, yes.

Alison: Are these E.T.s appearing as humans on Earth?

Quan Yin: Some are and some aren't. E.T.s in the flesh walking on Earth, it's rare for that to happen. It does happen, but it's rare.

Alison: So the Nordic Pleiadians are putting in that rare appearance?

Quan Yin: They're more known, yes.

Alison: But how would the E.T.s communicate with the scientists if they're not appearing as humans?

Quan Yin: Telepathically.

Alison: Is telepathic communication similar to tapping into information that has been sent on Earth?

Quan Yin: It is, however, sometimes telepathic communication is more intimate, more one-to-one, whereas what I was referring to in tapping into ideas, there is more of the information that's in the collective consciousness or that's in a stream of consciousness on a particular topic that the E.T.s are contributing to. And anyone who got into a relaxed enough state in a moment of quiet contemplation or meditation might be tapping into that stream of consciousness.

Alison: The person needs to be in a slightly higher vibration to access the stream of consciousness?

Quan Yin: Yes.

Alison: And then in telepathic communication, E.T.s would be more deliberately sending that information?

Quan Yin: At times, they will be targeting someone who can understand what it is that they want to transmit. And they will seek that vibrational harmony with that human being, so that human being can be on that same wavelength to pick up the bits of information that they would need to make an advancement in whatever their field is technologically.

Alison: Do the scientists know who they're communicating with, or do they just pick up the message without asking?

Quan Yin: They pick up the message. They understand telepathic communication. The E.T.s are also able to communicate by using your technology, by putting images on screens and working with formulas and numbers, and such to communicate what's needed to bring the science to the next level.

Alison: But do the scientists know that they are communicating with a non-human being?

Quan Yin: Yes, and some are receiving the downloads. It depends on the scientist and their readiness for contact.

Alison: A lot of channelers talk about getting downloads. It happens in a flash, but they receive a lot of information that they can unpack later.

Quan Yin: That's true. That is how information gets passed along, yes.

Alison: So scientists can get a download from E.T.s if they have the intention and they're in the right frequency?

Quan Yin: Yes. Most of these scientists are toiling in obscurity, so to speak. They're not well known. They shy away from the spotlight.

Alison: Oh, but they'll come up with the ideas that are important for a scientific breakthrough?

Quan Yin: Yes.

Alison: Are there any famous scientists who are E.T.s?

Quan Yin: No, they are still humans.

Alison: That's so fascinating. I guess these scientists would not acknowledge publicly that they're communicating with an E.T. being, and they're doing so telepathically?

Quan Yin: That's correct. A lot of these scientists are working with the military, so they know that they have to keep it under their hats. Others would never reveal their sources, so to speak, or their inspiration because they know they'd be discredited, they'd be laughed out of their fields, and whatever they would bring forth to the scientific community would not be accepted. So they're not openly talking about connecting with E.T.s as part of their work.

Alison: In Atlantis, I recall you said that E.T.s didn't show up in physical form or work directly with the Atlanteans.

Quan Yin: No, some Atlanteans communicated with the E.T.s, but they were not walking amongst the Atlanteans.

Alison: The E.T.s seem to be working more directly with us?

Quan Yin: Well, it's a very, very small number of people, percentage-wise.

Alison: Aside from assistance in science and technology, there are also many physical and nonphysical E.T. beings who are actively giving us guidance for spiritual transformation towards Ascension.

Quan Yin: Yes, Bashar is one of them.

Alison: Yes, I listen to Bashar all the time, but only the messages he's given in the last few years. I know Bashar and Darryl Anka have been doing this for almost four decades. When did the E.T.s start to turn up their communication to help us evolve our consciousness?

Quan Yin: It was in the '80s. That's when we saw Bashar coming in and Lyssa Royal Holt's channeling of E.T.s, and Barbara Marciniak channeling the Pleiadians. A lot of channelers emerged in the 1980s to help. Some were channeling E.T.s, of course, and others just channeling higher-dimensional beings like Abraham and Seth. But in the 1980s, there was a huge step-up in the delivery of this type of information.

(Note: Abraham, a twelfth dimensional master, has been channeled by Esther Hicks. Seth is also a master from the twelfth dimension, and he was channeled by Jane Roberts.)

Alison: E.T.s' involvement with us is as much technology as it is spiritual teaching. The most active teachers to me are the Arcturians, Pleiadians, and Sirians, but I know there are many others.

Quan Yin: Oh, absolutely, yes. That's always been the intention to help you shift your consciousness for the upcoming Ascension. There's been a lot more activity in the skies at this time than there was during the time of Atlantis, and there's been a lot more contact, but there are a lot more people on the planet.

Alison: And for all the sightings we have had, which are many, we see them because they want to be seen. Is that a correct statement?

Quan Yin: Yes.

Alison: And they do have the technology to shield their ships if they don't want to be seen.

Quan Yin: That's correct, too.

Alison: Recently in November and December 2024, there were reported sightings of "drones" in small or large numbers in the skies of New Jersey and New York. The difference this time was that it went on for a few weeks. This attracted widespread attention on Unidentified Anomalous Phenomena (UAP) or Unidentified Flying Objects (UFO). Politicians were raising concerns about national security and public safety, and they were calling for the government to explain what was going on. The government kept silent for a while and then maintained that there were no security concerns.

Quan Yin: It's not realistic for people to think that the E.T.s wouldn't have already just taken over if that was their aim. They already have these capabilities. They have the technology to disable all your weaponry all at once. They don't need to wait. They're not biding their time until the energy is right to attack. They are looking to help, and they've always been looking to help, and of course, they've been misunderstood by so many.

Alison: And they're going to be landing on Earth in the not-too-distant future (7), and that's different in Atlantis because they never did that.

Quan Yin: No, they did not.

Alison: It wasn't time for Ascension in Atlantean times, but it is for us.

Quan Yin: Correct.

With Power Comes Responsibility

Nuclear technology has been both beneficial and challenging to us since its arrival in the last century. Its immense power is daunting, especially in its destructive capability. This double-edged sword is true of many leading-edge technologies we have under development today, such as bioscience and artificial intelligence. What do these powerful technologies really mean to us? What is their true purpose in our evolution?

Alison: Nuclear technology is a monumental technology because of its unlimited power. Is there a special significance there?

Quan Yin: Yes, to see how something could not only help advance the civilization, but to see what the civilization then would do with the added responsibility of having more power. So you need new problems in order to grow. You need new challenges. You can't just have the same challenges over and over and over again.

Alison: It was known that there could be a major risk in giving this knowledge to humans who did not have and still haven't had a strong spiritual foundation to apply this technology?

Quan Yin: Yes, it was known. And again, it was a challenge, a problem, an issue that you would then be facing in your development to see what you would do with that knowledge, to see how you would use it.

Alison: There has been good use of it and there has been bad use of it. You spoke about the collective trauma of seeing the explosion of atomic bombs in Japan in 1945. So this is a continuous trial and test for humanity, given how many nuclear weapons we still have on this planet and how badly things could go wrong with a nuclear plant malfunction.

Quan Yin: There are, of course, limitations placed on what you can do so that you don't blow yourselves up and cause a ripple effect throughout the entire Universe with a major explosion or a major meltdown. But that is the help that you are being given at this point, the prevention of really cataclysmic type of events from occurring based on the knowledge that you were given by the beings who helped you in the first place.

Alison: It's really reassuring to hear that. So we are learning from our challenges, but there is a real level of shepherding by E.T.s to make sure we don't go astray.

Quan Yin: Correct.

Alison: The fast growth in genetic science, I guess, is part of the recycling of the Atlantean experience where they devolved to a lower-consciousness use of the technology. They had used their AI technology to create a slave race of androids as well, but I suppose they had not completed the full cycle of the AI challenge because the androids weren't that smart and self-aware yet. These are still the challenges for us today?

Quan Yin: Yes.

Alison: We'll have to explore our AI challenge in greater depth in the future because there are already so many concerns about the unchecked development of AI. Geoffrey Hinton, known as the Godfather of AI, is a major advocate of the potential risks of AI, and he received the 2024 Nobel Prize in Physics.

Quan Yin: Right.

Alison: Despite these tough challenges, I feel that nuclear technology, quantum physics, and space exploration all served the purpose of getting us closer to our cosmic roots. Other new technologies are also unveiling previously unknown possibilities for us. It's almost like it's preparing us for Ascension, for knowing how it feels to be in the fifth dimension, to lose our physical and cognitive limitations, and to access Universal knowledge.

Quan Yin: That's exactly what it's going to be doing. Everything is about Ascension.

Notes

1) "How Do We Launch Things Into Space?" (https://spaceplace. nasa.gov/launching-into-space/en/) by NASA. This is a short explanation and illustration of the traditional technology of launching a rocket for a non-technical audience. "When a rocket burns propellants and pushes out exhaust, that creates an upward force called thrust. To launch, the rocket needs enough propellants so that the thrust pushing the rocket up is greater than the force of gravity pulling the rocket down."

2) In Chapter 6, Quan Yin explained the antigravity technology: "It's an understanding of how to use the force that is the gravitational pull and coupling that with the electromagnetic energy that is present all around to reverse that gravitational pull and instead create the opposite of that gravitational pull, which is a polarized effect of it to cause the machine to fly. It wasn't reliant upon a huge amount of fuel being burned out of the jets or the rockets in order to propel them that high into the sky."
This basically means that this E.T. technology can somehow cancel the gravitational pull and lift and move the craft with electromagnetic energy.

3) According to Bob Lazar, an ex-government employee and whistleblower, he worked on a downed E.T. craft in Area 51 for a reverse-engineering project. He described an antigravity reactor the size of a basketball in the craft that would generate its own gravity field when turned on, but at his time in Area 51 in the

early 1980s, they were not able to reverse engineer the technology yet. He stated it was a top-secret project and only two people were assigned to each E.T. craft for reverse engineering. He recalled seeing 8-9 fallen alien crafts in the government's possession in Area 51 in the 1980s.

Sources:

"Joe Rogan | Bob Lazar Talking About Antigravity Reactor" (https://www.youtube.com/watch?v=CeGGn6F9Og8) on YouTube.

"Joe Rogan Experience #1315 - Bob Lazar & Jeremy Corbell" (https://www.youtube.com/watch?v=BEWz4SXfyCQ) on YouTube.

Additionally, Google AI's explanation of antigravity technology stated that "Antigravity technology is a hypothetical concept that involves creating a place or object that is free from the force of gravity. It's a complex area of study that involves both innovative science and speculative theory." It also stated that "Antigravity has the potential to revolutionize transportation, space exploration, and our understanding of physics. However, the science isn't there yet to lessen the effects of gravitational pull on an object."

4) According to Wikipedia – Replicator (*Star Trek*), "In Star Trek, a replicator is a machine that can create (and recycle) things. Replicators were originally seen to simply synthesize meals on demand, but in later series, much larger non-food items appear. The technical aspects of replicated versus 'real' things are sometimes a plot element."

5) "Israel's Former Space Security Chief Claims Aliens Exist, And Trump Knows" (https://www.youtube.com/watch?v=j6iE62jovMo) | NBC News NOW. 2020

6) *Imminent: Inside the Pentagon's Hunt for UFOs*, by Luis Elizondo, 2024, available on Amazon.
   U.S. Congressional hearings on UAP/UFO in 2023 & 2024, available on YouTube.

7) Bashar put the potential open contact with E.T.s in the 2026-2027 or the 2028-2029 timeframe, depending on our readiness and consciousness level.
   Source: "Echoes of Sedona" (https://tv.bashar.org/programs/echoes-of-sedona?category_id=195561), channeled by Darryl Anka, on bashartv.com

CHAPTER 15

$$\infty$$

THE EMERGENCE OF NEW HUMAN HYBRIDS

In the last two chapters, we learned that the parallel Earth humans had a significant impact on Earth life in our recent history. They inadvertently left us a treasure trove of advanced technologies. They became the iconic E.T.s in our minds because of the publicity of the UFO crash in Roswell, New Mexico. They came to our Earth with the intention to create a new species of hybrids using our and their DNA. They wanted to ensure that their race would survive.

In this chapter, we'll take a closer look at the creation of this new hybrid species. These hybrids were first born in the 1940s. The method used by the parallel Earth humans to collect our genetic material was not always pleasant, and it resulted in many abduction stories, including traumatic experiences for some involved in the incidents. These stories were amongst the first reported E.T. contacts in our time by ordinary people who had no prior knowledge or interest in extraterrestrials.

Because of how E.T.s were portrayed in these stories, especially in dramatic re-enactments in movies or documentaries, many people labeled E.T.s as nefarious and maleficent, and a great deal of fear and hostility was developed toward them. But we know the parallel Earth humans didn't represent the many benevolent E.T.s that have been working with humans throughout our history. As we learn more about the parallel Earth humans and their efforts to sustain their race, we'll see that they also weren't as malevolent as people have projected them to be.

Furthermore, encounters with E.T.s or a UFO in our modern era did not always result in a physical exam or collection of biological specimens. There have been numerous documented visitations that were friendly in nature with E.T.s from different star systems giving the contactees a tour of the ship, information about Earth, or an E.T. technology (1).

After many publications and documentaries describing the E.T. and UFO encounters in the past few decades, many people can agree that E.T.s are no longer a figment of someone's imagination. They have become very real for many people, and the awareness of E.T.s and UFOs has been raised for believers and nonbelievers alike. More truths about E.T.s are needed now more than ever, so we can have a fair and balanced view of our interactions and relationships with them.

As for the hybrids who were the main reason for the visitations by parallel Earth humans, there has been a deep fascination with them in the lightworker community and the UFO enthusiast circles. The hybrids are the latest development in the long history of human hybridization. In keeping with past traditions, they are meant to exemplify higher consciousness and intelligence for humanity on this planet, particularly in this age of Ascension. In this chapter, we will learn about their history of development, their upcoming visits with humans, and the future they hold for the new Earth.

Humanity's History of Hybridization

Before finding out more about the new hybrid species, let's quickly review how we as humans have transformed historically from a genetic and consciousness perspective. It has undoubtedly been a dynamic and continuous process of hybridization.

Alison: Humans on Earth now are really a mixture of E.T. and human species. We have received genetic coding from E.T.s, and we are a product of the mating between E.T.s and humans, and also between various human races.

Quan Yin: Yes.

Alison: And that's why we are a washed-down version of the Lemurians at their peak consciousness level, because of all the genes that permit higher or lower consciousness?

Quan Yin: Correct.

Alison: Our consciousness level has not come very far since the reset triggered by the fall of Atlantis?

Quan Yin: You are getting less and less so every day. In Lemuria, you had a uniform type of awareness where people were around the same type of frequency. On Earth today, you have people with very different levels of consciousness occupying the planet.

Alison: Bashar talked about the hybrids a lot, and his audience has asked about the hybrids a lot. He has spoken about the future sixth or seventh generation of hybrids. Did the first five hybrids come from the historical evolution of humans?

Quan Yin: The hybrids that Bashar is talking about, that whole program didn't start until the 1940s when the parallel Earth humans started to come and take DNA and sperm and eggs to create those hybrid races of which Bashar is one, and the Yahyel are another. Those are the hybrid races he was referring to.

In a sense, you are all hybrids because it stretches back a ways, of course. And as you know, there were original hybrids between humans and Pleiadians, and original hybrids between humans and Zetas, the real Zetas from Zeta Reticuli. But everyone has E.T. DNA. Everyone has genes that are not of this Earth. So, the long evolution of consciousness that has occurred with the help of E.T.s, that's a different type of hybridization that has been going on since the first humans came, and humans are essentially hybrids of many different races.

Alison: Right. Maybe it's just semantics. The truth is we are all hybrids because of our genetics, and Bashar is talking about the specific new hybrids that have been created since the 1940s.

Quan Yin: Yes.

Creation of New Hybrids and Alien Encounters

How were the new hybrids initially created by the parallel Earth humans? We know that the parallel Earth humans collected genetic material from us, and some humans were exposed to undesired experiences when they became involuntary genetic contributors. These encounters are frequently referred to as alien abductions. What can we make of these unusual situations and experiences?

Alison: So the crashes in the 1940s originated from the parallel Earth humans trying to collect human DNA to create a new hybrid species to sustain theirs. Did they mix human sperm and eggs with theirs?

Quan Yin: Yes, they used theirs too. The women were still producing eggs, so the eggs were the important part in this, and they got some help from females of Earth as well with your eggs. And some of the men still could produce sperm, enough viable sperm to be the donors as well. So, yes, they created test tube babies just like you do there on your planet as well.

Alison: Did they always create the embryos in the test tube? Is it possible that they could inseminate a human female or a parallel Earth human female and then remove the embryo or fetus?

Quan Yin: Yes, those are rare, but they have happened.

Alison: Did they use artificial gestation chambers to let the fetuses grow in them?

Quan Yin: Yes.

Alison: Their genetic science is more advanced.

Quan Yin: Yes.

Alison: Since the parallel Earth humans lived on ships, have the hybrids been living on ships?

Quan Yin: They have, yes.

Alison: And is that a large population?

Quan Yin: Millions.

Alison: Oh my. So they have created a lot of test tube babies.

Quan Yin: They have, yes.

Alison: Did this go on for decades since the 1940s?

Quan Yin: Yes.

Alison: And all those alien abduction stories, they were kind of true, weren't they?

Quan Yin: They were all true, every single one of them.

Alison: Did they always have to take humans into a ship to get the genetic material?

Quan Yin: Not all the time, no. They could extract what they needed to from the person's body while the person's body is lying in bed and while the soul, the soul's consciousness, is out astral traveling.

Alison: Is this type of extraction not physical?

Quan Yin: It is. It is physical, yes.

Alison: There were reports of biological harm in some of the encounters.

Quan Yin: Sometimes people would awaken during the procedure. They would wake up and they would move. And it would be the movement that would cause the harm. Or other times, it was psychosomatic. So when you have these fears and people don't know how to deal with their fears, don't know how to process the trauma of having awakened during one of these procedures, then yes, that can have a negative impact on the person physically.

And certainly, the parallel Earth humans didn't perfect their implant technology right away, and some of those implants could be annoying to people, but those implants were later removed. Certain implants that were less intrusive were placed within the energy fields or in places in the body where people wouldn't feel any harmful effects. But what I am saying is that there's no negative intent.

Alison: Were the implants used for tracking and monitoring physiological changes related to reproduction?

Quan Yin: No, the implants have been placed to study more of the thoughts and the emotions of humans so that the parallel Earth humans could understand better what it was they were getting themselves into by mating with humans of Earth.

Alison: Oh. There are people who had the experience of abduction, had genetic material extracted from them, and then later found a tracking device or implant in their bodies. But the implant wasn't placed for monitoring their hormonal level and things like that.

Quan Yin: Well, it can be when that's relevant to the thoughts and feelings of the person that they are studying, observing.

Alison: This was only done by the parallel Earth humans, or was it done by the other E.T.s as well?

Quan Yin: There are other E.T.s who have their own genetic programs going on, and when they are monitoring the Earth humans, it can be for a variety of reasons.

Alison: I see. And for the humans whose eggs and sperm were taken, I assume these cases were not voluntary.

Quan Yin: No, they're not voluntary. The people don't know what's happening or didn't know what was happening when it happened. They weren't volunteering.

Alison: Did their soul agree to it?

Quan Yin: Yes, that part of you agrees to everything that you experience.

Alison: Including the abductions.

Quan Yin: Yes.

Alison: I see. So the hybrids were created basically, well unfortunately, by abductions or by the extraction of genetic material without the conscious consent of the involved humans, as they were not fully aware of what their souls agreed to have them experience.

Quan Yin: Experiences that some people had with the parallel Earth humans were not unfortunate for them. They were remarkable, life-changing in a good way, putting them on a path of always being interested in E.T.s and wanting to connect with them. Some were terrified, of course, and for those, it was an unfortunate but necessary experience because they and their souls wouldn't create it for themselves if it wasn't going to help them in some way. Then for others, again, it was a pleasant experience.

Alison: Yes, there is a study that surveyed hundreds of people who had a UAP or E.T. contact experience (2), and the majority of respondents considered it a positive experience and wanted more contacts with E.T.s. But for those who didn't have a good experience, in what sense was the unfortunate experience necessary?

Quan Yin: As far as the human experience on Earth goes, you had then a trauma involving E.T.s that would help you to clear different traumas you've experienced in the past with E.T.s in other incarnations. And by in the past, I mean in other incarnations where E.T.s came to different planets that you were on. So this is an opportunity for people to experience E.T. contact differently and perhaps in a better way than in other incarnations of their soul, where those E.T.s just came in like locusts and took whatever they wanted and destroyed so much in their path and then left. That's very difficult for anyone to see in a positive way, and very challenging to make oneself feel better about an experience like that.

Alison: The word "locusts" reminds me of the Reptilians. But I understand they may not have been the only ones. A lot had happened to us before we began to experience life on Earth. So the abductions brought out the traumatic feelings, but most people have healed from the experience and continued to live their lives. This is how the previous trauma was released from their soul memory?

Quan Yin: Correct.

Alison: I know the creation of all experience is very much the doing of our higher self. So again, there is always another perspective and reason for anything that happens to us?

Quan Yin: Yes.

Alison: And for that matter, is the abduction also a co-creation between the human and E.T.s, with respective souls agreeing to be the abductor and abductee? So from a higher perspective, there is really no victim here?

Quan Yin: That's correct.

Alison: Have the abductions stopped? I assume millions of hybrids are happily living on board their spaceships now.

Quan Yin: Not the same ones, no. The parallel Earth humans are not alive anymore.

Alison: Oh, I see. You did say that other E.T.s have genetic programs they're carrying out.

Quan Yin: There are others, of course, who are also interested in creating hybrids, and the hybrids Bashar talked about are just one program that involves those parallel Earth humans.

Alison: Did the parallel Earth humans engage in more of this work than the others? Bashar is certainly a famous representative of that hybrid program.

Quan Yin: Yes, they did the most of it.

Alison: I don't know if people will be excited or scared when they hear that the hybridization programs are still ongoing.

Quan Yin: It's good for people to know that E.T. contact is still happening and is happening in a physical way, because if they then have their own experiences, they will be able to realize it wasn't just their imagination. "I wasn't just dreaming. I'm not just crazy. There was an actual physical being in my room, and they were touching me and poking at me." So sometimes people just need that validation to know there's still a lot going on as it pertains to humans and extraterrestrials. However, nothing harmful is being done. It's just the reactions, it's the fear that becomes harmful to the human being.

Alison: I presume, as always, their souls agree to this experience for the benefit of clearing or growth.

Quan Yin: That's correct.

Alison: We are focusing on the activities of the parallel Earth humans in this chapter, but the UFO and E.T. encounters are not limited to them.

Quan Yin: No, not at all.

Alison: In fact, I've seen descriptions of a variety of encounters with beings of different appearances that are humanlike, humanoid-like, or even insectoids or mantid-looking, and not all the encounters were about biological exams or genetic extractions.

(Note: The study cited in Note 2 offered this multi-faceted view of the E.T. encounters.)

Quan Yin: Yes, you have all kinds of E.T.s visiting with you all the time for different reasons, not the least of which are the familiar E.T. beings that have been with you and are observing and helping you.

The Seven Generations of New Hybrids

Bashar spoke of seven generations of new hybrids. There seemed to be a progression from creating hybrids that could really carry the torch for the race, to then creating hybrids that could live on Earth, and they are still in this creation process. I described the different generations of hybrids to Quan Yin and asked for additional insights.

Alison: I'd like to get a better understanding of these hybrids. Bashar has defined seven generations of the hybrids (3). The first generation was actually the original mutated parallel Earth humans, who we know have all died out by now.

Quan Yin: Correct.

Alison: The second generation is the first real hybrids carrying our human DNA. He said these hybrids could continue the race, but they're not a sufficient version of the hybrids envisioned by their creators.

Quan Yin: So the earliest created hybrids, of course, were more prone to sickness and less intelligent and perhaps even less emotionally intelligent than the younger ones are now, but since then, much learning has gone on to perfect the process of hybridization.

Alison: These test tube babies were the result of an artificial form of crossbreeding. Did the parallel Earth humans also apply genetic intervention in the creation of these embryos?

Quan Yin: Yes.

Alison: In what direction were they applying the genetic science?

Quan Yin: To correct for the problems with their own genetics that were coming from the fact that they were so toxic.

Alison: Ahh, I see. That's why these early hybrids were still not very healthy or intelligent. Then the third generation is the Sassani, Bashar's race, and their DNA is 50/50 between parallel Earth humans and humans on this Earth. They look more like the parallel Earth humans with huge eyes, a bigger head, a smaller body, and about five feet tall. Bashar and Darryl Anka showed pictures of the typical male and female Sassani in the book *The Masters of Limitation* and the documentary *First Contact* (4). The typical Sassani males have no hair, and females have white hair.

Quan Yin: It was the parallel Earth humans' genes that caused the males to have no hair.

Alison: Ahh, I see. But they seem like a healthy and intelligent race. Was this generation created by fusing Earth and parallel Earth human DNA, but also by applying more successful genetic manipulation?

Quan Yin: Yes.

Alison: The fourth-generation hybrids, according to Bashar, are more human in appearance but still have the E.T.'s bigger eyes and slender physique. The fifth generation is the more known Yahyel race. They are very humanlike, and Bashar said if they passed us on the street, we wouldn't be able to tell they're not fully human. They are being groomed by the fourth-generation hybrids for open contact with humans. I assume these two generations have also been created using the same test-tube method, but benefiting more from advanced genetic expertise. The Yahyel in particular are the perfect hybrids to meet and mingle with humans.

Quan Yin: Yes.

Alison: This means they'll likely come to Earth to meet and be with humans?

Quan Yin: Yes, they are in the process of coming to Earth.

Alison: How are they coming to Earth?

Quan Yin: Well, they have ships, so they can come in, drop in, and blend in.

Alison: When the genetic material was collected from Earth humans, did the parallel Earth humans include all human races on Earth?

Quan Yin: Yes.

Alison: There was no over-allocation to one or certain races?

Quan Yin: No.

Alison: So the hybrids, especially the later hybrids, can have different hair and skin colors?

Quan Yin: Right.

Alison: The sixth generation after the Yahyel, according to Bashar, is the hybrid children that will bring harmonization to Earth and help with Earth's evolution. And the seventh generation will be a blending of humans with other hybrids, including the sixth-generation hybrids, and they will complete the evolutionary cycle for Earth. Do these hybrids exist yet?

Quan Yin: No. These hybrids are in the future. The sixth and seventh hybrid races will start being created when you start mating with the other hybrid races.

Alison: Okay. It is a continuation of the tradition of Earth humans mating with E.T.s and E.T. hybrids?

Quan Yin: Yes, you'll be co-creating the race with them.

Alison: Will it be after we get into the fifth dimension?

Quan Yin: No, that's going to start before you complete the Shift. The sixth-generation hybrids will come from your merging with the hybrids with whom you have that similar genetic makeup so that coupling is possible.

Alison: Oh, so the sixth hybrid race will begin to be born before Ascension, and they will be the children of the Yahyel and humans.

Quan Yin: Yes.

Alison: And the seventh hybrid race will be created after Ascension?

Quan Yin: Yes.

Alison: Okay. Very interesting. And these hybrids eventually will stay on Earth and become the fifth-dimensional humans after Ascension?

Quan Yin: Some of them, yes.

Alison: Oh, will some of them go elsewhere, like another planet?

Quan Yin: Some of them will prefer life on the ship. That's what they know. Or a space station, or another world.

Alison: It sounds like the creation of the sixth and seventh generations of hybrids will become more natural, and no artificial genetic science will be used.

Quan Yin: The creation will be energetic sometimes, sometimes not even using science, but an energetic soul type of coming together, so more of a fifth-dimensional form of reproduction. That is the current fifth dimension that has evolved from the time when you were there.

Alison: The energetic type of creation will be for the future sixth and seventh generations?

Quan Yin: Not every time, but sometimes in the more advanced years of that generation's emergence, the energies will have been used.

Alison: I guess this means it is a reproductive method made possible after Ascension, so it'll be quite a long time into the future?

Quan Yin: Yes. The seventh-generation hybrids will arrive about 1,000 years after Ascension.

Alison: Wow. I see. So this is way into the future, but perhaps a blink of an eye in the higher realm?

Quan Yin: Yes.

Alison: Are the hybrids generally more intelligent than humans?

Quan Yin: Yes, they are because of the intellect of those humans from a parallel Earth.

Alison: What I'm curious about is why there is such a meticulous plan to create all these generations of hybrids. Why did they want to create the Yahyel who would mate with Earth humans?

Quan Yin: What you're asking about is a very pragmatic way you're thinking about it. You're not thinking in terms of love. The Yahyel are, first of all, very appreciative of the earthlings of your planet. They love you. They have highly advanced emotions now, which the parallel Earth humans didn't have. They are full of love and appreciation, and you could call it an agenda, but really, it's a desire to have experiences with you and to have a planet to call home. The end result of that will be falling in love and mating and creating that hybrid race, but they're not thinking about that as their overall agenda. That's just going to be the end result. (5)

Alison: So perhaps more genetic methods were involved in the creation of earlier generations of hybrids. But for the Yahyel and Earth humans, it'll definitely be a natural way to birth the sixth-generation hybrids?

Quan Yin: Yes, because of the feelings. In other words, it's hard and challenging sometimes to understand why two people have fallen in love with each other when you look at them on Earth and you think about the differences that exist between them. So there's a bigger story going on, and the bigger story has to do with the souls.

Alison: In what sense?

Quan Yin: The souls have a relationship to one another, where when they lock eyes in the physical, they're going to fall in love, they're going to want to mate eventually. And so that's how these new races are created. It's not because everyone's sitting around going, "Well, how do we further the consciousness now? Let's make these two groups come together and create another race." It's just going to happen naturally.

Alison: So it isn't like there is a well-defined plan to roll out sixth and seventh generations of hybrids after the Yahyel come to Earth. Future hybrids will be created not for survival or as a consciousness experiment. It'll be done for love, and it'll happen naturally.

Quan Yin: Yes, indeed.

Suppression of Emotions by the Parallel Earth Humans

Quan Yin mentioned that the parallel Earth humans did not have the same emotions as their hybrid offspring do. While asking about the intelligence of the hybrids, I uncovered something surprising but fundamental about the personality, or the mental and emotional states, of parallel Earth humans. Their civilization ended up on a destructive path, but it was not caused by a lack of morality. It was something else. And amazingly, it was their attempt to root out the source of all evil, which in their view was their emotions. They made a conscious decision based on their spiritual belief, but the decision would woefully seal the fate of their civilization.

Alison: There are a lot of human genes, our human genes, in the new hybrids. The later generations will likely have even a higher percentage of human DNA because they will be mating with humans. You said the hybrids are more intelligent than humans. Is it because the parallel Earth humans were superior intellectually?

Quan Yin: Yes, intellectually and spiritually.

Alison: Where did the parallel Earth humans get their spirituality? I thought they were not high vibrational.

Quan Yin: They are spiritual. It's a different kind of spirituality. It's a spirituality involving the mind, involving focus, but they do have an understanding of who they really are, and that everything is connected. They have a sort of hive mind mentality. They take care of each other. That was the way of the parallel Earth humans.

Alison: It sounds like they did possess key elements of spirituality, such as connectedness of all things and knowing who they are as soul beings. What were they missing?

Quan Yin: Yes, they just disconnected from nature and their emotions because they thought that was a good thing to do. There are a lot of such misperceptions and not great ideas in the spiritual and new age teachings as well. Of course, it is quite possible not to be on a good trajectory or the best trajectory, even though you're applying your spiritual beliefs to everything that you're doing. And that would be the case with these parallel Earth humans because they were very disciplined, but that discipline came from seeing, for example, that people would do things out of an emotion, a lower vibrational emotion, that would be harmful to others.

So they knew, for example, that if a person is angry or afraid, they're more likely to act out in these ways that are harmful to others. And the experiences that you have there on Earth right now are also really the by-products of these types of emotions. The negative systems you have in place that perpetuate greed and reward, narcissism, and those sorts of things, those are born out of fear, anger, and even loneliness and feelings of separation.

So the parallel Earth humans, knowing this, were basically saying, "Well, what if we eliminate these emotions, then won't we be more level-headed in our decisions? Won't we make decisions that are for the best of all? And won't we eliminate violence and hatred and these sorts of things?" And that's what their aim was. So it was a very spiritual aim that they had that allowed them to be those who had a great deal of focus and awareness, and who were tuning in and meditating. They were able to tune into these thought streams about technology that allowed them to make the advancements in technology that they did. So while it was a misguided type of spirituality in the sense that they thought by eliminating emotion, they could become even more spiritual, it was a type of spirituality.

Alison: Well, this reminds me of people in our world who are very disciplined, rational, well-intentioned, and successful. And many of them meditate as well to sharpen their focus and be super productive. But this type of spirituality didn't help the parallel Earth humans in the end. They had to abandon their planet, and they couldn't sustain their race on their own.

Quan Yin: Well, because you need your emotions, you need a balance, you need to be able to feel everything, including love and especially unconditional love. And they were missing that through their elimination of emotions from their lives.

Alison: They weren't guided by the feeling of love in their decisions, and they probably lacked self-love. That could have explained how they made themselves an endangered species.

Quan Yin: Right.

Alison: Did it change for the hybrids?

Quan Yin: Yes, because the hybrids had your emotionality woven into their DNA.

Alison: Oh, that's so interesting.

Quan Yin: Yes. So the DNA of the parallel Earth humans was affected. It was affected by their desire to move away from emotion.

Alison: I see. That was another reason why humans were a good genetic match for them. We have the emotionality that was turned off in their DNA. So the later hybrids have a good balance of high intellect and rich emotions.

Quan Yin: Yes.

Purpose and Impact of the New Hybrids

The new hybrids saved the parallel Earth human race from extinction. They carry the parallel Earth humans' DNA in their physical bodies. Their existence also serves a purpose for us on our Earth because they will contribute to our evolution.

Alison: For people who are so fascinated by the hybrids, is it just because they represent a future to us?

Quan Yin: It's because it's fascinating. But yes, some people do have memories that they're starting to tap into of their visitations or abductions, whichever it was.

Alison: And I realized just now why people always ask Bashar if they have hybrid children. Their DNA is probably in some of the hybrids.

Quan Yin: Yes.

Alison: There are also people who like hybrids because they seem to be an advanced species. But we are all ascending to be fifth-dimensional beings, and we are all going to be advanced.

Quan Yin: You're all evolving, and the infusion of their consciousness into what's going on there on Earth will help. It will help people expand their consciousness. Think about all the people who will have to reconsider their beliefs because of the landing of ships and the emergence of these E.T.s in the future; now they'll have to recognize that they don't know everything. The hybrids will make a similar contribution. So that's going to open people's minds to so much more.

Alison: And when the hybrids come, they're part of the effort to expand our consciousness?

Quan Yin: Yes, and it's all coming together in this culmination point of human and extraterrestrial consciousness converging in a harmonious way.

Alison: And in the bigger scheme of things, this is the higher purpose in the creation of these hybrids, even if humans and the Yahyel will come together primarily because of love?

Quan Yin: Yes, the higher purpose is to expand consciousness, and to create something new, a new experience, something that has never been before.

Alison: I see. It's also about the creation of the new and the excitement of it all.

Quan Yin: Yes.

Bashar's Home Planet and A Visit from the Future

The hybrids live on spaceships. Bashar and the Sassani have been on ships, visiting with us and talking to us through Darryl Anka in the past 40 years. It was thus puzzling to hear Bashar describing their beautiful home planet of E'sassani and his family life in his book, The Masters of Limitation. *Even more importantly, he has described his race as fifth-dimensional beings. Things seem to have moved at lightning speed since the 1940s for the Sassani to shift to the fifth dimension and settle on a new planet. I posed this question to Quan Yin.*

Alison: Bashar described his home planet E'sassani as green, lush, and beautiful. I believe he and some of his fellow Sassani are living on a ship stationed close to Earth. So where did that home planet come from?

Quan Yin: The home planet, there are some who live on the home planet. They discovered it. It's what's called the Goldilocks planet. The atmosphere is just right for humans to dwell on, and they made it their own.

Alison: Is that planet far from Earth?

Quan Yin: It's far, yes, in Orion's Belt.

(Note: According to NASA, the closest distance from Earth to Orion's Belt is about 800 light years.)

Alison: Oh, okay. I guess that's why. I was going to laugh because we're so crazy about moving to Mars, but this planet is much more suitable for humans, except that it's too far.

Quan Yin: Yes, it is.

Alison: And also, Bashar said the Sassani are fifth-dimensional. The parallel Earth humans were third-dimensional, and we were also third-dimensional when human DNA was taken and the new hybrids were first created. How did the Sassani become fifth-dimensional in such a short time?

Quan Yin: Now, this is going to get more confusing. The Sassani that Bashar is a member of are from the future. They're from your future, so they're able to time travel obviously. The Sassani are able to time travel back to where you are now.

Alison: So they exist in the future?

Quan Yin: Yes.

Alison: Now I remember that's what Bashar said in the book *The Masters of Limitations*. They are from the future. I didn't put two and two together. He said they're about 3,000 years ahead of us in development. They are fifth-dimensional because they're in that future where Ascension has already taken place.

Quan Yin: The Yahyel that you'll be meeting in a few years, no, but the Sassani, yes.

Alison: The Yahyel are concurrent fourth-dimensional hybrids?

Quan Yin: Yes.

Alison: So it seems the Sassani are hybrids that have been producing their own offspring, and that's how they have formed a new race and continued on during this long period of time?

Quan Yin: Correct.

Alison: Have they had any infusion of other DNA since their creation as the third-generation hybrids?

Quan Yin: No.

Alison: They were and are the ideal hybrids to carry on the heritage of the parallel Earth humans. So simply for the continuity of the race, there was no need for the later hybrids.

Quan Yin: Correct.

Alison: So the Sassani are future beings, post-Ascension beings. And they're coming back, visiting us, working with us to help with our Ascension?

Quan Yin: Yes.

Alison: This doesn't mean our Ascension is 3,000 years away. It just means they have developed further since their first entry into the fifth dimension. I know timing-wise, Ascension is not that far away for us.

Quan Yin: Correct.

Alison: Does this type of visit from the future happen often in our Universe?

Quan Yin: Yes.

Alison: Oh, okay. And that's why they were able to find their home planet and settle there from their ships. They had time to do it. They couldn't have gotten to where they are now from the 1940s because it would have been way too fast. It would be incomprehensible how they could have already ascended when Ascension hasn't happened in our reality yet, but they have ascended because they are from the future. Wow. Whenever I think I'm clear about something, there are always more surprises.

Quan Yin: Yes. It's more than the mind can really comprehend.

Alison: Right. Exactly.

Quan Yin: You're just scratching the surface, really, of what's possible, what's out there to be experienced.

Alison: I understand. And in the Sassani's development, they must have gone through the fourth-dimensional stage like we are now. That means there must be fourth-dimensional Sassani living on ships in our reality?

Quan Yin: Yes.

Alison: But we're not experiencing that. We're experiencing the future Sassani and particularly Bashar.

Quan Yin: Yes. The fourth-dimensional Sassani are not visiting you now, but they will be connecting with you all on Earth at some point.

Alison: Would that be after Ascension, and they would join in with the creation of the sixth or seventh generation of hybrids?

Quan Yin: Yes.

Alison: Okay. There were many E.T. beings that came to Earth in our past. For instance, in ancient Egypt, the Lyrans, Pleiadians, and Sirians were present to teach the Egyptians, and they were mostly third-dimensional beings. They were not from the future?

Quan Yin: Some.

Alison: Some were from the future as well?

Quan Yin: Yes.

Alison: Okay. We are being taught something about "time" here. Past, present, and future all exist simultaneously. They are just different points on a continuum of realities for us to experience what we want to experience. We live in and experience our present reality. However, we can go back to the past or the future using a time machine or in a dream state because those realities are always there, happening at the same time. But in the third and fourth dimensions, we choose to experience time and see our realities in a linear way.

Quan Yin: Yes. As you ascend to the fifth-dimensional consciousness, you'll naturally have this understanding. You'll know then that there is only "now," and what's most important is what your experience is right now.

Notes

1) Many books on alien abductions or UFO encounters have been published. A recent example is *The Extratempestrial Model* by Michael Masters (2020) available on Amazon. In this book, there were two case studies describing incidental encounters with a UFO and E.T.s, where the contactees were given a tour of the spacecraft. In "Case Study 1 Leo and Mike Dworshak North Dakota USA 1932", the contactees were told of what was to happen on Earth, including WWII. In "Case study 2 Udo Warterna Montana, USA 1940", the contactee was shown the anti-gravity technology on the ship.

2) "A Study on Reported Contact with Non-Human Intelligence Associated with Unidentified Aerial Phenomena" (https://www.researchgate.net/publication/326151576_A_Study_on_Reported_Contact_with_Non-Human_Intelligence_Associated_with_Unidentified_Aerial_Phenomena), Journal of Scientific Exploration, Vol. 32, No. 2, pp 298-348.

3) "The First Five Hybrid Races" (https://tv.bashar.org/programs/five-hybrid-races-video), a channeled session with Bashar, by Daryl Anka (2017), on bashartv.com

4) *First Contact*, a documentary about Bashar, E.T.s, and UFOs, produced by Darryl Anka (2016), available on YouTube

5) "Dear Mom and Dad" (https://tv.bashar.org/programs/dear-mom-and-dad), a channeled session with Bashar, by Daryl Anka (2016), on bashartv.com, where Bashar spoke about the feelings of the Yahyel who are being readied to come to Earth.

CHAPTER 16

❧

UNDERSTANDING OUR E.T. FRIENDS AND CONCLUDING THE EARTH EXPERIMENT

As the last few chapters have informed us, we have had a long and complicated history with E.T.s. They have been our progenitors, and through both good and sometimes bad deeds, they have been integral to our Earth experience. More and more E.T.s are lending a helping hand to our evolution today, and the E.T.s that have long been friends with us are also upping their engagement level. One conspicuous sign of such development is the increasing sightings of UAP or UFO. These sightings have been recorded and posted on social media and have even made it into mainstream media all over the world. The E.T.s are ready for mass contact when we are.

It is time to have a deeper understanding of the E.T.s, not just for what they have done but for what spirit or cause they represent. Quan Yin shares a unique vantage point, which is to learn the mission and purpose of the major E.T. races that have been intertwined with our evolution since antiquity. This educational process was endearing and inspirational. It is as if we finally see the true nature and character of a friend after knowing them for a very long time.

The E.T.s masterminded the Earth Experiment back in ancient times, and they have been the participants, observers, and shepherds of the Experiment. We, the humans, have lived through the Experiment across hundreds of reincarnations, collecting unique and valuable experiences that we desired to have. With Ascension on the horizon and our journey in the third and fourth dimensions drawing to a close, has the Earth Experiment fulfilled its promise as a study of the evolution of consciousness? As souls, have we completed what we set out to accomplish when we made that exciting decision to come to Earth?

Why Are E.T.s More Advanced Than Us?

Throughout human history, E.T.s have always been more advanced, whether it's in intelligence, technology, or spiritual gifts and capabilities. Being more advanced is generally true of beings of higher dimensions, but when I checked on the dimensionality of E.T.s visiting us in our past, they were mostly third-dimensional beings. Invariably, their civilizations were always way ahead of ours. Why is this the case? What did they do that we haven't been able to match?

Alison: This is a question about the dimensionality of E.T.s that have frequented Earth. Were all the E.T.s who were participating in the Earth Experiment fifth-dimensional beings or higher?

Quan Yin: It depends on how you look at it. From the higher dimensions, you have more of the nonphysical help including, of course, the 12th dimension. But the beings who originally seeded the Earth were third-dimensional.

Alison: Why were these third-dimensional E.T.s so advanced, especially technologically?

Quan Yin: If you stick around in the third dimension long enough, you can do these things. You do grow, you do evolve, you do advance, and you do create technology. Of course, those beings were channeling a lot of what they were getting, but when a civilization stays around for a while, they are making such advances that they're able to achieve space travel, they're able to have the technology that helps them terraform the world. It's within the realm of possibilities right now for humanity to do that, too. It's just not a high priority because you are working on evolving your consciousness as well and not just on evolving your technology. And you really haven't been around for very long in comparison to the Lyrans, the Sirians, and the Pleiadeans.

Alison: How long could their civilizations have lasted in the third dimension?

Quan Yin: Millions of years.

Alison: Ahh, I see. So these E.T.s were in the same third dimension as humans were, but they would have evolved to the higher range of frequencies in the third dimension and thus had higher vibration, consciousness, and knowledge than humans?

Quan Yin: Yes.

Alison: And that's the same for the fourth-dimensional E.T.s that are visiting us today. They are just more evolved and have higher vibrations.

Quan Yin: Yes.

Alison: How did the higher-dimensional E.T.s get involved with us?

Quan Yin: It depends on how you look at it. You could say they were involved all along in that they also wanted this to happen and were feeding their third-dimensional beings information that helped them with the project, and that channeled information came from somewhere above. So they were involved, just not hands-on.

Alison: Were the hands-on E.T.s always third-dimensional?

Quan Yin: Well, not always. There were those in the fifth dimension who had bodies and could have interfered in a variety of ways.

(Note: In the fifth dimension, beings have a physical body, but it is less dense than the third-dimensional body. This means our body will be able to hold more light after Ascension.)

Alison: I know even third-dimensional E.T.s would have been considered gods. These fifth-dimensional E.T.s most definitely were worshiped as gods.

Quan Yin: When those beings came to Earth from the fifth dimension, they lowered their vibrations enough to be seen, but they were still holding such a high vibration that they appeared as God, and they had access to those fifth-dimensional capabilities.

Alison: If our civilization started in earnest with the Lemurians about 300,000 years ago, we have not had a third-dimensional civilization for very long. This has been a fast journey.

Quan Yin: Yes.

Alison: So was that by design? We knew that the journey would be very short and very intense, unlike a typical third-dimensional E.T. civilization. We all knew it, and we willingly signed up for this intense human experience?

Quan Yin: Yes, you did.

The Themes of E.T.s from Different Star Systems

In Chapter 12, when we probed the intent of the Reptilians in their quests in the galaxy, we found they were clearly driven by selfish and malevolent interests. But we know most E.T.s participating in the Earth Experiment had genuine intentions to assist humans in our evolution. So, how much do we know about the E.T.s that have maintained a close relationship with humankind? What are their proclivities and their identity and purpose relating to the star system they belong to?

Alison: We usually identify E.T.s with the star system they come from. So they are Pleiadians or Arcturians, for instance, but they may be of different physical forms, from different dimensions, and they may have different agendas and intentions. Since there can be differences even within the same E.T. groups, what really unites them as the E.T. race of a star system?

Quan Yin: There are general themes within each star system that are being pursued. So Pleiadians tend to be more about channeling and teaching and healing, and Arcturians tend to be more about developing spiritual gifts and abilities that allow the physical and nonphysical to merge and become of one same intention. And Andromedans tend to be about expression, self-expression, and creativity, use of color, art, sound, and those types of things. So what unites them is the commonality of their origin and the themes of their star system, even though they'll have different forms and slightly different agendas, depending on their dimension.

Alison: What about the Cassiopeians? I know they have been sending us positive and beautiful energy.

Quan Yin: They're more about love and expressions of love and ways of knowing love, ways of feeling love, creating through love, healing through love. They're about "in the power of love" in Cassiopeia.

Alison: Wow. That's incredible. We don't hear from them much in the channeling world, but their energetic presence can trigger our hearts.

Quan Yin: Yes.

Alison: So the higher the dimension, the more they are in the teaching and guiding roles. But the beings in the lower dimensions would take more actions.

Quan Yin: They would be doing experiments.

Alison: What about the Orions? I know they stirred up trouble on Earth energetically, though for the ultimate benefit of our diversity.

Quan Yin: They're exploring the dichotomy of experience, polarization, being the villain and the victim, being the oppressor and the oppressed. So there's a lot of enslavement that's gone on there in the Orion system. There's been a lot of manipulation by those in power, giving out false information to manipulate and to control. So that's really a theme of dominance and submission.

Alison: And that was the cause of the Orion Wars?

Quan Yin: Yes, because the Orion Empire wanted to dominate all others throughout the galaxy.

(Note: The Orion Wars were an intergalactic war that happened in the fifth dimension millions of years ago. Please see the note on Orion Wars in Chapter 2.)

Alison: Are the Orions still trying to dominate others today?

Quan Yin: No, they're not.

Alison: They have evolved?

Quan Yin: They have. They've become more integrated. They still have their issues just like humanity does, and still are healing and clearing from the Orion Wars, from some of the traumas. But they are operating more as an Earth-like society now.

Alison: Hmm. An Earth-like society?

Quan Yin: That's correct.

Alison: Oh. But I think we have those issues too. We still have dominance and oppression here, and aggression.

Quan Yin: You do, and so do they, but to a much, much smaller scale.

Alison: Oh, really? Wow. We're doing better than I thought.

Quan Yin: Yes indeed.

Alison: What about the Sirians?

Quan Yin: Well, their theme is service, how to be of service, how to help without over-helping, without interfering and intervening to such an extent that the people are thwarted in their development.

Alison: That may be why they received some negative references about not being the best-intentioned sometimes, whereas they were only trying to find that balance in the way they assisted.

Quan Yin: That's someone's projection. That's a human being's concept of the Sirians. That's not real.

Alison: How about the Zetas of Zeta Reticuli who visited and lived with the Asians?

Quan Yin: They primarily wanted to explore the extent to which mind and technology could be used to alter reality and to get closer to Source ultimately.

Alison: I see. That explained why they wanted to infuse the Asians with their genes and knowledge to help them develop faster. What about the Antarians?

Quan Yin: Well, the main theme for the star system was to explore the relationship between that which is natural, naturally occurring body, naturally occurring mind, and that which is technological, which is created for use by the conscious beings.

Alison: That's a great theme too and somewhat connected to the Zetas' theme, but with an added interest in what natural evolution could lead us to versus what technology could. However, this theme was not embodied in the Antarians that landed in Africa 100,000 years ago. I guess these themes are a high-level abstraction of the E.T.s' developmental path, but there are many races and many planets in each of these star systems.

Quan Yin: That's correct.

Alison: What about the Lyrans?

Quan Yin: Genetic manipulation, hybridization, and the exploring of the theme of "Is it interference or is it helping? Is it intervening or is it playing God?" Those are the themes they had to face when going out into the other parts of the galaxy to see whether their master geneticist skills were really helping or harming the beings they were working with.

Alison: Their story in Lemuria was sad and tragic for all involved. But have they had more success elsewhere in the galaxy?

Quan Yin: Yes, much more so.

Alison: And is it because they have learned not to interfere outright with the evolution of other beings?

Quan Yin: Yes.

Alison: But what would they have done differently by using genetics in a more helpful way?

Quan Yin: In a way where they were able to do it more slowly and see the reattachment of strands of DNA happening over time with their help, but not trying to get beings to evolve all at once.

(Note: Quan Yin has said that as we evolve to higher consciousness, additional strands of DNA beyond the two we have now will be connected and activated.)

Alison: So they were still applying genetic science, but they were more patient and trying to be non-invasive facilitators?

Quan Yin: Yes, right.

Alison: So what they have learned then is they could do some intervention sometimes, as long as it's not overt or forceful interference?

Quan Yin: Yes, and that they needed to stay in the background and not allow themselves to be seen and ultimately then to be worshipped and have all of the empowerment or authority taken from the beings and given to them, because they saw how that ultimately doesn't allow for the beings to make a choice for themselves.

Alison: Do they think this revised approach would mitigate their interference and still bring the beings more benefit than cost?

Quan Yin: Yes.

Alison: Okay. And for the beings that they helped with, do they feel the same way?

Quan Yin: It varied quite a bit.

Alison: Do the higher realms consider their work to be an acceptable practice?

Quan Yin: The higher realms are accepting of everything. Because in the higher realms, there's a knowing that everything works out in the end, and everything leads to more expansion and more knowing of the self. So there's no saying, "Well, that's a mistake," or "That's a sin," from those higher realms. It's just, "Oh, look what these ones are doing. Let's go see how that goes."

Alison: I see. That is the theme and journey for the Lyrans. They may have made mistakes, but that's how beings in the galaxy were able to have so many different experiences.

Quan Yin: Yes.

Alison: Is there a theme for Earth? I know we are part of the solar system.

Quan Yin: Emotions. You're all about emotions. Emotions and creativity, because you derive a lot of your creativity from your emotions.

Alison: This is a clear contrast to the parallel Earth humans.

Quan Yin: Yes.

Alison: In Chapter Three, you told us that a major reason we chose to come to Earth is the range and intensity of emotions that are only available on Earth to experience. Even if we focus so much on the cognitive and rational side of us these days, emotions are the main theme we've been exploring on Earth?

Quan Yin: Yes. Some people come in to experience the mind rather exclusively and will not be very emotional at all. They will come in with a mind that will be more highly developed, and the emotions will not be utilized or even accessible to that person in that lifetime. And that's just a choice that the soul is making to have that type of experience.

Alison: That is still part of the exploration of the theme of emotions, by experiencing the lack of them while being surrounded by people who are emotional?

Quan Yin: That's correct.

Concluding the Earth Experiment

When we ascend to the fifth-dimensional frequency and consciousness, we graduate from the third and fourth-dimensional experience on Earth. Will we graduate from the Earth Experiment as well? As Quan Yin said, the Earth Experiment at its core is really an experiment of consciousness. Will we be able to prove we've successfully completed the Experiment?

Alison: Will the Earth Experiment continue after Ascension?

Quan Yin: The Experiment will be a success for sure when you've ascended. So it will no longer be an experiment in that regard. You will be more consciously collaborating with E.T.s rather than having E.T.s intervening, interfering, tinkering with DNA and all of that.

Alison: This will be in the fifth dimension?

Quan Yin: Yes, when you complete the Shift.

Alison: And so then, when we've ascended, what will humanity and other E.T. beings have learned from the Experiment?

Quan Yin: Well, there are options for so many different takeaways from what has transpired since the beginning of time on Earth, and each being will take what they take from it based on their ability to learn and their ability to see all of the wonderful outcomes as a result of what has transpired there. And so I cannot say that everyone is going to learn the same thing. It will depend on their perspective and their readiness, and what they're interested in. So some will be very focused on the emotional side of life on Earth, others will be focused on survival, and others will be focused on the artistic side. And some will be focused on relationships and family, and the relationship to God and Source, and how that has changed over time. It really does depend on the beings, what they're going to focus on and see as important.

Alison: It would be whatever stands out in these hundreds of lifetimes in terms of what we have benefited the most?

Quan Yin: Yes.

Alison: If we look at the umbrella themes of the Experiment, they are about emotions, diversity, and change of consciousness in the immensely diverse and polarized environment on Earth.

Quan Yin: Yes, that allows for there to be so many different experiences of that turmoil and the chaos of at first not getting along with others who are different, who look different, who believe differently, and who worship differently, and then moving into the time of being able to get along despite those differences. That's a large portion of what this has been about.

Alison: We as souls have all incarnated on Earth for hundreds or more lifetimes, and it's probably hard to say in a few words exactly what we have collectively gained from the experiences.

Quan Yin: Well, yes, it's easy to say that you're gaining consciousness evolution, that you're going through all of these experiences in such a way that you can come to a place of being awake and being in this time of Ascension. That's a pretty big accomplishment.

Alison: So all of us have chosen different roles, different lifetimes, different experiences, but our general path on this planet is somewhat similar because ultimately, when we look from the higher level, it's about going through the wild swings in consciousness evolution but still managing to ascend from the third to the fourth and then to the fifth dimension.

Quan Yin: Yes, that's exactly it.

Alison: It feels emotional that we'll soon be finishing up this Earthly journey. The sentient human part of the journey is only about 300,000 years. It is relatively short compared with the experiences on other stars and planets, but it's been a magnificent journey, and it's incredibly hard as well.

Quan Yin: Yes, but you'll have a lot to look forward to, particularly after E.T.s land their ships here. You don't even have to wait until Ascension for the excitement to begin.

Printed in Dunstable, United Kingdom